THE TWELVE
ZODIAC SIGN SYNDROMES
OF MEDICAL ASTROLOGY

Expanding Our View of the Seasonal Wheel

JUDITH HILL

Stellium Press™

The Twelve Zodiac Sign Syndromes of Medical Astrology
Expanding Our View of the Seasonal Wheel
by Judith Hill
Editor: Mark Polit
Assistant Editor: Melissa Behm
Book design: Leah Kent

ISBN: 978-1-883376-28-4   Revised edition

Disclaimer
The author is not a licensed medical practitioner and is providing astrological opinions only and not medical or psychological diagnosis, established medical fact, or advice. The author is not advocating the use of this content as an exclusive or primary medical model or psychological model or tool. The intent of this book is educational, historical, and to revitalize the energetic approach to astrology. Although this book's content is derived and extrapolated upon two plus millennia of empirical observation, one may consider the contents as generally hypothetical. Personal medical concerns are strictly the province of your personal health practitioner. The author and publisher are not responsible for student or reader misuse of this educative and historic content.

Cover illustration: *Urania*, with armillary sphere, from Johannes Stabius' *Prognostication*, 1503-1505, designed by Albrecht Durer, Nuremberg, 1502

Interior illustrations: English allegorical illustrations of the twelve zodiac signs from an A 186 calendar, anonymous. All other diagrams are created by the author.

STELLIUM
PRESS

DEDICATION

This book is warmly dedicated to my lifetime friend, research colleague, wise advisor, intrepid editor, and consummate mensch, Mark Polit.

IN APPRECIATION

Who first observed the circle of the tropical zodiac imprinted upon the linear body of the human being? This ancient genius bequeathed to humankind a golden key of healing! It works, and yet, it still needs work. May today's medical astrologers, and those of future times, continue to research, observe, polish, and build upon the edifice of this important ancient medical discovery.

CONTENTS

Preface ix

Foreword xiii
by Matthew Wood

Introduction xv
How Does Astrology Work?

1: Melothesia 1
2: Zodiac Sign Syndromes 11
3: Aries Syndrome 19
4: Taurus Syndrome 37
5: Gemini Syndrome 51
6: Cancer Syndrome 71
7: Leo Syndrome 97
8: Virgo Syndrome 127
9: Libra Syndrome 163
10: Scorpio Syndrome 191
11: Sagittarius Syndrome 215
12: Capricorn Syndrome 247
13: Aquarius Syndrome 271
14: Pisces Syndrome 295
15: The Twelve Zodiac Sign Syndromes
and their Relevant Herbs 321

Epilogue 339
Bibliography and Suggested Reading 341
Author's Books, Academy, and Biography 357

PREFACE

The contents of this book flowered within a fascinating course that I had the pleasure of co-teaching with renowned herbalist Matthew Wood entitled *Medical Sun Signs and Their Herbs*. [1]

Together, we worked our way in significant depth through the twelve signs. I presented the first hour on sun sign idiosyncrasies and body systems. Matthew tackled the second hour, focusing on their related herbs. This turned into a mutually delightful and pioneering effort, resulting in the chapters of this present book, and Matthew's significant new writings as well!

Preparing for each class invariably turned into a goose chase down dark alleys unexplored by existing sources. We soon discovered how much was missing. For instance, it's an understatement to assert, rightfully, that Aries "rules the head", without further embellishment on this theme. The head is a complex place, home to a multitude of brain hemispheres, senses, fluids, vessels, cranial nerves, teeth, palate, and bones of the ear and skull. For example, empirical experience allowed ancient researchers to note that Mars-ruled Aries tended to be "hot and dry" with energy swiftly rising upward towards and in the head. However, ancient writers did not know anything about the Mars-ruled adrenal cortex and its function!

H.L. Cornell, and other moderns of the twentieth century did their best to sort this out and upgrade our astrological knowledge to reflect the discoveries of modern medicine. But in truth, there has been an explosion in knowledge of the body. Therefore, the sorting

---

[1] Available at Judith's Academy and Matthew's Institute

has just begun! Thus, we put our field boots on, wading forth into our class investigation. The field is ripe for new inquiry.

This work is necessarily incomplete, as there is so much more to explore with the assistance of the discoveries of modern medicine. However, it is hoped that this book establishes a new foundation for the empirical use of astrology in modern medical practice.

"For, who without Astrology would know
The Art of Healing, does but blindfold go,
By dull Conjectures they are wandering led,
Into a Labyrinth without a Thread."

Lancelot Coelson

From his forward and tribute to Richard Saunder's

The Astrological Judgement and Practice of Physick, 1617

FOREWORD

There are some great Sun Sign books, but mostly we expect superficial treatments of astrology because the twelve sun signs are only one element of the vast array, marrow, and pith of astrology. This book, however, leads us in the opposite direction: to the powerful physiological and energetic depths of the twelve sun signs which have remained hidden down through the centuries until right now.

First of all, Judith shows us that the twelve signs are not to be routinely associated with the elements, qualities, or categories which we habitually associate with them. We are in the habit of thinking of Taurus, Virgo, and Capricorn as the "Earth Signs" and therefore associate them with the Earth element of old Greek medicine, which is cold and dry--or only cold--depending on whether you follow Aristotle or Plato. But no! Taurus is not cold or dry, though Capricorn certainly is. Aquarius is not damp and warm—the attributes of the element of Air in Greek philosophy and medicine. That is, according to Aristotle; Plato would have Air as dry. Judith shows that the signs are energetically (and physiologically) a product of many components—in fact, a composite of season, planetary ruler, element, and modes.

A more complex background in energetics needs to be grasped as a backdrop to Judith's groundbreaking work. Each sign personifies or incarnates an important, deep, underlying physiological process. For instance, Aquarius is associated with oxidation--or pathologically, sub-oxidation, a concept originated by the old astrological doctor, William Davidson, MD. Additionally, Judith shows that each sign is associated with weaknesses that characterize the

opposite sign, also the sign that falls behind it, and the two quincun-
cial signs—so houses 6, 7, 8 and 12 from the sign itself. So, Aquarius
would have a weakness with the heart and cardiovascular system
(Leo) that brings it oxygen.

Altogether, these characteristics of energy, physiology, and
stressful relationships create what Judith calls a *Zodiac Sign Syn-*
drome. This remarkable material is described here in depth for the
first time in the age-old literature of our tradition. But it does not just
add depth to astrology--also to physiology and pathology itself,
which have not been presented in a holistic form to any great extent.

It was exciting working with Judith in the Sun Signs course,
cross fertilizing as we explored together the rulerships and remedials related to the various sun signs. In this way, I am pleased to have
contributed a little to Judith's process and be present as she reframed
the understanding of the sun signs in medical astrology.

I cannot overemphasize the importance of this book. It is seldom
that one gets to be present at a ground-breaking event, but that is the
case here with the publication of this book.

- Matthew Wood, MSc (*Herbal Medicine*)
Martell, Wisconsin

INTRODUCTION

Zodiac Sign Syndromes

Alternative and institutional medicine have both categorized and documented all manner of body type-oriented health syndromes. Ancient medicine provides us with our "choleric", "phlegmatic", "sanguine" and "melancholic" types and their symptoms. We have the famous three Ayurvedic doshas (Vata, Pitta, and Kapha). And there are the Western "Ectomorphs" versus "Mesomorphs", and "Endomorphs", and the like. This study unveils twelve distinct and hitherto neglected physical types and symptom sets relevant and correlative to the twelve zodiac signs of the seasonal wheel: the Twelve Zodiac Sign Syndromes. The observant practitioner, natal chart in hand, will find these syndromes reliably true, thus deserving their rightful place in medical evaluation and remediation. This is the first text defining these twelve medical syndromes as entities distinct to themselves.

Intentions

One of my intents in crafting this sign-targeted book is the elucidation of an insight revealed in the opening paragraphs for each sign's chapter: *The character of the signs, both famous and infamous, appears intimately linked to their assigned body zones, physical functions, and associated glands, vessels, organs, nerves, et al.*

As an example, classic Aries behavior is noted as "impulsive, positive, athletic." But why? This is partially explained because Aries, and its warlike ruler Mars, govern the adrenal glands' "fighting" hormone epinephrine. Conversely, the famously dreamy, vague sign Pisces governs the parasympathetic "rest and relax" response! The understanding of these relationships allows a far deeper awareness of the signs than would otherwise be possible.

The second intent of this book is to see individual signs not as static "things," but gestalts in motion. Traditional sign character is composed in part from a sign's angular relationship to all other signs on this great wheel of life, as opposed to just being "Taurus," for example. As the proverb goes *"no man is an island,"* and neither is a sign! Certain signs support a fellow sign, while others stand averted to it, unable to exchange beams. Each sign will behave as if weakened, or deficient in the qualities of the signs *standing at averted angles to it.* We will learn how to recognize all supportive, stressful, and averted angles per each zodiac sign in the following chapters. Considering how each season exerts unique energies, we propose that various energies are indeed deficiently supplied, or conversely strongly so, for each sign. We will learn how this all works throughout the chapters for each sign.

My final intent for this book is to demonstrate the following: Signs are *conflations* of many types of energies, *pranas*, or *ethers*, as some old texts say. First, each sign is sorted by *female* (centripetal) and *male* (centrifugal) signs. Six per gender. Next, signs are grouped by *element* (either Fire, Earth, Air, or Water). Then grouped by *mode*, three types of rates of motion of a particular element (either Cardinal, Fixed, or Mutable).

Finally, every sign possesses a *ruling planet* and a planet that is in *detriment* when placed in that sign (because it rules the opposite sign). Some signs have a helpful planet that is *exalted* in them, whereas others have a planet that *falls* therein. This all contributes to the overall sign portrait and physical personality! There is more, but this is the most basic structure of negative and positive energies that conflate in the birth sign character.

It is essential to realize that signs are not in themselves elements, modes, "humors," seasons, or planets. Rather, they meld these diverse energies within their character, - think of a celestial stew. This explains why an individual sign character can greatly vary from the descriptors assigned to their element alone. For instance, physically, Aquarius is our coldest sign. It is governed by the cold planet Saturn and sits at mid-winter in the Northern Hemisphere, opposite the hottest sign, the Sun's sign Leo. Although Aquarius is an "Air" sign, we cannot physically assign to it the warm, moist qualities associated with the element Air! Moreover, all of Aquarius's classical symptoms run cold, creating the chilly *Aquarius Syndrome*.

Most texts focus on sign character and basic assignments. My approach is to *also* look under the sheets, at each sign's more subtle energies, because these, above all else, define the health portrait of each sign! In this manner, we awaken to the abundant health information available to anyone who comprehends what planets are in fall or detriment per sign!

An astute study of medical horoscopes will prove useful in proving the efficacy of this system for oneself. A good random example is included below.

Example:

Recently, I needed to find a new chart for our academy's "monthly mystery chart". American singer-songwriter Jimmy Buffett was suggested - a chart I'd never seen before. He had died just days prior of a rare form of skin cancer known as Merkel-cell carcinoma.

Before finding his chart, I construed the possibilities in my mind's eye. Capricorn governs the skin, secondarily Libra, and Saturn. Capricorn is a famously weak sign for the moisturizing Moon, and Jupiter (the planet ruling oils, which falls in this sign).

Although the publicly cited list of medical causes for his disease did not include such planetary portraits, I felt sure that astrology held a valuable key.

There it was! Jimmy's Sun and Moon were *both* in the skin sign Capricorn, clustered together with the malefic, hot, dry planet Mars standing right between them (causing irritation). Buffett's Ascendant sign was the secondary skin sign, Libra. Furthermore, Mars-in-Capricorn is famous for an insufficient elimination of toxins at the skin surface and here it was afflicting both Jimmy's Lights in this sign.

The chart was replete with multiple additional testimonies for skin issues. The ruling planet of Capricorn is Saturn, which co-rules the skin with this sign. Where was Saturn in the scheme? In what condition? Saturn, as you would have it, was in detriment in Leo, and also standing in an angle of aversion (no contact) with its home sign Capricorn. This meant that skin planet Saturn was also in aversion to Buffett's Sun, Moon, and Mars, tenanting there. Thus, two malefic planets afflicted the skin sign Capricorn, while his two centers of life (Sun and Moon) were there as well. Was there any hopeful balance in this chart? No, because the Moon, the bringer of balancing moisture, was also in detriment, being in dry, hard, Capricorn.

Could the ruler of protective oils, Jupiter, help out? No, Jupiter, or lipids, was in the same sign of the South Lunar Node, indicating a possible lipid distribution problem. And the whole chart scheme sang "trapped toxins at the skin," and insufficient waste removal at the colon, combined with excess alcohol consumption. The latter was widely known in this case. Jimmy Buffett appeared to suffer from *Capricorn Syndrome*, produced by multiple testimonies of afflictions involving Capricorn and Saturn - and much else - as you will discover within this book.

This example is not mere chance. These remarkable correlations happen in most (but of course, not all) cases, an observation strongly seconded by several historical physicians.

HOW DOES ASTROLOGY WORK ANYWAY?

In this section, we try to give an answer for the following question: **How does the one-dimensional horoscope reflect the influence of the planets and signs upon the human body?**

Ah...there are so many profound theories and delicate answers to this enduring mystery. As simply as possible, allow me to describe my personal vision. I mean this literally - this vision flashed before my mind following days absorbed in this question!

Even if true, no one theory could be an exclusive explanation of the mechanism for the planetary and zodiac sign influences we experience. There are many paradigms to entertain.

This paradigm considers a three-dimensional tube model of the one-dimensional horoscope and describes a mechanism whereby we might receive vibrational imprints and effects from the planets in the zodiac signs and degrees they tenant at our birth. This is especially useful within the field of Medical Astrology, but also of supreme service to all astrological genres.

First, let us explore five puzzle pieces that led to my wholistic view.

1) Antenna

In his tiny pamphlet on *Stellar Healing*, C.C. Zain postulates the existence of an innate reception 'antenna' for each planet, located within the body region governed by the sign that specific planet tenants at birth. This fascinating idea rang true for me, although something felt missing.

2) Twelve-fold Cyclic Process

Each sign represents a stage in the circle of life between infancy and death. These phases, in turn, are nearly perfectly matched to the *Measure Formula* proposed by significant physicist Dr. Arthur Young. In his seminal *The Geometry of Meaning*, Arthur Young discusses the Measure Formula: the twelve-fold cyclic process, demonstrated on a pendulum's swing, for all matter in motion known to physicists. This cycle transparently corresponds to the known character of the twelve zodiac signs, which is a fact brought forth by Young himself in various texts.

Young's work awakened within me the insight that *because* all cycles are circles, and, conversely, all circles are cycles, that <u>everything</u> in the Universe is *cycling in circles* and *circling in cycles*. These cycles in motion all revolve in the same continuously unfolding twelve-fold process that Young describes! This alone explains zodiacal effects, but not the actual *planetary* reception we empirically observe while working with horoscopes. We will address that problem later in this section.

Simplistically, every object in motion, every cycle or circle, moves through twelve demonstrable phases that correlate beautifully with the twelve cycling zodiacal signs! For instance, the first sign, Aries, starts the pendulum's swing. Young named this state "acceleration," marking 0°, or "start" on the seasonal wheel, the spring equinox. Halfway through the pendulum's swing, at Libra, the autumn equinox (or 180° on the seasonal wheel), the pendulum pauses and looks back at the start point! Libra, the 7th sign is depicted by a set of weighing scales. Libra's character is noted as observing, rational, thought-before-action. Much as "God rested on the 7th day," the zodiac cycle-circle pauses at the 7th sign, Libra.

Simultaneously, all parts of the twelve-fold cycle comprise but a phase of the whole circle. In this manner, *one no longer thinks of a zodiac sign as a stationary entity*, but rather as a *stage in the process of cyclic change on the great, endlessly revolving seasonal wheel*.

In this way, the whole cycle-circle, rolling continuously through twelve stages, or processes, can be further sub-divided according to our classical astrological principals:

- 2 genders
- 4 elements
- 3 modes
- 6 'male' signs and 6 'female' signs
- 12 zodiac signs
- 360 (zodiacal) degrees of the whole circle

Young describes how all this fits neatly into the Measure Formula, but that is not our focus here, but rather, what are the mechanics behind Medical Astrology, aka *Melothesia*?

3) *Melothesia* and the *Twelve Horizontal Zones*

As described in detail in Chapter One, ancient medical astrology describes the circle of twelve signs reflected as *twelve horizontal layers* down the human frame (think of a chocolate layer cake). This is an extraordinary concept. Typically, in acupuncture, prone distribution theory, and neural tracts, we envision *vertical* meridians, vessels, and nerves. However, the ancient discovery of *Homo Signorum* (aka *Zodiacal Man)* and his twelve horizontal body zones, became a mainstay for medical astrology. Charts of this figure were carried in the satchels of Renaissance physicians and decked the walls of the era's surgeon's quarters and barbershops (regretfully, the same place!). Perhaps this was because it worked so well! Personally, I've found this design of inestimable value. Over millennia and into the modern era, this system has been, and continues to be, refined and improved.

Note: The term "Twelve Horizontal Zones" is original to this author. She has found that the old terms "Zodiacal Man," "Homo Signorum," and "Melothesia", do not in fact, state this out front. Although first alluded to in writings as early as 10 BCE, the earliest images appeared in Europe in the late Medieval period. Typically, they display an image surrounded by pictographs of the twelve zodiacal signs, pointing to twelve body regions. We can further divide *the Twelve Horizontal Zones* into 36 zones of 10 degrees each, and of greater importance to this article, *the 360 zodiacal degrees*. Envision 360 'slices' of our chocolate layer cake now, each attributed to a quite precise region of the body <u>within</u> their larger body zone of 30 degrees, (or one twelfth of the vertically stacking horizontal body zones).

There are partial exceptions to this horizontal zone stacking model which are described in the chapters on Cancer and Scorpio. However, for most purposes, this manner of envisioning Zodiacal Man is useful.

Brief History of Melothesia

10-30 BCE: Cuneiform tablet is discovered with complete table of *melothesia* (12 signs linked to specific twelve bodily zones). *from article by John Z. Wee*

14 CE: Marcus Manilius writes the first known exposition of *melothesia* (Zodiacal-Body Zone correlation). See earlier reference for 10-130 CE, above.

1150-45 BCE: French scholar Jean-Francois Champollion discovers papyrus scrolls from the tomb of Ramses V, explicating correlations between ascending constellations (by the hour) and body parts. Though unproven, these scrolls could be a predecessor of the later Greek tradition of *melothesia*, (zodiacal sign-body part correspondences), or, conversely, a link to a potentially far earlier

Mesopotamian origin for the practice. To date, the origin and date of this tradition remains unconfirmed.

4) *Receptor Sites*

Physicians know that cells have 'receptors' designed for the reception of hormones that have 'key codes', in the form of a uniquely shaped key that precisely matches their receptor site. For instance, many body tissues and organs possess estrogen receptors! No hormone except for estrogen can access these estrogen sites. Nature's best designs are commonly found to be repeated throughout nature. *This universal "receptor lock and key" principle must certainly work as well for my proposed receptor sites for planetary energy!* We will soon see how this idea can help us comprehend how the birth chart works.

In recent years it has been discovered that cell membranes are intelligent receivers of all manner of signals and information via the *extracellular matrix* (ECM), and perhaps through other more elusive channels. Bruce H. Lipton, Ph.D.'s groundbreaking book *The Biology of Belief* is conceptually important to understanding the hitherto unrecognized possibilities of cellular intelligence and signal reception.

Receptor sites and their matching keys is another ubiquitous phenomenon, witnessed in sex, magnetism, and many other universal processes.

5) Fractals

"A fractal is a never-ending pattern. Fractals are infinitely complex patterns that are self-similar across different scales. They are created by repeating a simple process over and over in an ongoing feedback loop." Quote extracted from *fractalfoundation.org*

If we understand fractals, we know that Universal principles fractalize throughout all creation.

Cycles are circles is a truth witnessed everywhere in creation from the giant swirling galaxies down to the tiniest atom. This is also true within each cell of the body. In my estimation, a tiny circle template of 360 degrees exists within each and every cell of the body. This can be understood as a fractal of the 360 degrees of ecliptic longitude, or any other circle-cycle.

HOW ASTROLOGY WORKS: PUTTING IT ALL TOGETHER

In crafting a new hypothesis, let's put all these discussed ideas together on the table.

What do we get by melding Zain's stellar antennae, Young's twelve-fold universal cycle of motion, the ancient Greek *Twelve Horizontal Zones* of Homo Signorum, cell receptor sites, and the reality of universal fractals, with the endlessly repeating circle-cycle fractal of all creation?

Let's repeat the question posed at the beginning of this section: **How does the one-dimensional horoscope reflect the influence of the planets and signs upon the human body?**

The Sign Circle and Body Circle Fractal (Figures 1-a & 1-b)

Let's envision the human frame again, as segmented by 12 horizontal body zones, each representing one zodiac sign (Body Zone 1 is Aries the head; Body Zone 2 is Taurus, the mouth and neck, etc.).

The circle of seasons is subtly reflected as an energetic fractal upon the human frame. This is a great discovery of the ancients.

Envision the human frame as a stacked slinky toy, made up of 360 stacked slices. This reflects the 360 zodiacal degrees, and the 360 degrees of any circle. For example: horizontal slinky slice 0-1°

would relate to the very top of Zone 1, the *crown of the head*. Slice 360° would be located at the very end of Body Zone 12, the *tip of the toe.* Note: The twelve zones, however, are not all of equal length. For example, Zones 1 and 2 share portions of the head, whereas the entire calf and ankle comprise Zone 11.

The ancients postulated that the circle of twelve horizontal body zones, cycling through the body (like stacked layers of the chocolate cake), are a tiny, personal version of that larger *fractal* of the twelve cycling zodiac signs (or seasonal zones) of the ecliptic. We experience these as twelve seasons of thirty days each.

Regretfully, humans are inclined to envision fractals visually, not realizing that fractals also occur as cycles in space-time. It is difficult to notice something that is not easily seen! Hence, the enduring mystery of "how astrology works." However, endless repeating patterns, such as fractals, do occur in universally repeating cycles, processes, and vibratory patterns. Most of these aren't readily seen, without charting them out over time, because they are a *process*.

No one cycle is more basic to the universe than the circle in process. As discussed above, Arthur Young demonstrates this clearly through his revelations pertaining to the Measure Formulae for all objects in motion.

For example, the Measure Formulae declares that the second stage of matter-in-motion is 'mass'. The pendulum launches its swing at position 1, Aries, and soon, *gathers mass* in stage 2 of the cycle-circle. This universal principle comes <u>first</u>, fractalizing itself through all moving matter throughout the universe. Thus, the second stage of the zodiac seasonal cycle is also 'mass', the zodiac sign (stage) Taurus that eats, nurses, builds a body, and gathers mass, following the birth of stage 1, Aries, acceleration. In this way the second stage of the human body, Taurus, is mass.

Stage 2, Taurus, is linked throughout all cycles, throughout the universe. They are *one thing*. You ring the doorbell on the larger fractal (zodiac sign), and it rings through to the smaller fractal, the body. In this way, a planetary stimulus in the second sign Taurus rings the bell in zone 2 in the mouth and throat area of the body!

This cannot be directly seen, as yet, and therefore some scientists continue to scoff. The only means we currently have to see this working is through the empirical experience of observing horoscopes. We observe, we feel, we see.

Now, put on your mental high beams. This next step takes a moment of concentration to 'grok'!

Hypothesis. (Figures 1-a, 1-b, 1-c, 1-d, 2-a)

Each human cell of the body possesses energetic receptor sites for each planet, Sun, Moon, and Lunar Node. Planets emit specific vibrational keys to match and link up to their receptor site. This stimulates that site, and therefore, that exact body region! Similar to how hormonal sites within cells match to 'their' hormone, the proposed planetary receptors attune to only 'their' planet. However, the receptor sites are matched to planetary vibrations, rather than hormones!

Note: It is unclear as to whether we possess planetary receptor sites for all planets in all cells, or only <u>one</u> receptor site, positioned, one per planet, within <u>each</u> of our 360 body zone slices located in the *etheric* or *astral body*. These bodies, well known to metaphysicians, are believed to be composed of fine matter surrounding and interpenetrating the dense chemical-molecular physical body.

In the first paradigm, we would enjoy 37.2 trillion receptors for Mars, Venus, et al. This is because the human body contains that approximate number of cells! These receptor sites would *all remain latent unless stimulated by a natal position of 'their' planet on their body degree*, or a transit planet drifting through it.

In the second paradigm, we would have but 360 receptor sites for Venus, or Mars, et al. However, only <u>one</u> would "click in" through our natal pattern's planet placement degree, and a second receptor site would be stimulated by the current degree transit of its planet.

Because, at birth, a planet tenants a *specific zodiac sign*, its specific vibration is filtered *primarily through that sign*. Therefore, the planet will most powerfully link to its own planetary receptor site within the body zone matching that sign, and specifically to the tiny slice of the body indicated by the astrological degree of that planet at birth. The planet's rays are then extended to other signs and planets through an intricate series of geometric angles called "aspects," a pet fascination of the ancient Greeks still popular today.

<u>**Example:**</u> Cousin Moe was born with Venus in Cancer. Therefore, Venus will most strongly be experienced in his Body Zone 4, the stomach and breasts. Furthermore, Moe's natal Venus is located near the 9th degree of Cancer, or 99° on the cycle-circle of 360°. Cousin Moe's latent Venus energy receptor sites (located in each cell of his body) would be awakened mostly in Body Zone 4 and strongest on slice 99, reflecting the 99th degree of the entire zodiac and the 9th degree Cancer.

Now, envision the slinky again. In your mind, or crudely on a sheet of paper, imagine the planet receptor sites going down the slices of the slinky toy, representing the human body. Perhaps you have Mars in Aquarius - then draw your personal 'Mars Receptor' in Zone 11, the lower leg. Now check if it is positioned in an early or late degree of Aquarius? Approximate Mars' position by dividing the entire lower leg into 30 slices or reflected zodiacal degrees. Draw a dot there, representing Mars. *Do this with each planet.* For fun and easy viewing, you can give the planets different colors.

What do you see? You should see the slinky with a spread of colored dots running through it, poised on various slices! Each dot represents a receptor site for a specific planet's energy within the precise zodiacal degree and zodiac sign it tenanted at birth. Looking through the three-dimensional slinky approximates a view of the tube shaped, three-dimensional human body.

Visual aids are prepared for you in Figures 1-a, 1-b, 1-c, 1-d, and 2-a of this chapter.

Making the horoscope

There are two possible ways to achieve this.

(1) Take the slinky and attach the bottom (29° Pisces) to the top (0° Aries). You will see that the slinky now forms a circle. Pretend to lay it on the floor and look down on the slinky from above so that it appears as a two-dimensional circle. You can see the receptor site dots aligned around the circle, spaced according to their places in the signs. These are now the planetary placements in the body arranged in the two-dimensional horoscope. The natal chart is an ingenious device for displaying the location of all planetary receptors within the body and its twelve horizontal zones on a two-dimensional piece of paper.

(2) You can use an alternate, and perhaps more straightforward "tube model" (as shown in figures 1-a, 1-b, 1-c, 1-d and 2-a). To accomplish this, one **must first stagger the first degree for each slinky slice, (aka sign), exactly 30 degrees ahead of the previous, as depicted in Figure 1-d.** Remember, each sign is composed of thirty degrees of a circle, stacked horizontally. "0° Aries" marks the start of Aries; 30° equals the beginning of Taurus; 60° starts Gemini; 90° is the first degree of the sign Cancer, and so forth through all twelve signs.

If one were now to draw a line down through the twelve slices of our slinky model, connecting all thirty-degree spaced sign commencement points, this line would generate a gentle spiral through our metaphorical slinky slices.

The mystery faced here now, is *where* on the diameter of this invisible tube surrounding the body, would each of the sign commencement points begin? We don't know yet because as yet no way has been devised to see into the finer level of matter existing just above the physical matter. We do know however, that 0° Aries, our start point of the scheme should be located at the crown of the head. Dependent on the size of the diameter, we could postulate that 0° Taurus (which equals 30° on the wheel of 360°) should be spaced that amount distant, one zone below. Anti-clockwise or clockwise? This too is unknown, and both routes have good arguments because although the signs rise through the sky clockwise, they are traditionally ordered, and counted through the horoscope in an anticlockwise manner!

However, this method allows the entire "tube" of the human body, complete with its planetary receptor sites, to be readily viewed on a flat, two-dimensional diagram (once collapsed to a flat surface). *The natal chart is now revealed as an ingenious device for instantaneously viewing all planetary receptors within the tubular body field, within its twelve, zodiac sign-associated horizontal zones, upon a simple, flat surface.*

The following graphics will elucidate this process (Figures 1-a, 1-b, 1-c, 1-d, 2-a).

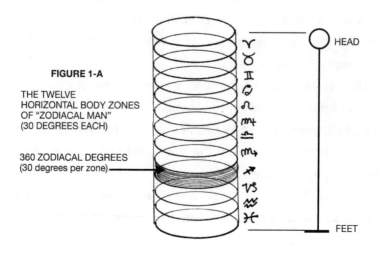

FIGURE 1-A

THE TWELVE
HORIZONTAL BODY ZONES
OF "ZODIACAL MAN"
(30 DEGREES EACH)

360 ZODIACAL DEGREES
(30 degrees per zone)

HEAD

FEET

The Twelve Horizontal Body Zones: 30° each = 360°	ECLIPTIC PLANE Twelve 30° "Signs" = 360°

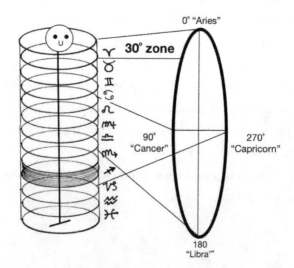

0° "Aries"

30° zone

90°
"Cancer"

270°
"Capricorn"

180
"Libra"

Figure 1 B: Homo Signorum / Melothesia

FIGURE 1 C: ETHERIC MODEL

'planetary vibration receptor sites' situated within each of the twelve horizontal body zones through all 360 levels (30 per zone), corresponding to twelve zodiac signs (of 30 degrees each) and total 360 degrees of ecliptic

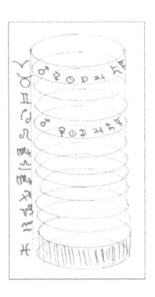

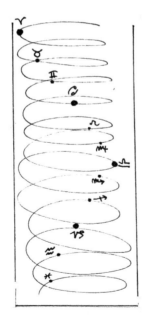

FIGURE 1-D

FIGURE 2

Depiction of how the astrological natal chart depicts a one dimensional "collapsed" view of a three dimensional, horizontal grid of twelve, 30° "body zones", *corresponding to the twelve zodiac signs*; further subdivided into 360° degrees, *corresponding to the 360 degrees of ecliptic longitude* (the total zodiacal degrees). Hypothetically, "receptor sites" keyed to each planet's distinct vibration may exist on each degree within either the hypothetical etheric body template of fine matter, or astral body, or within the physical body's cells located within these traditional twelve zones, and their total three hundred sixty micro-zones. These proposed receptor sites are stimulated only by "their" planet's vibration in a similar manner as to how cellular hormone receptors are exclusively keyed to "their" hormone.

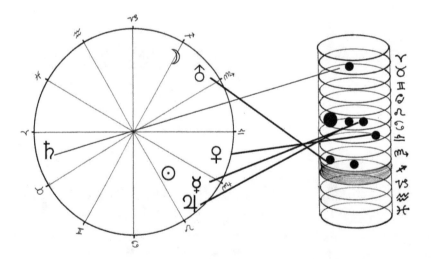

Chapter One:
MELOTHESIA

"...a Physitian is Nature's helper, or at least he should be so;
whosoever would help nature, must of necessity be acquainted with her..."
- Nicholas Culpeper, 1655
Renowned astrologer & herbalist

Ancient empirical astrologers discovered a remarkable fact: twelve ecliptic-linked horizontal body zones of zodiacal influence overlay the human form. The ancient Greeks gave the name *melothesia* to their science of zodiacal sign-body affinities. This term approximates "body part assignments."

Melothesia was first elucidated as a firm system by Marcus Manilius in 14 BCE. Researcher Markham J. Geller's paper *Melothesia in Babylonia* discusses evidence of a late Babylonian participation. There are also tentative links to an Egyptian melothesia based on *decans* (a decan is one third of a sign). There is also some evidence of far earlier roots.

French scholar Jean-Francois Champollion discovered papyrus scrolls from the tomb of Ramses V, (1150-45 BCE), describing by the hour correlations between ascending constellations and parts of the body. Though the link is unproven, these scrolls could be a predecessor of the later Greek melothesia, or even a link to a far earlier Mesopotamian origin for the practice. To date, the origin and date of this tradition remains a mystery. Also, see brief history of Melothesia on page xxii.

Zodiacal Man

The earliest extant melothesian maps of the body zone appeared in Europe in the 14th century. They were an indispensable tool of Jewish, Christian, and Muslim physicians. So much so, that local and national statutes appeared throughout Europe, poised to ensure Zodiacal Man's use for safer phlebotomy and surgery. However, despite the lack of earlier known depictions, it is clear that the ancient Greek and medieval Persian, Arab, and Jewish physicians were well aware of this paradigm.

Most of us have seen these depictions of a forward-facing naked man, often with guts exposed, surrounded by the twelve zodiac signs, each pointing at, or seated upon, a body region. Names for this popular figure are: Zodiacal Man, Homo Signorus, and the more rarely used Dominus Signorus and the *Ish ha* Zodiac.

How to Envision the Zodiacal Human

From Earth's viewpoint, the twelve zodiac signs comprise a 360° circle of seasonal time and celestial space. Picture this circle-cycle as a rope tied in a circle. The circle encompasses 360°, as all circles do.

Divide this rope into twelve equal 30° sections representing the zodiac signs. Now, snip the circle at the beginning of Aries, so that our circular rope dangles down and becomes a straight line.

Now, picture the linear body of a standing human. Place the cut rope with 0° (first degree of Aries) at the crown of the head with the rope dangling from the head to the toe, which is at 360°. Notice how Aries is at the top with Pisces at the feet and the other signs or *Body Zones* dangling in between. Now you have the basic system! Nevertheless, some zones are longer on the body than others, which is another empirical discovery of the ancient physician-astrologers.

When viewing illustrative depictions of traditional Zodiacal Man, one seldom "groks" the existence of the twelve distinctly horizontal zones. This is not because they aren't there, but because the illustrations were not designed to clearly display this fact. To remedy this significant problem, I have designed the first new Homo Signorus in two thousand years, aka *Zodiacal Human*, with twelve horizontal zones clearly shown, as well as history's first known lateral view of the system. (See the illustrations on page 6 and 7).

Twelve Horizontal Zones

In the West, we are more familiar with the Chinese acupuncture meridians and perhaps the more modern nerve-based dermatome maps. These twelve horizontal slices do not interfere with acupuncture points, dermatomes, spinal nerve pathways, or any other system one prefers to use. All these networks exist within the framework of twelve sign-associated zones. Neither does an origination point for nerves in any of these twelve body zones replace the sign rulership of that zone with the auspices of the origination zone. The twelve horizontal zones deserve our respect as a framework in their own right.

Role of Planets

When planets tenant signs at birth, the correlative zones of the body are imprinted with the temperature, color ray, speed, and moisture level of those planets.

Likewise, when transit planets pass through these signs, the correlating body zones also respond to those influences. Most of the time, the response is negligible or brings minor physical changes. For instance, a strong "watery" influence might express itself as an encounter with a delicious watermelon! But, as medical astrologers all know, results can sometimes be alarming.

Zodiac Signs are Not Constellations

As discussed in my previous books, the term *Sun Sign*, as in "What's your Sun Sign?", or worse, "What's your star sign?" refers to the sign that your birthday falls in. In the Western style tropical zodiac, a zodiac sign is a thirty-day season. The cycle of twelve signs, or seasons, begins at the Spring Equinox, or 0° Aries.

You may have heard that tired old skeptic's complaint about how the "constellations have drifted backward" so are no longer aligned with their astrological signs. This would be a valid criticism if we were basing our wheel on constellations. However, Western style astrologers are not using actual constellations and, surprisingly, neither are the proponents of the many "constellation based" *Sidereal zodiacs* favored in India! The Sidereal Zodiac is linked to the ecliptic drawn from a choice of eight or more possible starting points, and signs measured out in thirty-degree slices. Thus, the zodiac signs of both the Tropical and Sidereal systems are not precisely determined by the constellations. However, only the Tropical zodiac is created by the seasonal position of the earth-sun dance, with its eternal, unchanging starting point at 0° Aries. In this book, we are using the Tropical model.

It is a simple fact that the venerable *Tropical Zodiac* cycle has remained unchanged since the solar system began, eons ago. How can this be true?

The twelve-fold sign scaffold of the Tropical Zodiac is structured upon four pivot points provided by the year's two equinoxes and two solstices. A zodiac sign is a season of about thirty days situated in a unique angle in time from the main event: the spring equinox, or "0° Aries". Thus, each sign has 30 degrees, denoting roughly 30 days in the 365-day year. For example, a Leo native is one born between 120 and 149 degrees (or days) *after* the spring equinox, and only 30-59 degrees (or days) *following* the summer solstice. It matters not that the constellation Leo has drifted backward over the last two thousand years.

Let's put this into a real-life scene. Pretend that every year on July 4th you visit your favorite pizzeria, knowing that on that day, you will receive a free cherry cola. Three decades pass. Due to global warming, the weather changes. The neighborhood changes. The people change. But there is always a free cherry cola on July 4th! All that matters to you is the cherry cola, not the changes going on around it. This is similar to how to view the Tropical Zodiac vs the background star clusters that once loosely accompanied them (very loosely indeed). Yes, the clusters have crept slowly backwards over time, but July 4th still dispenses a precise, unchanged type of "Cancer" energy to those born on this day, regardless of constellational drift.

Summary

Ancient cosmologists bequeath to us the seminal discovery that the twelve zodiac signs align with *twelve distinct zones in the human body*. Through further observation down the centuries, practitioners observed that these twelve zodiac types correlated with unique physical idiosyncrasies, temperaments, character types, preferred careers, and select disease proclivities.

My decades long empirical observation of bodily responses to both natal and transit charts has taught me the striking efficacy of the system, but also its deficiencies. Additionally, my years of obsessive statistical research into astro-genetics showed me, as Einstein once remarked when asked about God, "Something is moving". Every horoscope, plus influential transits, empirically proves the validity of *melothesia*.

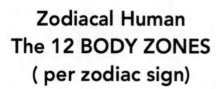

Zodiacal Human
The 12 BODY ZONES
(per zodiac sign)

Graphic by J. Hill extracted from book *"Medical Astrology for Health Practitioners"*

ARIES =1	LIBRA=7
TAURUS=2	SCORPIO=8
GEMINI=3	SAGITTARIUS=9
CANCER=4	CAPRICORN=10
LEO=5	AQUARIUS=11
VIRGO=6	PISCES=12

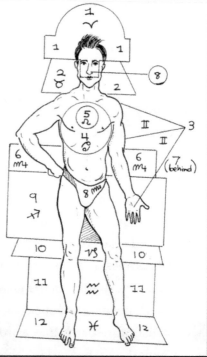

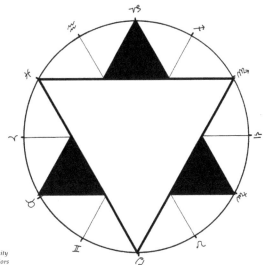

"FEMALE" SIGNS
(CENTRIPETAL)
form building
nourishing/excreting
retaining/excreting
retains imprints
Earth - *astringent; bones*
digestive organs
Water - *moist, fluidic, flesh,*
lymphatic, ECM, excretive,
reproductive

Vital force moves
inward, toward center,
and often downward.

WATER (white) fluids
Cancer
Scorpio
Pisces

EARTH (black) bone
Taurus
Virgo
Capricorn

Note: white and black colors are for clarity
only, and are not the sign-associated colors

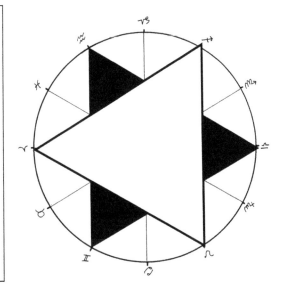

"MALE" SIGNS
(CENTRIFUGAL)
vivifying

Vital Force moves
outward,
and upward,

AIR: (black) venous
circulation, peripheral
nerves, ideation.
Gemini
Libra
Aquarius

FIRE: (white)
muscles, motor and
voluntary nerves,
arterial circulation.
Aries
Leo
Sagittarius

ELECTRICAL AND MAGNETIC CURRENT THROUGH THE TWELVE TROPICAL SIGNS

Copyright © 2020 by Judith Hill

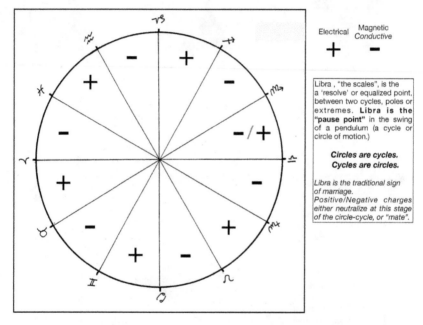

Electrical   Magnetic *Conductive*

+   **–**

Libra , "the scales", is the
a 'resolve' or equalized point,
between two cycles, poles or
extremes. **Libra is the
"pause point"** in the swing
of a pendulum (a cycle or
circle of motion.)

***Circles are cycles.
Cycles are circles.***

Libra is the traditional sign
of marriage.
Positive/Negative charges
either neutralize at this stage
of the circle-cycle, or "mate".

PLANETARY AND SIGN SYMBOLS

PLANET		SIGNS	
Sun	☉	Aries	♈
Moon	☽	Taurus	♉
Mercury	☿	Gemini	♊
Venus	♀	Cancer	♋
Mars	♂	Leo	♌
Jupiter	♃	Virgo	♍
Saturn	♄	Libra	♎
Uranus	♅	Scorpio	♏
Neptune	♆	Sagittarius	♐
Pluto	♇ , ⚵	Capricorn	♑
North Lunar Node	☊	Aquarius	♒
South Lunar Node	☋	Pisces	♓
Pars Fortuna	⊗		

Chapter Two:
ZODIAC SIGN SYNDROMES

You can tell in the twinkling of an eye if you use astrology; to the doctor it gives great insight. The quickness, the speed of it is unbelievable; it's like reading a piece of music. After all, that's what a horoscope is: it's music of the soul projected into the body...

- Dr. William Davidson
The great medical astrologer, regarding the use
of the medical natal chart.

Expanding Our View of the Seasonal Wheel

We tend to think of signs as static "things" or entities. As the proverbial "no man is an island" saying goes, neither do the twelve zodiac signs exist as isolated cosmic arenas. We can expand our understanding of their nature by viewing the signs as phase angles in an ever-revolving seasonal cycle-circle, and further as being composites of strong and weak angular influences holding forth at their precise turn of the revolving dial. A sign is just as much its strengths as its weaknesses!

In other words, Leo is not just Leo. Rather, Leo is a composite of fixed, fiery, and solar energies; weak on Cancer, Pisces, Aquarius, and Capricorn vibrations; and deficient or incompatible with Saturn's rays; and strengthened by its fellow fire signs and its ruler the Sun. Leo is a gestalt! As are all signs.

Discovering Zodiac Sign Syndromes

During our classes, Matthew and I researched the functions, glands, and physical mysteries traditionally associated with each sign. It occurred to me that certain symptom sets, or *syndromes*, reliably occurred among clients born in the same sign. I noticed how well these observed symptoms matched tradition, as well as being supported by the empirical observations of fellow researchers of this realm. These include the great Renaissance medical diarist Joseph Blagrave, plus some of my favorite moderns: C.C. Zain, Max Heindel, Dr. William Davidson, Dr. Howard L. Cornell, Eileen Nauman, and more.

For example, the symptoms of GERD, gallstones, hypertension, overheating, plus volatile temper, all *combined* in at least five people I know with quite similar horoscopes. Armed with this knowledge, and a horoscope, it was easy enough to later guess who had gallstones and GERD, exclusively by viewing their charts. I won't spoil the fun and reveal the "gallish" sign signature here, because you will learn all about it in the appropriate zodiac sign chapters!

These sign-related syndromes were reliable enough to declare the existence of the twelve *Zodiac Sign Syndromes*. Thus, unintentionally, our class (*Medical Astrology by Sun Signs*) and our resultant research forays together opened a new day for melothesian studies and the medical itemization of twelve, very real, Zodiac Sign Syndromes.

This book studies the zodiac signs as *entities in themselves, yet intimately connected in an angular process on the seasonal wheel.* Envision a zodiac sign as one would a wave on the ocean. The wave is a unique form yet connected to the "all" of the ocean. It takes a medically oriented spy glass to understand the nature and manifestations of each zodiac sign in their own right.

Uses

The discovery of Zodiac Sign Syndromes is an epiphany for medical astrology. Remediating the causes of the syndromes, by supporting the affected body zones and functions, can act to bring the body back to balance, diminishing the syndrome. Thus, understanding the tendencies of a natal chart can be used in this way to mitigate the development or severity of a symptom set. After all, foreknowledge is the handmaiden of preemption.

Awareness of the twelve Zodiac Sign Syndromes empowers the health practitioner in a multitude of other ways. Based on the doctrine that specific organs, body systems, and pathways are emphasized for each sign, any match found between a known emphasis in a sign and listed symptoms of the sign's syndrome allows a deeper insight into the underlying processes of a patient's complaint.

For example, let us take a case of chronic fatigue. This condition is common to sleepy Pisces, but rare enough to be alarming for active Aries. Furthermore, the seat of the issue varies considerably between birth charts. In Pisces, we suspect lymphatic sluggishness and glandular imbalance. In Aries, we would first look to the adrenal gland, brain, kidney function, electrolyte balance, motor nerves, insomnia potential, and possible dehydration! The skilled practitioner nuances this further by looking at the whole chart with a detailed assessment of element and mode imbalance as well as planetary participation by placement and aspect. By looking at the onset of the symptoms, the timing tools of transits and progressions can be especially helpful.

A confident knowledge of the twelve Zodiac Sign Syndromes is indispensable to physicians, healers, and astrologers alike.

WHAT CAUSES A ZODIAC SIGN SYNDROME?

This book studies how *an emphasis in a sign can manifest as a Zodiac Sign Syndrome.* So, what are some of the emphases we look for? These contributions to the syndromes are described below and will be explored with specific detail as they apply to each sign in the chapters that follow.

Sign Emphasis

The study of solar and lunar influences comprises the entry floor to astrological medicine. The Sun and Moon are the great *hylegs* or life-giving points of the horoscope. This is also true of the *Ascendant,* the degree rising (ascending) on the eastern horizon at birth. Any of these three provide the greatest emphasis to a sign and can partake of the symptoms and quality of the sign they were tenanting at the birth of the native.

Harmonious and **disharmonious** signs both contribute to a syndrome. **Harmonious** signs (same element or gender) in excess create too much of a good thing, pushing the syndrome over the edge! The Lunar Nodes and the malefic planets, Mars and Saturn, can add to a sign syndrome. **Aversion** means any two signs placed on angles "unseen" to one another (150°, 210°, and 330°). In this book, the term *"quincunx"* is sometimes used to describe *aversion.*

The Weak Houses

The sign ascending at birth represents the body. Quite naturally, any planetary excess or deficiency in this sign or affecting this sign can be expected to manifest physically.

The signs inhabiting the 6th, 8th, or 12th angles of the natal chart (counted counterclockwise from the ascending sign, counted as "1") so often display **weakness** in the body zone governed by these signs. These angles constitute the traditionally malefic 6th, 8th, and

12th houses in the ancient and recently re-popularized Whole Sign House System. But more specifically, these angles are *averted* to the Ascendant, residing at 150°, 210°, and 330° from the ascending sign.

Due to the nature of aversion, the ascending sign has difficulty receiving the energies from these body zones, in part because they share with it neither mode nor element. The body zone ruled by the sign opposite (180° from) the Ascendant could also indicate a bodily weakness, due to its opposition to the sign ruling the body.

The important Ascendant sign, positioned at angle "1", swings either way - but certainly, and strongly emphasizes the body zone and general traits of this sign (the "rising sign")!

For these reasons, the placement within these whole sign houses of the Sun, Moon, Ascendant Ruler, Saturn, a Lunar Node, or other significant planetary placement may contribute to the presence of a symptom set for that zodiac sign or for the ascending sign.

Note that a significant planetary placement in a weak whole sign house (6, 8, 12) could contribute to the assigned syndrome of the ascending sign, but could also indicate a deficiency, or excess in the body zone or sign inhabiting the weak house. *Remediating and supporting the relevant body zones and functions, with these characteristics in mind, acts to bring the body into balance.*

The Weak Angles

The houses and angles discussed above are weak because they are averted or in a quincunx relationship from the ascending sign. The same principle applies to all angular relationships between all signs in the natal chart, regardless of their placement. For instance, should Taurus be natally positioned in the happy 5th house of the chart - it will still be positioned opposite Scorpio (180°) and in a difficult quincunx relationship to Libra (150°), Sagittarius (210°), and Aries (330°).

Useful Tip: Any singular sign that is poorly positioned to all three primary Hylegs, or life-giving points (Sun, Moon, and ascending sign) will, if unremediated, tend toward problems within that body zone. This rule bears out more strongly should a malefic planet tenant that sign.

How Planetary Dignity Contributes to Sign Syndromes

Traditionally, the Sun, Moon, and all major planets, each enjoy <u>two</u> specific sign *Dignities* termed: <u>***Rulership***</u>, and <u>***Exaltation***</u>. These two "Dignities" assist the nature of their specific planet, but also sometimes act to push a 'Zodiac Sign Syndrome' into extremity, being "too much of a good thing!"

Conversely, we have <u>two</u> *Debilities*. The Luminaries and planets *Fall* in signs *opposite* their *Exaltation*; and experience *Detriment* in signs *opposite* their home "Rulership". Debility acts to convert, weaken, or subvert the nature of the said Luminary or planet.

Dignity and Debility both contribute to a sign's overall syndrome portrait. E.g. Mars governs testosterone, whereas Venus governs estrogen. **Natives of each zodiac sign inherently possess the strengths and deficiencies of their native "dignity" profile, regardless of the actual sign position of the planets in the natal chart.** However, the planetary ruler of the ascendant and/or sun's sign will strongly influence the syndrome if found to be in dignity or debility. *Planetary Dignities and Debilities will be detailed for each sign in their respective chapters.*

Signs are Not the Elements!

There are four elements in classical astrology: Fire, Earth, Air, and Water. It is easy to think of a sign as <u>the</u> element, but this is not so. For example, although Leo is indeed a fiery sign, it is not <u>the</u> Fire element. Rather, the season of Leo is a vibrational *composite* of the fire element in its *fixed* state, plus solar forces (the Sun rules Leo), plus midsummer energy, and just as important, the weak, missing or deficient energies, as discussed above.

An Element represents one of the four levels of matter's density, plus a distinct type of real energy. The four elements are: *Fire, Earth, Air* and *Water*. Water <u>is</u> water, fire <u>is</u> fire, and so forth.

The Three Modes are: *Cardinal, Fixed,* and *Mutable*. These represent three *rates of matter in motion*: initiating, concentrating, and dispersing (modulating).

Four Humors vs. Four Elements

The *Four Humors* (body fluids) are <u>not</u> identical to the Four Elements, which came first. However, these two groups were regretfully conflated by Aristotle (to the point where excepting for specific uses, the four humors medically preempted the four elements). Neither are the signs identical to their assigned humors but partake of them in their make-up (as they do with their element). The Four Humors hold an esteemed place in medical astrology. However, to avoid confusion, this book will use the original Four Elements.

Cautions

The reader must beware of incorrect use of this material. Being born in a specific sign does not imply that someone will have all or any of the symptoms listed in their chapter. Nor is it requisite to be born in a specific sign to evince that sign's specific symptom set. The Moon or Ascendant sign perform just as well, as can the placements of Lunar Nodes, Mars, and Saturn!

Traditionally, one requires *three chart testimonies* to be confident in any interpretive direction. Nevertheless, one or more symptoms associated with a sign are curiously common, if not typical, to those born therein.

PHYSICALLY WEAKEST ANGLES in the NATAL CHART: (DEFICIENT VITAL FORCE ABSORPTION)

Angles: 6, 7, 8, 12
(sign angles moving anti clockwise, counting the Ascendant as "1".)

Angles 6, 8, 12 are the **"quincunxes"** that produce deficiencies. *Angle12 is also especially important For mental health.*

NOTE: Angle **2** is also a quincunx, but physically, can produce a nourishing and building-up influence. It is not reliably negative, (hence its rulership over "Money" and "Food", and the mouth.)

ANGLE 7
Angle **7** stands *opposite* to the Ascendant sign, and can sometimes indicate a "missing" species of Vital Force

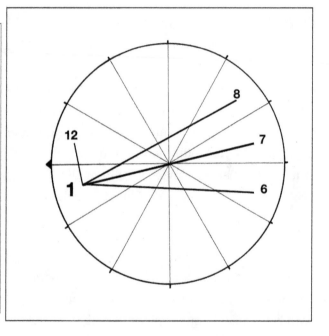

Chapter Three:
ARIES SYNDROME

Have a care therefore, where there is more sail than ballast.

- Old Quaker proverb

Dining with Aries

When considering Aries, think adrenaline! Shopping or dining with this type is rarely a chore. Their typically high metabolism demands fuel (now!) and grows impatiently ravenous when hungry. The Aries folks I know dash frequently into the supermarket to grab their favorite high fuel items, and leave. In restaurants, they order quickly, eat fast, and laugh, jest, or argue while eating. There is no sitting around discussing the tedious details of menus with this sign!

Fundamentals Refresher

Aries Syndrome is a set of collaborative symptoms, consistently appearing together, which are typical for natives of the sign Aries.

The symptoms associated with Aries Syndrome can be experienced by people with other sun signs when there is a particular emphasis in this sign. Zodiac sign syndromes can occur in seriatim, first one symptom, then another, weeks, months or years later. Few experience all symptoms. However, two or more of these symptoms are frequently observed clustered together at the same time.

An Aries native may have few if any of the symptoms associated with Aries Syndrome. Indeed, many Aries are specimens of perfect health. However, this symptom set often, but not always, evinces itself when a native's Sun, Moon, or Ascendant tenants Aries and displays certain astrological conditions which are discussed at length in this chapter.

This chapter describes the astrological conditions that may aggravate the syndrome. With this knowledge, practitioners can explore the underlying condition when symptoms consistent with the syndrome present themselves in a patient. Understanding the energetic cause is the first step in remediation.

THE SIGN ARIES

In Classical Western Astrology, with use of the Tropical Zodiac, an Aries is someone born from the Spring Equinox through the thirty days (or longitudinal degrees) immediately following it. Aries is not defined by constellations in the sky. Conversely, zero degrees Aries marks the beginning of the Tropical Zodiac and the seasonal wheel.

As with all other signs, we cannot think of Aries as an isolated single entity or a static constant. "Aries" is a gestalt of strengths and weaknesses based on its angular relationship to the other signs of the interconnected solar cycle. In turn, each of the twelve phases of this cycle is influenced by the unique planetary configurations at birth and throughout the life. Aries is a unique phase-state, with its interactions peculiar to the first stage of the twelve-fold cyclical process.

Element and Mode: Aries is of the element Fire. The advent of Aries initiates the spring season and, thus, is a member of the *cardinal quadruplicity* of signs.

Life Cycle Phase: In the seasonal cycle, life cycle, and all cycles, Aries is the beginning, the burst of energy accelerating outward. The sign of beginnings. In this way, Aries is the infant born, springing into life! As an infant appears headfirst, then gasps for air, Aries is the head of the year, and of the body, and governs many life-igniting processes.

Aries Superpowers: "I can do it"

Because we are explaining the syndrome itself for those who encounter its symptoms, we have paid less attention to positive traits. Therefore, it is useful to balance this emphasis with a short discussion of Aries' superpowers.

A typical Aries is naturally positive and self-reliant. Once dedicated to their own cause, there is little they cannot achieve. (However, taking the doctor's advice is another issue!) Preference for the sunny side of life is rarely a challenge, and few Aries natives are preoccupied with their past.

Fun loving Aries is typically quick to laugh. At a memorable dinner with two Aries born friends, we laughed all night!

Aries is noted for strong hearts, directed wills, surplus energy, and good muscular-skeletal constitutions and coordination, often being natural athletes. The innate Vital Force is superbly strong in this sign - readily displayed by a fast, if not excessive immune response! Aries heals speedily. Except for those who kill themselves through foolishness, Aries natives tend to be long lived.

Many Aries are excellent surgeons. Aries' courage and physicality are legend.

Physical Appearance

Exhaustive detail with illustrations is provided in this author's *The Astrological Body Types*.

ARIES BODY RULERSHIPS AND FUNCTIONS

As described in Chapter One, a body zone is a general box that overlays many organs, functions, vessels, and their sub-rulerships. Anything within this zone will feel the influence of Aries.

Aries, Body Zone 1

The Adrenal Type: On observation, it seems obvious that many of Aries' classic symptoms, listed later in the text, correlate with abundant adrenalin. The Aries-Libra axis, in concert with planet Mars, governs the adrenal gland.

Aries holds a general dominion over the eyes, sense of vision, cranium, skull, facial bones, forehead, upper jaw and teeth, motor nerves, and the upper brain lobes. The latter coexists with multitudinous sub rulerships. Sun, Moon, and Mercury also strongly govern the brain; and Taurus is influential to the brain stem.

The crown of the head, upper teeth, and all cranial nerves are heavily influenced by this sign and transits to it. Aries also governs the upper facial bones and the mandible (this last is co-ruled with Taurus). It is of interest that Aries natives frequently incline toward either very narrow or conversely extremely wide mandibles (jawbones). The pituitary and pineal glands, although given to other signs and planets, obviously must be co-influenced by transits to this sign. The quintessentially "martial" adrenal glands sit atop the kidneys in Aries' opposite sign Libra (Body Zone 7).

In response to alarm signals sent from the amygdala (in the brain), the hypothalamus (also in the brain), informs the adrenal glands (atop the kidneys) to release epinephrine (adrenalin). Blood is channeled away from the internal organs to the muscles; arteries tense, heartbeat accelerates, and pupils constrict, as the body readies to spring into fast action. For some Aries, this condition is to some extent a daily constant. One observes in Aries natives the instantaneous need to leave the house, office, desk, or luncheon, now! And walk! The physical type also reflects these processes.

Davidson offers that natives with Sun or Mars in Aries should avoid heat to the head. This is because heat is fast rising, and through the head in this sign. I second his opinion having more than once witnessed the devastating effect of radiation directed to the head of Aries types.

ARIES SYNDROME

As discussed in Chapter Two, a Zodiac Sign Syndrome is a cluster of symptoms associated with the body zones and functions of a zodiac sign and the signs positioned on the seasonal wheel opposite (180°) and quincunx (150°, 210°, 330°) the sign. Remediating and supporting these body zones and functions act to bring the body into balance, diminishing the syndrome. These symptoms may manifest when there is an emphasis in one or more of these signs. Planetary dignity plays an important role, and, in the case of Aries, harmonious signs may also influence the syndrome.

The Weaker Signs for the Aries Vital Force
Quincunx Signs

Virgo, Scorpio, and Pisces are quincunx Aries, as they are positioned 150°, 210° and 330° distant from this sign on the seasonal wheel. These signs represent the 6th, 8th, and 12th *averted* angles from the sign Aries (see the illustration for this chapter). This averted condition makes it difficult for Aries to absorb the cosmic rays that feed these signs. Thus, Aries natives may have trouble absorbing the vibrational and light "nutrients" of these signs. Likewise, these signs may have trouble absorbing the rays from Aries.

Virgo rules Body Zone 6 which includes the upper intestines, duodenum, liver, pancreas, immune system, sympathetic nerves, and spleen. Being prone to hyperinsulinism, we might suggest a connection between production of excess insulin at base. Both Aries and Virgos are prone to diabetes but hypothetically for different reasons. Aries' formidable adrenal response may be at fault. An excess of glucocorticoids released by the adrenal glands impairs glucose tolerance by causing, over time, insulin resistance. Secondly, the adrenal hormone epinephrine increases sugar in the blood, and another adrenal hormone cortisol frees up stored glucose, creating higher blood sugar levels.

We also postulate a high incidence of hypoglycemia, especially when Mars tenants this sign. The Aries Sun, as a rule, rapidly channels the Vital Force into the adrenal axis, muscles, and motor centers of the brain. Do they require more immediately available sugars than other sign types? Plausibly. This would explain the intense, sudden hunger experienced so often by natives of this sign, and equally sudden fatigue when this need is not hastily met.

We also have the vagus nerve originating in Aries and strongly influencing Body Zone 6, Virgo. Another interesting thought, both Virgo and Aries appear to have a hyperactive immune system response. Could insufficient intestinal (Virgo) and/or stomach mucus and/or general acidity allow less protection against ingested pathogens in the Aries type? The problem here is that the reaction is usually in the skin.

Scorpio rules Body Zone 8 which includes the sacrum, coccyx (with Sagittarius), colon, bladder, rectum, genitals, nose, sweat glands, and excretions. Excessive androgens are noted in Aries, possibly due to the Zone 1 hypothalamus and pituitary connections to the sex glands. Conversely, one notes deficient female hormones, virilization, balding, and excess or deficient sweat. Androgens are under Mars, ruler of both signs. Sense of smell, hormonal imbalance to the masculine, and libido extremes are often observed when natal planets are in both signs. Disturbances of taste, hearing or smell are sometimes noted.

Pisces rules Body Zone 12 and the mysterious 12th angle in relation to Aries. Thus, Aries syndrome involves fear of Pisces. For example, this can include terror of non-individuality, entropy, breakdown of self, unconsciousness, sleep, weakness, restriction, imprisonment, lack of self-propulsive powers, and receptivity. Many Aries types resist sleeping.

Opposite Sign, Libra

When the Sun is in Aries, the opposite sign, Libra, "sleeps." **Libra rules Body Zone 7**, which includes the kidneys, ovaries, adrenal axis, and balancing of salt and fluids. When there is a stressed planet in Libra, it appears to fuel the syndrome, as Libra is not able to balance the intense energies of Aries. Davidson cited kidney issues as often the hidden cause lurking behind an Aries headache.

Signs Aggravating Aries Syndrome - Squaring Signs

Cancer and Capricorn are the two signs positioned 90° from, or square to, Aries (see chapter illustration). These squares create friction, for good or ill. Aries can reflex with these signs, as well as its opposite sign, Libra.

Cancer rules Body Zone 4 which includes the lower lungs, thoracic duct, stomach, mucus membrane, moisture, breasts, elbow, armpit, pleura, and pericardium.

One so often notes chronic or spontaneous nausea and vomiting when Moon is in Aries. This may be due to overacidity and/or lack of mucoid protection of the stomach lining.

Capricorn rules Body Zone 10 which includes the knees, skin, and gallbladder (with Leo). One can get the hot, flaring rheumatic conditions with afflictions between Aries and Capricorn, relating to lack of moist protection of the joints and sinews.

Harmonious Signs

Signs that are trine or sextile Aries can also play a role in the expression of Aries syndrome!

The two fellow fire signs, **Leo and Sagittarius**, are at 120°angles (or trine) to Aries (see chapter illustration). Thus, they stimulate all Aries processes and can easily push them to extremes. The heart system in Leo is strong, if not excessive, as are the arterial and muscular systems governed by companion fire sign Sagittarius (with Jupiter and Mars). However, in a sign as strong as Aries, the fire element gone wild, can be deadly.

The two fellow Air signs **Gemini and Aquarius** are the two signs at 60° angles from Aries or sextile the sign on the seasonal wheel. Fire thrives on air. In the same way, these Air signs can ignite the fire of Aries, enhancing the natural energy of Aries natives.

How Planetary Dignity Contributes to Aries Syndrome
Strongest Planets

The traditional ruler of Aries is the hot, dry, fighting planet Mars. The Sun is exalted in Aries, and Jupiter is friendly here. The strong energetics of these planets when located in fiery Aries can lead to an excess of their color rays, exciting the brain, heart, and arterial system.

Mars governs Aries and rejoices in his home domain! He rules iron, red blood cells, available muscular energy, pizzaz, adrenal response, motor portions of the brain (with Aries), immune defense, and ready sexual virility. However, Mars' hot, dry ray can bring all manner of dehydration problems, inflammation, and acute episodes, including accidents. I've known few Aries who haven't left a trail of head accidents in their wake!

The Sun is exalted in Aries, adding terrific vital force and will-fulness to this sign. The heart is strong, though prone to excess "hot, dry" symptoms, such as palpitation and racing pulse. Vital force is supremely strong in this sign, as is immune resistance. Disease and accident recovery is fast!

Jupiter is a friend of Mars and the Sun. He co-governs with his buddy Sol the fiery triplicity of which Aries is a member. Jupiter governs the arterial system (with Sagittarius). Arterial strength is in Aries, but also arterial pressure which in excess can lead to problems.

Weakest Planets

Saturn and **Venus** are weaker in this sign. Thus, the native may require a boost in the violet and indigo color rays of these planets.

Venus, the pain reliever of the pantheon, is in her *detriment* in Aries because she rules the opposite sign, Libra. Passion is fast, excited visually, and if unbalanced, trends towards impulsive romantic choices. A deficiency of Venus ruled parts (estrogen, veins, kidneys, copper, mucus, Vitamin E) may contribute to Aries syndrome. One often sees the iron-strong but copper-deficient Aries type. Watch for a bright, focused and fiery spark to Aries eyes! In Aries, the arterial system dominates the venous. The Aries type may lack mucoid protection and moisture.

Saturn falls in Aries and is notably weaker unless very well placed in the natal chart. Saturn's strength and self-reliance are actually very high in Aries! Nevertheless, Saturn rules boundaries, not a quality that the spontaneous Aries always appreciates. Saturn's wisdom and passion regulating qualities are reduced in this birth season. One must learn anew from experience, crashing around like an unguided toy truck.

Note that Saturn, the "law of God" is exalted in the sign of the scales, Libra, opposite on the seasonal wheel to Aries. Conversely, Saturn's fall in Aries symbolizes the person who is either a law unto themselves or must learn by their mistakes. The weakness of Saturn in Aries seems to apply more to behavior and self-control regulation than to bone integrity, which is ruled by Saturn. One rarely sees an Aries struggling with osteoporosis. Davidson observes the tendency of Aries, and Saturn in Aries or Libra to have kidney issues, kidney-related headaches, and gravel.

Planetary and House Positions that Enhance Aries Syndrome

(1) **Sun, Moon, or Ascendant sign in Aries**

(2) A weakness in a body zone governed by the signs opposite or quincunx Aries on the seasonal wheel, as discussed above under *The Weaker Signs for the Aries Vital Force.*

(3) The Aries symptom cluster is accentuated when one or more of the Sun, Moon, Ascendant, Ascendant Ruler, Saturn, and the South or North Node is in Aries in the native's birth chart. This is compounded by the testimonies below:

- Aries inhabits the 1st, 6th, 8th, or 12th house in the native's birth chart. (See discussion of Weak Houses in Chapter Two).
- Saturn or Jupiter square an Aries Sun or Moon.

- Jupiter or Mars is in Aries (or another fire sign), especially in the 1st, 6th, 7th, 8th, or 12th houses. This is even stronger when the Sun, Moon, Ascendant, or Ascendant Ruler is likewise in another fire sign.
- South or North Node rising in Aries, or conjunct an Aries Sun, Mars, or Moon.
- Day birth, with Mars above the horizon in a fire sign.
- Venus in Virgo, Scorpio or Aries

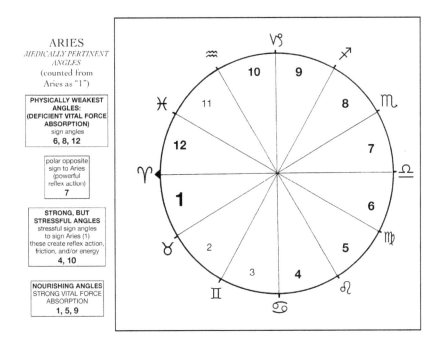

ARIES
MEDICALLY PERTINENT ANGLES
(counted from Aries as "1")

PHYSICALLY WEAKEST ANGLES:
(DEFICIENT VITAL FORCE ABSORPTION)
sign angles
6, 8, 12

polar opposite sign to Aries
(powerful reflex action)
7

STRONG, BUT STRESSFUL ANGLES
stressful sign angles to sign Aries (1)
these create reflex action, friction, and/or energy
4, 10

NOURISHING ANGLES
STRONG VITAL FORCE ABSORPTION
1, 5, 9

SYMPTOMS OF ARIES SYNDROME

The following is a list of symptoms and traits associated with Aries Syndrome. Aries Syndrome is a set of collaborative symptoms, consistently appearing together, which are typical for natives of this sign. These symptoms can occur in seriatim, first one symptom, then weeks, months or years later, another. However, two or more of these symptoms are frequently observed clustered together at the same time. These do not pertain to "Aries people" per se, but those born with prominences in this sign that <u>actually do suffer the syndrome</u>. These symptoms are not listed in any order, but simply as a list of collected observations common to Aries.

- hyperthyroid
- dehydrated brain
- dehydrated tissues, organs, joints
- deficiency of protective mucus
- inflammation of the brain or eyes
- sore or itchy dry eyes
- conjunctivitis or other eye infections
- flushed face (in fair skinned individuals)
- itchy skin
- dry skin conditions: dandruff, cradle cap, eczema, psoriasis, scabies
- eruptive skin diseases and complaints (measles, erysipelas, shingles)
- prone to sudden fevers (fast accelerating, high)
- hard, dry, sinewy muscles
- hyperactive (physically)
- possibly manic or bi-polar
- hyperinsulinism/hypo or hyperglycemia (irritable, always hungry, sudden hunger) Blood sugar issues, diabetic leanings
- anger management issues, impatience
- accident prone, especially to head

- head injuries, concussion
- ADHD
- sudden strident or aggressive motions
- sudden decisions
- abrupt need for muscular exercise "now"!
- overactive adrenal response, fast reactions (yet fearless)
- prone to high-risk behavior, adrenaline addiction
- risk-taking, athletic
- impulse control issues
- requires aerobic action to feel good
- rises early, eager to plunge in the lake or go running
- loves morning exercise (running, fast walking, swimming, et al)
- extreme dislike for being "trapped inside" in good weather
- excessive testosterone
- excess androgens (in all genders) and/or deficient female hormones
- flash tempers over seemingly trivial matters to others (but not to them)
- acidic stomach and PH
- acidic digestion, or heat in the intestine, liver, gall
- chronic nausea (often seen with Moon in Aries)
- vomiting, sudden or projectile
- dry, unprotected stomach lining
- premature ejaculation
- All genders are sexually assertive
- headache (usually sharp, sudden neuralgic pains in head/eyes/teeth/ears)
- dental issues
- tinnitus
- dizziness
- itchy, dry ear canals
- hearing issues
- skull or facial bone anomalies (rare)
- fast or racing pulse
- heart palpitations
- attraction to alcohol
- enjoys hot sun and morning hours

- loud attention-attracting clothes, shoes, shirts, hats, hairstyles
- preference for red or pink clothing
- attracted to stimulants and "uppers", like caffeine
- some Aries types enjoy laughing and/or loud and aggressive, high rhythmic music
- enjoyment of fast motion through space (for example, race cars, motorbikes, and skiing)
- claustrophobia
- weak or dehydrated kidneys
- aversion to water (prefers coffee, carbonated beverages, whisky, etc.); or fails to drink
- bilious, "choleric"
- hair loss or balding, especially in the front (all genders)
- hot, yet loses heat quickly
- prone to hypothermia through rapid loss of heat through shivering, lack of subcutaneous fat or directly through the head
- head gets very cold in winter, but too hot in summer (hence the love of various hats)
- prefers outdoors
- hyperactive immune response or the reverse
- acne
- stroke prone (not in all cases)
- brain tumors (rare)
- brain related palsies, tremors, fits
- epilepsy
- hypertension
- neuritis, typically in head, teeth, ears or eyes
- insomnia
- glaucoma (with strong Taurus contribution)
- hyper-responsive adrenals
- adrenal exhaustion
- grating or shrill voice (loud)
- head or facial marks or scars
- deafness or ear complaints
- hearing damage from loud music

- blood shot eyes, burst vessels in eyes; eye stroke (rare)
- facial birth marks
- outward turning feet, strident walk
- protruding ears (sometimes)
- prone to anaphylaxis

REMEDIATION TIPS

Please note that these remedial tips are for interest only. The author is not suggesting that any person use these without the evaluation and consent of their personal healthcare practitioner.

Caution on Treating Aries Types. For the Aries type, it is extremely important to know how to modulate the fast, upward, rising of dry heat from the interior towards the surface and the head and brain. *Is the sympathetic or antipathetic cure best, or a combination?* In other words, should we work with this fast rising, hot energy or combat it? Specifically in the case of Aries and Mars, the absolute suppression of this irrepressible Martian force could drive it inward, potentially ravaging the patient. Thus, the purely antipathetic treatments so useful for other signs and planets is not the approach for Aries-Mars people and their classic problems. Yet, allowing a fire to run through in a case of low vital reserves or dehydration is equally deadly. The vital force can also burn off! So, what to do?

Traditionally, to treat hot, dry conditions with cold, where Mars is deduced as causative is to place a sufferer in grave danger (Blagrave). The correct approach was to assist Mars, allowing "fire to chase out fire" while simultaneously not allowing the fire to kill the patient! This tricky business requires great skill to combine specific heating and cooling remedies together. Joseph Blagrave gave very specific instructions on how to handle this Martian conundrum. This approach is hypothetically useful for working with Aries type patients expressing high fevers, rampant inflammations, or hot, eruptive ailments.

What to Strengthen? With Aries, it is not so much a matter of strengthening as *balancing*. Aries is red, hot and dry - so think green, cool and moist. The Vital Force is very strong but can hastily burn off or out! As the old Quaker proverb suggests: *"Have a care therefore, where there is more sail than ballast"*. However, never fail to support Mars as well. This is the one planet that one must never entirely suppress!

Support Brain and Eye Hydration. Johann Grander's magnetized water is worthy of investigation. The brain requires an adequate supply of appropriate cold pressed oils, such as the traditional favorites sesame, olive, and walnut oils. Cooling oils, such as avocado and coconut oil, may also work well. Also, protect the eyes, as they are sensitive to sun and glare.

Reduce Acid. The Aries type runs acidic. Herbs that alkalize the body and assist kidney function are worthy of consideration, such as alkaline fruits and vegetables, Chickweed (Stellaria), cucumber water, carrot juice, and Cleavers (Gallium).

Sweeten and Cool the Stomach. Marshmallow and Peach Leaf are two herbs that seem specific to *Aries Moon nausea*.

Support the Adrenals. Matthew Wood suggests Oat Straw and Borage Leaf, combined, for exhaustion of the adrenal cortex, and cases of wholesale exhaustion (confirmed in one recent case). Licorice is a renowned adrenal tonic.

Antidote or Reduce the Excessive Yellow and Red Cosmic Rays of Mars and the Red Ray of Sol. This can be done by a skilled and adjudicated selection of gems for use in water, tincture, or jewelry. (Discussed in depth in the author's *Astrology and Your Vital Force*).

Accident Protection. Turquoise and the more affordable Malachite are famous gems for protecting the body from accidents.

Hormonal Balance. Reduce excessive androgens or testosterone in the blood. Spearmint is one herb demonstrated to assist in clearing excessive testosterone from the blood stream.

Cool the Spinal Sheath and Cord. What does this mean? Astrologically, the planetary heat of Mars can occur anywhere. Aries types seem uniquely prone to a sudden rising of astral heat in the spinal cord, sheaths, and brain. One must be on the alert for strong aspects from Mars to an Aries Sun, Moon, or Ascendant. In fact, we can't underestimate Mars' transits to any planet in this sign.

The Venusian metal copper, the Green and Blue Cosmic Rays and their gems, or blue and green light, may be combined with the correct use of cooling oils and water to prevent this dangerous occurrence.

Work with the kidneys - the balancing organ zone for Aries, and opposite sign Libra.

Eruptive Medicine. The sick Aries type is apt to experience red, irritating skin eruptions. It is beyond the scope of this book to consider all herbs for these maladies because each malady is different. However, we could surmise the involvement of a hot dry mucus membrane throughout, biliousness, and hot, dry and overloaded kidneys resulting in acidic blood. For Aries natives, Mars hurls toxins suddenly upward, and outward, mostly toward the surface and face!

Curiously, Renaissance practitioners had success in smallpox infection with the "red cure," used, in fact, on Queen Elizabeth I. All windows were draped in red cloth, and the sick swathed in red blankets. Red drinks were provided, such as pomegranate. This cure was believed to prevent death and disfigurement. Niels Finsen (1769) discovered that red light sped the healing of smallpox lesions, whereas ultraviolet aggravated them. The old "red cure" provided a shielding effect on the ultraviolet rays that empower the variola virus responsible for smallpox!

Traditionally, all three of the "choleric" fire signs benefited by cooling bitters and herbs that cooled the liver and cleared the gall-bladder.

See also Chapter 15, *The Twelve Zodiac Sign Syndromes and their Relevant Herbs.*

Chapter Four:

TAURUS SYNDROME

So, the key to disease is the simple diagram IN-MIX-OUTGO...
So, you've got the in-mix-out, and when you think of that, you've got
a simplification of the whole business of disease, or most of it other than
that of a psychological nature...

- Dr. William Davidson,
Davidson's Medical Lectures

Oral Taurus

In middle school, I offered Michael, my first known Taurus-born friend, a taste of my mini-ice cream cone. He immediately put the entire cone in his mouth and grinned. We would spend happy hours together raiding his mother's stash of epicurean delights. Although no etymological connection exists, the root word "Taur" appears in the word "restaurant". It's still a great way to remember the basics of this sign that governs eating!

All my many Taurus friends do indeed enjoy eating well, except that one rare exception who prefers drinking instead! Governing the mouth, this sign is the zodiac's ultimate gourmand and food acquisitive, or as the psychologists put it, "oral." Spouses of an overweight Taurus Sun or Moon native will find it far easier to add a cholesterol clearing clove of garlic than to remove or hide their favorite cheese!

The entire physical problem of Taurus (and, in essence, its solution) is condensed in the above quotes from Dr. Davidson! As we shall see in this chapter, this sign is the strongest of all signs for nutrient intake, retention, and assimilation, yet weak at the other end - the excretion process through the bladder and colon. Food "In" versus waste "Out". The whole problem of Taurus' health rests upon this principle, and its sanative balance.

Fundamentals Refresher

Taurus Syndrome is a set of collaborative symptoms, consistently appearing together, which are typical for natives of the sign Taurus. The symptoms associated with Taurus Syndrome can be experienced by people with other sun signs when there is a particular emphasis in this sign. Zodiac sign syndromes can occur in seriatim, first one symptom, then weeks, months or years later, another. Few experience all symptoms. However, two or more of these symptoms are frequently observed clustered together at the same time.

A Taurus native may have few if any of the symptoms associated with Taurus Syndrome. Indeed, many Taurus natives are specimens of perfect health. However, this symptom set often, but not always, evinces itself when a native's Taurus Sun, Moon, or Ascendant displays certain astrological conditions which are discussed at length in this chapter.

This chapter describes the astrological conditions that may aggravate the syndrome, and their postulated underlying cause. With this knowledge, practitioners can explore the underlying condition when symptoms consistent with the syndrome present themselves in a patient. Understanding the energetic cause is the first step in remediation.

THE SIGN TAURUS

In Classical Western Astrology, with use of the Tropical Zodiac, "a Taurus" is someone born between thirty to fifty-nine days (or longitudinal degrees) following the spring equinox. In the Tropical Zodiac, the zodiacal signs are not dependent on constellations in the sky.

As with all other signs, we cannot think of Taurus as an isolated single entity or a static constant. "Taurus" is a gestalt of strengths and weaknesses based on its angular relationship to the other signs of the interconnected solar cycle. In turn, each of the twelve phases of this cycle is influenced by the unique planetary configurations at birth and throughout the life. Taurus is a unique phase-state, with its interactions peculiar to the second stage of the twelve-fold cyclical process.

Element and Mode: Taurus is of the element Earth. It is in the center of the season of spring and, thus, one of the fixed group of signs.

Life Cycle Phase: In the life cycle, while Aries is the infant being born and springing into this world, Taurus is the infant eating, gathering mass, and growing stronger. At Taurus, the infant nurses. Note how the motherly Luna stands exalted in this sign!

Taurus Superpowers: The Power of the Tortoise

Excellent intake and storage of prana combines with slow expenditure of both calories and the Vital Force. Much like a battery, Taurus natives seem able to attract and store Earth magnetism and life force. (However, the same quality of hoarding Vital Force creates an equal tendency toward hoarding toxins!)

Taurus possesses the greatest reserve of magnetism of all the signs, providing an exceptionally long life for many of its natives. In two separate longevity studies (that, regretfully, I cannot cite), Taurus was the number one sign for octogenarians.

Taurus unflappability in the face of danger is legendary, as this sign would rather preserve calories than to fly into needless action. Easy going and slow to anger, they are notably slow to excite, provoke, or stress out, thus saving calories. They just don't sweat the small stuff. My intrepid Taurus Academy Director can sort difficult, tedious work for twelve consecutive hours and yet remain pleasant and calm - even singing! That being said, Taurus natives are infamous for the "big blast" once consistently provoked.

Endurance and reserve stamina are epic in this sign. Plenty of Taurus folks are perfect athletes. This sign mends wounds fast and strong, readily building bone and muscle. In the Western Hemisphere, mid-spring is the perfect and most natural time to be born, offering abundant food and magnetism! Habits are also built to last, and incredibly hard for natives of this sign to break or change. It is wise to guide a Taurean child into good habits at onset! In particular, the Taurus birth Moon is especially inclined towards rich deserts and may require healthy substitutes. Taurus is a supremely healthy sign if the native monitors their intake and supports their outflow!

Physical Appearance

Exhaustive detail with illustrations is provided in this author's *The Astrological Body Types*.

TAURUS BODY RULERSHIPS AND FUNCTIONS

As described in Chapter One, a body zone is a general box that overlays many organs, functions, vessels and their sub-rulerships. These sub-rulerships are especially common in the head region. Yet, anything within Body Zone 2 will feel the influence of Taurus. For example, Aquarius and Venus have a general dominion over veins. However, the jugular vein in the neck still receives a large influence from its zone landlord, Taurus!

Taurus, Body Zone 2

Taurus will typically be seen in natal charts, or by current transit, when one observes accidents or symptoms in this zone.

Generally, Taurus governs the lower head and base of brain; ears (with Mars and Saturn); hearing (with Mercury), lower jaw, chin; lower teeth (with Saturn), salivary glands, gullet, pharynx, vocal cords; tongue (with Scorpio, Venus, Mercury and Mars), upper esophagus, swallowing reflex, epiglottis, lower palate, mouth; gums (with Cancer), neck, cervical vertebrae, brain stem, jugular veins and carotid arteries. It is important to note that the preceding sign Aries maintains a strong co-influence over the entire head. The atlas and axis bones appear co-ruled between the two signs.

Taurus holds a considerable influence over the thyroid, (with Uranus, Venus, Mercury), parathyroid (with Saturn?), and thymus gland (with Venus - Edgar Cayce).

TAURUS SYNDROME

As discussed in Chapter Two, a Zodiac Sign Syndrome is a cluster of symptoms associated with the body zones and functions of a zodiac sign and the signs positioned on the seasonal wheel opposite (180°) and quincunx (150°, 210°, 330°) the sign. Remediating and supporting these body zones and functions act to bring the body into balance, diminishing the syndrome. These symptoms may manifest when there is an emphasis in one or more of these signs. Planetary dignity plays an important role.

The Weaker Signs for the Taurus Vital Force

Quincunx signs

The signs Libra, Sagittarius, and Aries are positioned 150°, 210° and 330° distant from Taurus on the seasonal wheel. These signs represent the 6th, 8th, and 12th *averted* angles from the sign Taurus (see the illustration for this chapter). This condition makes it difficult for Taurus to absorb the cosmic rays that feed these signs. Thus, Taurus natives may have trouble absorbing the vibrational and light "nutrients" of these signs. Likewise, these signs may have trouble absorbing the rays from Taurus.

Libra rules Body Zone 7 which includes the kidneys, ovaries, lumbar spine, acid-alkaline balances, salt-water balances, and the adrenal axis (with Aries, Mars). Tonsilitis (Taurus) has been linked to kidney complaints (Libra). This is an example of the remote causation of which quincunxes disclose.

Sagittarius rules Body Zone 9 which includes the hips, femurs, thighs, arterial system, expiration of breath, Central Nervous System (CNS), lower spinal cord, coccyx (with Scorpio), sciatic nerve, and strongly influences voluntary muscular movement, ligaments, and muscles of back and legs.

Aries rules Body Zone 1 which includes the head, skull, brain, motor nerves, adrenal firing, and upper jaw and teeth. Aries is also the mysterious 12th angle to Taurus. Thus, Taurus syndrome involves "fear of Aries," for example, discomfort with fast reactions, releasing waste, energy expense, temper, extravagance, and letting go of food, money, calories, or toxins!

Opposite Sign, Scorpio

When the Sun is in Taurus, the opposite sign, Scorpio, "sleeps." Scorpio rules Body Zone 8, which includes the colon-anus, removal of toxins from the body, nose, bladder, genitals, and diaphoresis (sweating). When there is a deficiency in Scorpio, it appears to fuel

Taurus syndrome. Sometimes Taurus evinces chronic colon issues, especially if natal Saturn or the Lunar Nodes are in Taurus or Scorpio.

Signs Aggravating Taurus Syndrome - Squaring Signs

Leo and Aquarius are the two signs squaring (positioned 90° from) Taurus (see chapter illustration). The effect of a square is to create friction, good or bad. Taurus can reflex with these signs, as well as its opposite sign Scorpio.

Leo rules Body Zone 5 which includes the thoracic spine, heart, aorta, spinal sheaths, and strongly influences the entire spine, gallbladder, wrists and forearms (with Gemini). Taurus's rich eating habits can lead to cardiac issues via hardened or clogged arteries. Dental bacteria can lead to heart (Leo) complaints via infected teeth (Taurus).

Aquarius rules Body Zone 11 which includes the ankles, shins, "electrical body," veins and venous circulation, oxygenation of blood, quality of blood cells, and lower spinal nerves (with Sagittarius). Venous stagnation (Aquarius) is common to Taurus and may contribute to their tendency towards boils and other toxic accumulations and edema.

How Planetary Dignity Contributes to Taurus Syndrome
Strongest Planets

The traditional ruler of Taurus is the temperature normalizing, relaxing, and pain allaying planet **Venus**. The **Moon** is exalted in Taurus.

Venus gives an abundance of magnetism, a sweet tooth and a gourmand's appetite. All this is very nice, although in excess, contributes a great deal to Taurus Syndrome. Venus is mucus building. One often notes mucoid obstructions in the ear, nose, and throat.

The Moon's exaltation role in Taurus assists absorption, contributing to swellings, obesity, and food (or other oral) addictions. While in Taurus, she also pulls energy to the ear, nose, throat, and vocal cords. Fluidic pressure at the base of the skull is typical, often producing strong headaches. Similar to Venus, the Moon is also mucus building, though more inclined to water retention. We also observe a strong tendency for water bloat, especially near menses.

We now see how both retentive, fluidic planets are potentized in this sign. Together they produce a Taurean tendency toward bloat, soft tumors, polyps, and fluidic or mucoid congestion in the ear-nose-throat area, female organs, breasts, and colon.

Deficient Planet

Mars rules Scorpio, the opposite sign to Taurus, and therefore this fiery planet is in detriment in Taurus. Thus, his toxin excreting powers are potentially slowed and suffocated. This by no means weakens Mars, rather it alters him. Rather than throwing energy upward and outward, as he does in home sign Aries, he hoards it in mighty Taurus. Instead of pushing toxins out of the body, as he does in his other domicile Scorpio, he turns retentive!

On the plus side, this Mars "reverse" produces slow energy burn, high stamina, and easy muscle and bone building. Yet it amasses toxins. Therefore, Mars' detriment in Taurus plays an essential role in producing many aspects of Taurus Syndrome.

Planetary and House Positions that Enhance Taurus Syndrome

(1) **Sun, Moon, or Ascendant sign in Taurus**

(2) A weakness in a body zone governed by the signs opposite or quincunx Taurus on the seasonal wheel, as discussed above under *The Weaker Signs for the Taurus Vital Force.*

(3) The Taurus symptom cluster is accentuated when one or more of the Moon, Sun, Ascendant, Ascendant Ruler, Saturn, and the South or North Node is in Taurus in the native's birth chart. This is compounded by the testimonies below:

- Taurus inhabits the 1st, 6th, 8th, or 12th house in the native's birth chart (see discussion of Weak Houses in Chapter Two).
- Saturn or Jupiter square a Taurus Sun or Moon.
- Venus, Jupiter, Saturn, or Mars in Taurus (or in an earth or water sign), especially in the 1st, 6th, 7th, 8th or 12th house, and especially with the Sun, Moon or Ascendant likewise in Taurus (or another earth sign).
- South or North Node rising in Taurus, or conjunct a Taurus Sun, Mars, or Moon.
- Sun, Moon, Ascendant Ruler, South Node, North Node, Jupiter, Venus, Mars, or Saturn, in the sign Taurus, in the 6th, 8th or 12th.
- Night birth, with Moon or Venus above the horizon in an earth or water signs.
- Natal Saturn in an earth or water sign, compounded by a night birth, and/or the natal placement of Saturn below the horizon.
- Earth and water sign emphasis

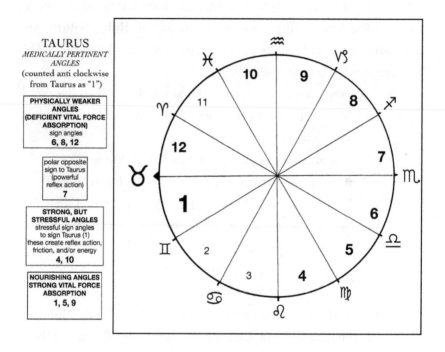

TAURUS
MEDICALLY PERTINENT ANGLES
(counted anti clockwise from Taurus as "1")

PHYSICALLY WEAKER ANGLES
(DEFICIENT VITAL FORCE ABSORPTION)
sign angles
6, 8, 12

polar opposite sign to Taurus (powerful reflex action)
7

STRONG, BUT STRESSFUL ANGLES
stressful sign angles to sign Taurus (1) these create reflex action, friction, and/or energy
4, 10

NOURISHING ANGLES
STRONG VITAL FORCE ABSORPTION
1, 5, 9

SYMPTOMS OF TAURUS SYNDROME

The following is a list of symptoms and traits associated with Taurus Syndrome. Taurus Syndrome is a set of collaborative symptoms, consistently appearing together, which are typical for natives of this sign. These symptoms can occur in seriatim, first one symptom, then weeks, months or years later, another. However, two or more of these symptoms are frequently observed clustered together at the same time.

Although commonly observed to be true, these symptoms do not necessarily pertain to "Taurus people" per se, but to those born with prominences in this sign that actually do suffer the syndrome. These symptoms are not listed in any order, but simply as a list of collected observations common to Taurus.

- hypothyroid
- sore throat
- ear, nose, throat congestion (usually thick, wet mucus)
- ear-nose-throat infections
- edema
- chronic infections of ear, nose, throat, vagina, bladder, urinary tract
- problems with swallowing reflex, choking, or throat-esophageal obstructions.
- swellings (typical to mouth, throat, tongue, but anywhere in body.
- excess mucus (more typical to ear-nose-throat, but anywhere in body)
- boils, carbuncles
- sepsis tendency
- slow metabolism
- auto-toxicity
- appendicitis
- tonsillitis
- chronic obesity
- affectless, dull expression (but friendly!)
- laconic (but enjoys socializing)
- excessive craving for fatty, meaty, fried and sweet foods
- tumors
- hearing complaints and deafness
- tongue issues
- tongue, mouth, and esophageal cancers (rare)
- soft palate swelling
- vocal cord anomalies or polyps
- full, magnetic, mellifluous, sonorous voices
- snoring, obstructive sleep apnea
- oral fixations, such as gum, cigars, and beer
- auto-sexual fixations
- excessive beer drinking
- lethargic, slow motion, yet hard workers!
- fixed habits, difficult to break
- chronic headache (dull pressure, anywhere in head but more commonly at base or temporal area, or nasal and ear related).

- headache related to pressure or subluxation of cervical vertebrae
- chronic, severe migraines
- "constipated" brain
- sluggish CNS
- dental issues (more common to lower teeth, but all included)
- fatty gullet growth
- goiter
- TMJ
- bruxism
- tinnitus
- vertigo
- head injuries, concussion
- gaseous fermentation
- acne
- lower brain tumors (rare)
- Glaucoma (with strong Aries contribution)
- neck injury or issues, stiff necked
- stiff trapezius
- weakness in hips
- sluggish kidneys
- constipation
- endometriosis
- candida
- delayed parturition
- breast or uterine tumors
- menstrual or uterine congestion, water retention
- nuchal cord (umbilical cord wrapped around neck of baby)
- colitis, Crohn's disease, colon polyps
- prostate swelling
- urine retention
- arthritis, rheumatism, gout
- chronic congestive, sclerotic, or fatty conditions of heart, colon, or liver due to gradual accumulations of toxins or poor intake habits
- scoliosis or spinal subluxations (reflex to Leo)
- high blood pressure (late in life)
- atherosclerosis and/or clogged jugular veins
- colon issues or stasis
- ear injury (cauliflower ear, deafness, et al)
- fatty deposits in neck vessels

REMEDIATION TIPS

Please note that these remedial tips are for interest only. The author is not suggesting that any person use these without the evaluation and consent of their personal healthcare practitioner.

The quotes from Davidson at the beginning of this chapter succinctly describe the physical problem of Taurus as well as its solution. Taurus is the strongest sign at intake and assimilation, yet weak on excretion processes. *Input-Output management is truly the Golden Key to Taurus health.* What exactly is entering the mouth, in what chemical combination, when (time of day), and how much? And what is exiting at the other end?

This sign excels at input and slows at output! Eating that nightly bowl of ice cream with chocolate syrup at bedtime is one typical example of what might gum up the health of a Taurus. This is especially true if exercise is wanting, sweating is poor, congested ear-nose-throat or constipation is noted. Watch for long term habits and/or addictions. For Taurus natives, the chemical combination of foods may be as, or even more, important than the food items themselves!

What to strengthen? In Taurus Syndrome, the colon, kidneys, uterus, skin, lymphatic system (inclusive of the brain's lymphatic system - recently cited as the "glymphatic system"), and blood can all use assistance with their toxin removal functions. Taurus holds on!

Additional remedies and herbal suggestions for Taurus are cited in Chapter 15, *The Twelve Zodiac Sign Syndromes and their Relevant Herbs.*

Chapter Five:

GEMINI SYNDROME

A man's mind may be likened to a garden, which may be intelligently cultivated or allowed to run wild; but whether cultivated or neglected, it must, and will, bring forth.

- James Allen from *As a Man Thinketh*

Where's Johnny?

Gemini types are rarely easy to find! They unexpectedly drop by with their latest book, toy, or device, chattering constantly, and then, waxing bored, abruptly vanish off to their next source of mental entertainment. The most frequently asked question about one Gemini friend is, *"Where's Johnny?"* Not all my Gemini friends behave this way, though far more do than don't!

How might these behaviors reflect the third stage of the cyclic pendulum's swing? We will soon see. This is the stage of branching and governs the peripheral nerves and communication. The mind, hand gestures, and speech develop during this stage of the yearly cycle.

Fundamentals Refresher

Gemini Syndrome is a set of collaborative symptoms, consistently appearing together, which are typical for natives of the sign Gemini. The symptoms associated with Gemini Syndrome can be experienced by people with other sun signs when there is a particular emphasis in this sign. Zodiac sign syndromes can occur in seriatim, first one symptom, then another, weeks, months or years later. Few experience all symptoms. However, two or more of these symptoms are frequently observed clustered together at the same time.

A Gemini native may have few if any of the symptoms associated with Gemini Syndrome. Indeed, many Geminis are specimens of perfect health. However, this symptom set often, but not always, evinces itself when a native's Sun, Moon, or Ascendant tenants Gemini and displays certain astrological conditions which are discussed at length in this chapter.

This chapter describes the astrological conditions that may aggravate the syndrome. With this knowledge, practitioners can explore the underlying condition when symptoms consistent with the syndrome present themselves in a patient. Understanding the energetic cause is the first step in remediation.

THE SIGN GEMINI

In Classical Western Astrology, with use of the Tropical Zodiac, "a Gemini" is someone born between 60 to 89 longitudinal degrees (or days) following the spring equinox.

As with all other signs, we cannot think of Gemini as an isolated single entity or a static constant. "Gemini" is a gestalt of strengths and weaknesses based on its angular relationship to the other signs of the interconnected solar cycle. In turn, each of the twelve phases of this cycle is influenced by the unique planetary configurations at birth and throughout the life. Gemini is a unique phase-state, with its interactions peculiar to the third stage of the twelve-fold cyclical process.

Element and Mode: Gemini is of the element Air. This is a late spring sign positioned at the gradual change from spring to summer and, hence, our first member of the mutable quadruplicity of signs.

Life Cycle Phase: The sign Gemini represents the stage on the human life cycle where the infant born (Aries), has fed (Taurus), and now becomes the toddler, wandering from drawer to drawer, curiously pulling everything out, and then, on to the next!

More than any other sign, Gemini has more to do with the development of the individual mind, speech, hand gesture, coordination of the two halves of the brain, and language. Thus, James Allen's advice, quoted above, is most apt.

Gemini Superpowers

Hummingbird Power: Flexibility and speed, like a hummingbird.

Random Flow: Geminian gifts include childlike playfulness and just not taking life's conundrums too seriously. This gift is bestowed upon Gemini natives by their ruling planet Mercury, Messenger of the Gods, depicted with wings on his heels and cap. Negatively of course, this same trait disposes to irresponsibility and late maturation. If any sign qualifies as puer aeternus, it's Gemini!

Gemini is perhaps the most "be here now" of all signs, rarely allowing social mores, mom, religion, or fear of the future to dictate their day. Their fun-loving nature and curiosity sustain them through health challenges that might weigh down stronger signs. From Gemini's point of view, death and disease are just another test of wits! When Death lurks at the door, the classic Gemini confounds him with riddles, changes identity, or just keeps roller skating. Their natural iconoclastic and apostate tendencies allow for a freedom of experiment and lifestyle that can work either for or against them, medically speaking. This is the sign of improvisation!

Shape and Habit Shifting: Gemini also has a curious ability to lose a great deal of weight in a short period of time (the reverse is also true). One might call this shape shifting. I've witnessed Geminis effortlessly and instantly abandon what for most people are binding habits. One fine day, a Gemini lady I know gave up her daily alcohol and ice cream routine and never looked back. They just don't get stuck! Many Gemini natives enjoy slipping into different personalities by changing hair styles, cities, jobs, outfits, opinions, and social scenes. These are just a few examples of their shape shifting powers! Only one sign can get the best of a Scorpio - and that's Gemini!

Similar to shape shifting, Gemini natives have the knack for communication shifting, the ability to adjust speech, conduct, or accent to fit the occasion.

Gemini types so often evince a buoyant sense of fun and humor, applying this to all things (much to the chagrin of a challenged spouse). This sign loves games, puzzles, and trying on new identities.

The Healthy Gemini: Gemini is a naturally healthy sign whose natives more typically ruin their own health through poor sleeping and eating habits combined with compulsive device exposure! They can often smoke cigarettes or pot and snack on anything handy "to do something with my hands." I've never understood why they don't just take up drumming, though, in fact, many do! Gemini was one of the three most statistically significant signs in my study of great jazz drummers.

Communication: Gemini and its ruler Mercury govern personal or brief communications inclusive of words, languages, messaging, and hand signaling. Perhaps this is why Gemini natives are famous for talking, writing, gesturing, mimicry and creating word puns.

The Gemini mind delights with new incoming information. The nerves are quick and the bodily coordination excellent, unless an affliction reverses that. Synapses and fingers are exceptionally fast, perfect for pinball wizards or the playing of musical instruments. And I have yet to meet a Gemini who didn't dream of becoming a writer or was one.

Gemini men are famously great talkers and game for conversation. As a sign, Gemini contributes to various spectrums... ADHD, Autism, etc. This potential neural hyper-conductivity makes these natives vulnerable to the electromagnetic field exposure of computers, phones, and the like. These devices may speed up the neurological system, because as primates, we are imitational creatures. Our nervous systems and speech centers attempt to imitate the speed of these devices. If you do not believe me, compare youth speech patterns and speed from 1950-80 with circa 2023.

It is interesting to note that the endothelial cells lining the traditionally Gemini ruled capillaries have been found to be signalers involved in constant communication with the cells of the vessels. *Gemini rules all manner of communication!*

Physical Appearance

Exhaustive detail with illustrations is provided in this author's *The Astrological Body Types.*

GEMINI BODY RULERSHIPS AND FUNCTIONS

As described in Chapter One, a body zone is a general box that overlays many organs, functions, vessels and their sub-rulerships. For example, Aquarius and Venus have a general dominion over veins. However, the venous system of the arms still receives a large influence from its zone landlord, Gemini! Gemini will typically be seen in natal charts, or by current transit, when one observes accidents or symptoms in this zone.

Gemini, Body Zone 3

This sign generally governs the upper lungs, bronchial tubes, and shoulders, but not the trapezius which is under Taurus. Gemini governs the arms, with the forearms and wrists shared with Leo (opposite Aquarius), and the fingers shared with sister Mercury-ruled sign Virgo. Gemini rules the upper thoracic vertebrae (with Saturn), scapula (with Cancer), and the mid-esophagus. Davidson asserts that Gemini influences the ureters, (normally the province of Scorpio, with co-influence of Libra). He also states that Gemini governs all "tubes", but this rule cannot be invariable because bodily tubes exert many functions and occur throughout all twelve body zones. There is more on this topic further on. However, Gemini absolutely influences the tiniest blood vessels (also tubes): capillaries, venules, and possibly the arterioles, working in tandem with Aquarius (veins) and Sagittarius (arteries).

While Aries still holds dominion over the brain in general (with Mercury, Sun, and Moon), Gemini rules the verbal centers of the brain, dendrites, and the peripheral and afferent nerves. Gemini may possibly govern efferent neural connections too, or co-govern these with opposite sign Sagittarius, the CNS. This is still being worked out. Neurologically speaking, it's easiest to envision all the voluntary "branches" as Gemini and the coordinating "tree" as Sagittarius (the cord). This is, however, simplistic but suffices for now.

Gemini and the Nervous System

Let's be frank. The ancients did not understand the components of the nervous system well (do we yet?). Nevertheless, we can broadly sculpt out a general picture of Gemini's provinces.

Gemini and its ruler Mercury hold a profound relationship to the speed of neural synapses and the conscious comprehension of data received from the peripheral sensory nerves. The typical Gemini native is a curious creature, ever thirsting for mental stimulus and new information.

Gemini rules the capillaries, speech, and neural coordination of the voluntary nerves. This sign also has a considerable influence over all bodily tubes (while not necessarily ruling them), notably the fallopian tubes and ureters, which are both under the general rulership of Libra-Scorpio.

Please note that the voluntary neural instructions moving from the CNS and brain outward to the muscles, are under the general auspices of opposite sign Sagittarius, who also has a significant hand in the coordination properties of the CNS.

Gemini and its opposite sign Sagittarius always work as a team. This is summarized here and discussed in greater detail in the chapter on Sagittarius. Sagittarius is the great coordinator, always working on a larger field than Gemini. To understand this, we will use similes. Gemini rules personal coordination, such as a writer, a circus juggler, or piano player. Conversely, Sagittarius rules universal coordination, governing the publisher, the circus producer, and the orchestral conductor. It is the same with the voluntary nervous system.

Sagittarius, a centaur firing an arrow from a bow, is in part symbolizing "one coming out of two" (the arrow comes from the horse and man). Here we have the spinal cord coordinating the incoming and outgoing data. Gemini is the twins, literally two coming forth from one. This is an apt symbol of the branching out of the peripheral nerves! Gemini governs all branching faculties, including the peripheral nerves and capillaries. Gemini and Sagittarius hold a dominant influence over the voluntary nervous system. Message reception, and the inspiration of the breath (inspiration!), are governed by Gemini. With help from Aries and Mars, Sagittarius coordinates sensory and motor input, and, in part, the voluntary nerves. The legs are especially dominated by Sagittarius. Aries governs the motor centers of the brain.

Ascending Sensory and Descending Motor Tracts of the Spinal Cord

As described above, the dendrites (receiving segments) of the neuron (nerve cell), are clearly Geminian in function. The axons (sending segments) are of the opposite sign polarity, Sagittarius. Following this picture, I'm working on assigning the ascending (sensory) track of the spinal cord to Gemini, and the descending (motor) track to Sagittarius. However, there is considerable interplay between these two signs, and in truth, they often mimic each other.

The ascending motor tracts affect position and balance. Here we have an astrological puzzle. Information heading toward the brain is typically Gemini's province, and the motor nerves are assigned to its opposite sign, Sagittarius (the motor center in brain is given Aries and Mars). Could the ascending motor tracts be of Libra?

I've always wondered how Libra partnered with its opposite sign Aries, in relationship to the nervous system. Libra is also the singularly least neural of the famously nervous Air Triplicity! Traditionally, Libra knows few neurological associations, other than the "sense of balance". Ascending motor tracts have everything to do with balance and position. And so does Libra's position on Arthur Young's pendulum model (*The Geometry of Meaning*). Libra's position within any circle or cycle (or pendulum's swing) is 180°. Here, the pendulum stops, considers, and looks back at the swing's starting point, Aries. Furthermore, Libra is represented by a set of scales, and is renowned as "the sign of balance" in all things. Because Libra is the Cardinal Air sign, it connects the Cardinal Cross (pituitary-adrenal axis) and hormone regulation with the Air triplicity, inclusive of Gemini. Thus, Libra represents a balancing point again, between different systems! The third and last decan of Libra, the last ten days of this sign, is co-influenced by Gemini. *Libra balances salt*, so necessary to neural conduction.

The Air Triplicity and Nervous System

What signs or planets govern synaptic processes, electrical, and neurotransmission? Mercury and Gemini are certainly top contenders, and no one seems more dedicated to forming new synapses than a good, solid Gemini native, cell phone in hand.

What signs or planets rule neural transmitters, and salt, so necessary to the conduction of electrical systems? We know that salt is allotted to Aquarius, that most electrical sign, and the homeopathic remedy Nat Mur (sodium). We also know that synapses can travel slightly faster or slower for different people.

Gemini maladies demonstrate the fastest synapses in the zodiac! Aquarius is rather slow, though highly sensitive, nervous, and prone to undiagnosable spasm and tetany. In Chapter 13, we discuss a plausible dryness of nerves common to Aquarian natives. These Aquarian-type folks sometimes show a curious symptom of receiving shocks from light switches, cats, or doorknobs, when nobody else does.

Gemini and Aquarius belong to the Air Triplicity, so often associated with nerves, and the mind. The third sign of the Air Triplicity is Libra. Libra governs the kidneys that, among other essential functions, balance the salt in the body! Discussed in pages 174-175.

The Mutable Cross and the Nervous Systems

The Virgo and Pisces polarity of signs squares the Gemini and Sagittarius polarity. I see this as clearly related to the sympathetic and parasympathetic systems (Virgo-Pisces) vs the somatic nervous system and voluntary nerves (Gemini-Sagittarius).

Pisces governs sleep, and its natives famously display this sleepy trait! No sign is better placed as the ruler of the parasympathetic system. Pisces typically have large and joyous appetites and rarely suffer as much the chronic digestive fussiness and allergies of their opposite sign Virgo.

Virgo, Pisces opposite sign, is awake, busy, and tense. The Vagus nerve runs from Aries (Body Zone 1) to Virgo's digestive organs (Body Zone 6). Virgos are alert and anxiety prone. Typically, they have selective appetites, order their food carefully, then push the food around, and take most of it home. If you don't believe me, take a few Virgos out to eat, and compare them with your Piscean dinner companions.

It is very clear that our two Mercury ruled signs of the mutable square (Gemini and Virgo) generate activation of the peripheral nerves and sympathetic system. Conversely, the Jupiter-ruled pair (Sagittarius and Pisces) govern a more wholistic function of the nervous system. You can observe this in gymnasts, tap dancers, and others who excel at small muscle coordination. Gemini and Virgo types are overwhelmingly noted in these fields, at least physiognomically. Sagittarius typically prefers large muscle sports, such as running, surfing, and group sports. Pisces can go either way!

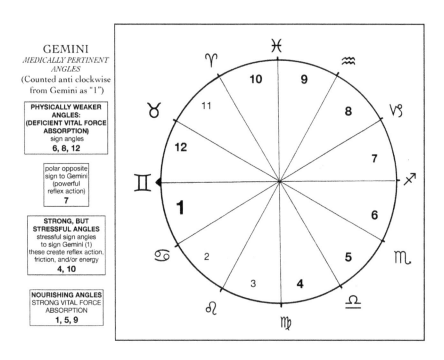

GEMINI
MEDICALLY PERTINENT
ANGLES
(Counted anti clockwise
from Gemini as "1")

**PHYSICALLY WEAKER
ANGLES:**
(DEFICIENT VITAL FORCE
ABSORPTION)
sign angles
6, 8, 12

polar opposite
sign to Gemini
(powerful
reflex action)
7

**STRONG, BUT
STRESSFUL ANGLES**
stressful sign angles
to sign Gemini (1)
these create reflex action,
friction, and/or energy
4, 10

NOURISHING ANGLES
STRONG VITAL FORCE
ABSORPTION
1, 5, 9

GEMINI SYNDROME

As discussed in Chapter Two, a Zodiac Sign Syndrome is a cluster of symptoms associated with the body zones and functions of a
zodiac sign and the signs positioned on the seasonal wheel opposite
(180°) and quincunx (150°, 210°, 330°) the sign. Remediating and
supporting these body zones and functions act to bring the body
into balance, diminishing the syndrome. These symptoms may
manifest when there is an emphasis in one or more of these signs.
Planetary dignity plays an important role.

The Weaker Signs for the Gemini Vital Force
Quincunx signs

The signs Scorpio, Capricorn, and Taurus are positioned 150°, 210° and 330° distant from Gemini on the seasonal wheel. These signs represent the 6th, 8th, and 12th *averted* angles from the sign Gemini (see the illustration for this chapter). This condition makes it difficult for Gemini to absorb the cosmic rays or the vibrational and light "nutrients" that feed these signs. Likewise, these signs may have trouble absorbing the rays from Gemini.

Scorpio rules Body Zone 8, which includes the colon, bladder; ureters and ovaries (with Libra, generative system, excretory system, and nose. I've noticed a propensity to prostrate problems for Gemini men. Asthma and bronchitis, so typical of Gemini, often pair with colon issues (Scorpio).

Do Scorpio's proverbial nasal problems create limitations of inspiration (Gemini)? Conversely, does bronchial stress lead to nasal drainage issues? Additionally, Scorpio tendency to smoke may relate to this quincunx.

Capricorn rules Body Zone 10, which includes the knees, and influences the gallbladder, skin, and bones in general (with Saturn). Asthmatics, so typical of Gemini, often have rheumatism, a Capricorn malady. Gemini types can sometimes suffer weakened or fine bones, or osteoporosis, especially in the knee, or shoulders, arms, hands, or clavicle. An insightful British woman, Julia Lawrence, at a recent talk of mine volunteered a brilliant idea for osteoporosis in air signs: "more space between the lacunae in the bones". Perhaps the old concept of "wind in the bones" has some merit.

Taurus rules Body Zone 2, which includes the ear, nose, throat, and neck. Taurus also occupies the mysterious 12th angle to Gemini on the seasonal wheel, the house of psychological health. Thus, Gemini Syndrome involves "fear of constancy." This type suffers stifling boredom with the same food, job, house, or romance. Lack of Taurean properties of proper self-care and nourishment is their undoing!

Opposite Sign, Sagittarius

When the Sun is in Gemini, the opposite sign, Sagittarius, "sleeps." **Sagittarius Rules Body Zone 9**, which includes the CNS, axons, voluntary muscular nerves, hips, and thighs. However, what we see in both signs is an enhancement of the entire polarity of the nervous system. It is often hard to tell these two signs apart. People of both signs so often resemble the other! The overall effect in these types is restlessness, as both the peripheral and muscular nerves are amped up, plus the mind and speech centers are activated.

Signs Aggravating Gemini Syndrome - Squaring Signs

The two signs squaring Gemini (positioned 90° from Gemini) are Virgo and Pisces (see chapter illustration). The effect of a square is to create friction, good or bad. Gemini can reflex with these signs, as well as its opposite sign, Sagittarius.

Virgo rules Body Zone 6, which includes the upper intestinal organs, sympathetic nerves, and the immune system (shared with Pisces, Cancer, and Mars). Unless intentionally strengthened, Geminis, as a rule, aren't noted for strong immune systems.

Pisces rules Body Zone 12, which includes the feet, general lymph system (thoracic duct shared with Cancer), the extracellular matrix (Hill), and fascia (speculative, Hill).

We often note the hyper flexible ligaments in prominent Sagittarius-Gemini and Pisces-Gemini squares, especially with Neptune involved. Lung and bronchial maladies are also common.

How Planetary Dignity Contributes to Gemini Syndrome

The weakest planet in Gemini is Jupiter. Thus, the Gemini native may need this planet's color rays (Primary Blue). The strongest planet is Mercury, which rules Gemini. Thus, the native may suffer an excess or disturbance of this color ray (green)!

Strongest Planet

Mercury, ruler of Gemini, is the speediest of planets. He/she (Mercury is hermaphrodite) was seen as the messenger of the Gods. It thus governs speech and communication.

Mercury governs the everyday thinking apparatus, the peripheral and afferent nerves (traditional modern), and possibly the dendrites (Hill), but also the general speed of neural transmission in efferent nerves too. This is quite apt because most Geminian pathology is of a neurological or mental origin. This is easy to remember if you consider that our nerves send along messages as speedily as possible, exactly as does their mythological governor Mercury, messenger of the Gods.

Gemini, and Mercury, represent the informational reception network - all messages coming from outside in, and from inside, moving out. The interpretation of signals, once received, is partially a Mercurial function too, in concert with the Moon (memory and memory related subconscious response) and Saturn (stable reality). The everyday thinking mind is attributed to Mercury, whereas deep scholasticism is more the province of Jupiter and Saturn. Mercury also sends and delivers messages. We must truly consider that all outgoing and incoming messages are under Gemini's and Mercury's auspices. However, the central post office, the spinal cord, is mostly a Sagittarian-ruled affair. Sagittarius, the great coordinator of the zodiac, stands exactly opposite to Gemini on the seasonal wheel.

No planets are exalted in Gemini. This is quite apt, as the classic Gemini native exalts no single opinion or viewpoint over another, preferring to test them all!

Weakest Planet

Jupiter rules Sagittarius, Gemini's opposite sign. Therefore, this booming planet is in detriment in Gemini. This by no means weakens Jupiter's expansive character, rather it alters him in such a manner as to work against the native's best interests. In Gemini, Jupiter blows wind around! This produces bibliomania, scribomania (compulsive writing), and an active zest for multiple topics. Half read books lay all over the house. Either entirely disinclined to religion or studies many paths but cannot pick one! In Gemini, Jupiter invests in pointless merriment, diversion, and incomplete studies; a "jack of all trades, master of none." Jupiter in this sign can, in some cases, divide the attention, lacking focus, as is now styled attention deficit disorder (ADD).

Planetary and House Positions that Enhance Gemini Syndrome

(1) **Sun, Moon, or Ascendant sign in Gemini**

(2) A weakness in a body zone governed by the signs opposite or quincunx Gemini on the seasonal wheel, as discussed above under *The Weaker Signs for the Gemini Vital Force.*

(3) The natal Sun, Moon, Ascendant, Saturn, South or North Node is in Gemini, compounded by the testimonies below:

- Gemini inhabits the 1st, 6th, 8th, or 12th houses in the native's birth chart. (See discussion of Weak Houses in Chapter Two).
- Saturn or Jupiter square a Gemini Sun or Moon.
- Mars in Gemini appears to reliably stimulate and irritate the nerves (Mars is an enemy of Mercury).

- The South or North Node rising in Gemini, or conjunct Sun, Mars, or Moon in Gemini.
- Sun, Moon, Ascendant Ruler, South Node, North Node, Jupiter, Venus, Mars, or Saturn in Gemini, in the 6th, 8th or 12th houses.
- Day birth, with Mercury, Sun, Jupiter, or especially Mars above the horizon in a fire or air sign.

SYMPTOMS OF GEMINI SYNDROME

The following is a list of symptoms and traits associated with Gemini Syndrome. These symptoms can occur in seriatim, first one symptom, then weeks, months or years later, another. However, two or more of these symptoms are frequently observed clustered together at the same time. These symptoms are not listed in any order, but simply as a list of collected observations common to Gemini.

These do not pertain to "Gemini people" per se, but those born with prominences in this sign that actually do suffer the syndrome. Many Gemini natives are specimens of perfect health. However, factually, Geminis are more likely to ruin their own health through irregular lifestyle and poor eating and sleeping habits!

Note: Observe how an excess stimulation of peripheral afferent nerves and/or the ascending sensory tract of the spinal cord, and/or sensory nerve disruption or sensory/motor discoordination is associated with many of the below symptoms noted for Gemini Syndrome. This is a profoundly mental sign, so several classic Gemini-style personality disorders are on this list. If you are a Gemini native, this does not mean you will be heir to any of them (all signs have their more "interesting" tendencies). Many outstanding and great personalities were born in this sign!

- ADD (does not always accompany a hyperactive body, sometimes purely mental)
- autism (Many testimonies are required).
- excessive chattering or mute
- discoordinated frontal gaze or one wandering eye (rare)
- stuttering or other speech impediments
- talking excessively fast
- delayed (or, conversely, precocious) speech and verbal development.
- excessive gesticulation
- autism spectrum
- schizoid spectrum
- ADHD
- jittery nerves
- tremors
- trouble processing information, learning disabilities, dyslexia.
- environmental restlessness or boredom, requiring frequent, new environments.
- jumping from job to job, unemployment, suffers from lack of clear direction in life
- extension of teenage behaviors into middle age
- incoming sensory disability or disruption (especially with heard information and language)
- dislike of fixed mealtimes
- whimsical snacking
- forgets to eat or grabs a quick meal of junk food
- media, gaming, music and/or phone addictions
- bibliomania
- annoying others through constant puns, word games, riling you up for fun or practical jokes
- breathing difficulties
- graphomania or scribomania (compulsive urge to write)
- insomnia
- asthma or frequent bronchitis
- bone, joint or teeth weakness (mineral deficiency?)

- lung weakness
- difficulty maintaining jobs or housing for a duration of time
- hand, shoulder, arm or finger problems
- epilepsy and other neural effective disorders relating more to brain wiring and nerves than to chemistry or hormones (but can involve them).
- disturbance or hyperactivity of speech centers in brain
- coordination issues (or excellent coordination). In particular, issues involving the discoordination of arms, speech, or two halves of the brain, and sense reception/ interpretation
- attraction to name changes and strange names
- festooning hands with multiple rings, bracelets, and/or tattoos
- disinterest in religious or spiritual disciplines
- hyper flexibility of joints

- love of small muscle coordinative sports
- kleptomania or compulsive shoplifting
- mythomania, pseudologia fantastica
- nicotine addiction, drug abuse
- neurological ticks, 'tweaking'
- multiple personality disorders or conscious enjoyment in the living of secret lives
- rare: problems with bodily tubes or capillaries (ectopic pregnancies, ureter issues, etc.)
- sudden 'shape shifting': easy loss or gain of a great deal of weight
- kinked ureter (rare)
- fallopian tube kink or anomaly (rare)

Gemini is but one prominent component in coordinative disorders of the peripheral nerves and neuro-muscular diseases. It therefore cannot be considered to exclusively rule them in entirety. Several signs and planets (and physical organs, plus the inherited DNA) are involved in most neurological conditions. However, you may find the Gemini-Sagittarius polarity prominent in the following disorders: Parkinson's, dysmetria, dysarthria, epilepsy, palsy, tremors, Friedreich ataxia, MS, ALS, autism, schizoid disorders, and all manner of problems involved with the coordination of the arms, speech, sense reception/interpretation, and disturbed communication between the two halves of the brain.

REMEDIATION TIPS

Please note that these remedial tips are for interest only. The author is not suggesting that any person use these without the evaluation and consent of their personal healthcare practitioner.

What to strengthen?

In Gemini Syndrome, the peripheral nerves and their sheaths require extra nutritional support and calming. The awake consciousness needs greater focus, as so often we see ADHD or other distractive mental disorders. Strengthen all neuro-muscular coordination (piano playing, juggling, etc.) Support spinal cord health.

The bronchial tubes so often benefit from relaxation and moistening demulcents. Balance breath inspiration with expiration. Gemini obtains its Vital Force from the Air! The diet is often irregular and lacking in vitamins and/or minerals. Typically, the diet is not well rounded, as this type snacks on the run.

Support excretions through the colon, bladder, and skin. The knees, bones in general, and the gallbladder may be either sensitive or weak spots worthy of extra attention.

See also Chapter 15, *The Twelve Zodiac Sign Syndromes and their Relevant Herbs.*

Chapter Six:

CANCER SYNDROME

I heard a thousand blended notes,
While in a grove I sate reclined,
In that sweet mood when pleasant thoughts
Bring sad thoughts to the mind.

- William Wordsworth

Centripetal Force

It seems that so often it is the Cancer-born child who is hesitant (or terrified!) to roller skate, preferring cello practice, a book, or a fairy tale instead. My friend's two little Cancerians are both content to solitarily play with coloring books for hours, while we adults visit sans the usual chaos accompanying most modern children.

Cancer is the most *centripetal* of all signs. Notice how Cancer's glyph perfectly depicts a centripetal, or inward curling spiral! Compare this with Aries' glyph - the outward moving, centrifugal spiral! Cancer draws the Vital Force inward towards the stomach, breast, and most especially, the personal feelings. Few other signs possess a greater capacity for a personal feeling-connection to the Divine.

Fundamentals Refresher

Cancer Syndrome is a set of collaborative symptoms, consistently appearing together, which are typical for natives of the sign Cancer. The symptoms associated with Cancer Syndrome can be experienced by people with other sun signs when there is a particular emphasis in this sign. Zodiac sign syndromes can occur in seriatim, first one symptom, then another, weeks, months or years later. Few experience all symptoms. However, two or more of these symptoms are frequently observed clustered together at the same time.

A Cancer native may have few if any of the symptoms associated with Cancer Syndrome. Indeed, many Cancers are specimens of perfect health. However, this symptom set often, but not always, evinces itself when a native's Sun, Moon, or Ascendant tenants Cancer and displays certain astrological conditions which are discussed at length in this chapter.

This chapter describes the astrological conditions that may aggravate the syndrome. With this knowledge, practitioners can explore the underlying condition when symptoms consistent with the syndrome present themselves in a patient. Understanding the energetic cause is the first step in remediation.

THE SIGN CANCER

In Classical Western Astrology, with use of the Tropical Zodiac, "a Cancer" is someone born between 90 to 119 longitudinal degrees following the Spring equinox, or the thirty days following the summer solstice. In the Tropical Zodiac, the sign status of Cancer is not dependent on constellations in the sky.

As with all other signs, we cannot think of Cancer as an isolated single entity or a static constant. "Cancer" is a gestalt of strengths and weaknesses based on its angular relationship to the other signs of the interconnected solar cycle. In turn, each of the twelve phases of this cycle is influenced by the unique planetary configurations at birth and throughout the life. Cancer is a unique phase-state, with its inter-actions peculiar to the fourth stage of the twelve-fold cyclical process.

Element and Mode: Cancer is of the element Water. The advent of Cancer initiates the summer season and, thus, is a member of the *cardinal* quadruplicity of signs.

Life Cycle Phase: The sign Cancer heralds the second quarter of the seasonal wheel, representing the fourth stage on the twelve-fold human life cycle. The infant born (Aries), has fed (Taurus), is next the babbling tot (Gemini), and now becomes aware of its place in the home and tribe (Cancer). At this stage, the soul is sensitized and must build a protective shield. Looked at in another way, the three previous stages of life are devoted to building the infant's body and initial equipment: birth and vital force (Aries), body and fuel (Taurus), then mind, language, and nerves (Gemini). These have prepared Cancer for family inclusion and clan awareness. This is the quintessential sign of Motherhood. In Cancer, we develop respon-sive feeling and bond to place and tribe.

About Cancer: In this season, energy moves towards the center (*centripetal*). To reiterate from the opening paragraph - this fact is immediately apparent in the Cancer *glyph* that is depicted with two inward circling spirals. This is in reverse of Aries, the *cen-trifugal* sign, where energy spirals outward, away from center! Extending the "horns" slightly on Aries glyph creates an obvious centrifugal spiral!

The keynote for Cancer is the centripetal movement of the life force. Sensitivity on all levels is developed at this stage of the season wheel, and necessarily, must be carefully shielded.

Energy moves inward, primarily toward the stomach and the personal feelings. One might say that this sign revolves around the stomach. The adage "the road to a man's heart is through his stomach" is precisely true for many members of this sign. Notice the connection here with Taurus, the mouth. Astrology has an answer for the fellowship between these two signs. Cancer's ruler, the Moon, is *exalted in Taurus*. In reverse, the Jyotish recognize a heightened directional power, or *dik bala*, for Venus in the 4th house, the natural house of Cancer. Both Venus and the Moon are strongly placed in this house.

We can further understand Cancer in relationship to its opposite sign Capricorn "awareness of the Universal Environment." Opposite signs are but opposite ends of a single pole, Cancer being "awareness of the Internal Environment." Cancer puts its ear to the tree to hear and feel the forest. Capricorn looks at the trees and plans a city! Cancer natives notably excel at small, focused work: research, miniature sculpture, cooking. I have two Cancer friends who were nearly impossible to drag out of their homes, except to movies or dinner. In fact, I've learned through experience never to book an outside event on a Cancer Moon! Folks prefer to stay home on that day.

Feeling and Velocity: It is cogent to recall how Cancer sits at the precise point in the twelve-fold cycle of motion which is described by renowned physicist Arthur Young as "velocity." This fourth stage of motion is where the pendulum reaches the bottom of its trajectory toward 180° degrees, Libra, where it will pause, look back, and prepare to return to start. When I asked why he called this fourth stage of the cycle-circle "velocity", Young replied, "You *feel* velocity".

This sign is all about personal feelings, memory, bonding, nourishment, and personal love. My mentor taught that Cancer was the sign representing *the awareness of the personal environment,* or more directly put, *"I feel."* Feelings and close personal bonds hold priority.

Sensitivity is developed in this sign. The seedling must be protected. My teacher taught me something that through experience I have found to be too true - he said: *"in Cancer natives, the self-protective instinct is working overtime".* The shell of the crab is an apt symbol of this highly attuned and necessary defensive mechanism. We hypothesize that many of this sign's physical and psychological problems are furthered by this very defense mechanism, *when experienced as fear.* This can be exacerbated when combined with poor mineralization plus an anguished memory. This is the sign governing the imprinting of personal memories.

Rhythm: The Sun is the Vital Force, and the Moon distributes this force. It is often overlooked how much the Moon relates to rhythm and beat. Her monthly trajectory about Earth is a delicate affair, full of subtle and continual perturbations. Yet it is quite regular at the same time. Luna plays a significant role in all cyclic and rhythmic processes in the body, such as the sleep cycle, menses, breathing, heartbeat, and circulation.

Moon-ruled Cancer natives appear most sensitive to even slight changes in temperature, hormones, or change in the bed-time hour. The healer should never neglect this essential sensitivity in their Cancer patient. Cancer Ascendant people I have known seem to be acutely temperature sensitive, frequently donning (or removing) jackets, hats, or socks. Musical healers have worked with specific keys and notes to heal various conditions. I wonder if specific rhythms would work well for Cancer natives!

Notably, dancing is a favorite of this sign. Cancerians often love emotionally expressive dance and music, as this is one of the most musically responsive of all signs. The receptive emotions are alive!

Keywords for Cancer Health: Sensitivity (physical and emotional), fear (because they are so sensitive), hyper-attachment (to family, parents, home), and the power of personal memories.

Cancer children nearly invariably evince a reluctance toward leaving home, risky sports, or hurdling fast through space. Typically, they will fear some sport and be the last to grasp it. For example, this Cancer boy won't roller skate or this Cancer girl is afraid of the bicycle. There are very sound reasons for their reluctance, so it is wise never to push them. Once comfortable, they may excel at a sport. One of the greatest Olympic swimmers ever born, Michael Phelps, is a Cancer with Cancer Ascendant (double Cancer), born with Mars (sports) rising in Cancer! Remember, this is a water sign. They excel when feeling secure and confident in their own space.

This sign is infamous for low vital force, rivaling only Pisces. Infants are notably delicate, especially when this sign is Ascending at birth. The young Cancer or Cancer rising child must be gently fostered and protected from harsh or spiritually detrimental external influences.

Cancer Superpowers
Closeness to Source

Cancer is *the* sign of personal and family love. This characteristic allows these natives perhaps the closest access of all signs to ancestor guidance, plant spirits, the Divine Mother (or Father), fairies, a favored saint, and more. Personal feelings can be extended to a special stone, pet, locality, or favored plant. Many Cancer natives evince true religious devotion felt in the heart. This sign resonates strongly with "place" and sacred space.

Cancer natives are so often sensitive to vibration, those unseen feelings emanating from persons, things, and places. This is a great asset for healers and patients alike. William Gray, the great healer who felt and utilized the astrological vibration of each person, was born in this sign, with Sun conjunct Jupiter. This trait makes for excellent vibrational, mantra and music healers of all kinds.

Cancerians are also quite receptive to inner guidance. Perhaps an intuition or dream alerts them to be proactive, thus preventing a later malady.

Cancer rules altars, sacred pools, personal fountains. These natives make excellent small space Feng Shui experts and temple guardians. Ancestors offer their assistance. One might say that natives of this sign have a direct supply line to the personal element of the divine.

The famous nurturing powers of this quintessentially motherly sign also pertain to the self. The sensitive Cancer native knows when to adjust themselves to external stressors, and when to convalesce. Their natural defensiveness protects them, if not taken too far. Often born with physical delicacies, they learn to go slower, becoming excellent self-care experts. Herbal medicine and cooking are natural fortes.

Shielding/Defense

The self-damage protection monitor of this sign is very sharp, allowing Cancer natives to withdraw quickly from physical threat. Naturally cautious, the Cancer type is much less likely than most other signs to be involved in foolish accidents. I doubt that many Cancer natives go sky diving for fun. A strong, prepared defense is the forte of this sign. The classic Cancer is rarely caught unprepared for emergencies. Doors are locked and the cupboard is well stocked.

Kindness

Through personal *love power*, parental Cancer is the wonderfully caring midwife, or hovering nurse (the one who remembered your name and favorite foods). Kindness is a superpower in reverse. Clue: "power", as we think of it on earth, is neither necessary or useful in the eternal realm, where there is no dense body to protect from earthly dangers - hence no need there for big muscles, weapons, teeth, money, or like accouterments of power.

Physical Appearance

Exhaustive detail with illustrations is provided in this author's *The Astrological Body Types.*

It is important to note that the New Moon Cancer is quite a different creature from the Full Moon Cancer. This is to be expected for a Moon-governed sign! After all, we have the Lunar Phases. Cancer is the Moon-responsive sign!

CANCER BODY RULERSHIPS AND FUNCTIONS

As described in Chapter One, a body zone is a general box that overlays many organs, functions, vessels and their sub-rulerships. Cancer will typically be seen in natal charts, or by current transit, when one observes accidents or symptoms in this zone.

Cancer, Body Zone 4

Cancer governs the breast, lacteals and milk, sternum, thoracic duct, upper lymphatics, the peristaltic action of the thoracic duct, rib cage; diaphragm (shared by Virgo), lower esophagus, fundus, stomach, pylorus, epigastric region, and armpit. Interestingly, Cancer rules the elbow, which is opposite to the knees (ruled by the opposite sign Capricorn). Cancer rules many organ coverings, including the pericardium, pleura, meninges, and womb (when pregnant).

Cancer holds a significant influence over personal and familial memory, attachment-bonding mechanism, imprinting of long-term personal memory, and extra sensitivity to light, diurnal rhythms, and temperature.

Cancer influences much within the Aries and Aries-Taurus border zones. Cornell states that Cancer governs the posterior pituitary gland (with Jupiter - Cayce, verified by Hill). It is obvious that the influence of this sign regarding long-term memory, memory establishment, and the visceral response to fear and satiation is seen in the amygdala, thalamus, and hypothalamus, as will be explained later in this chapter.

Moon-ruled light sensitivity and optic lens accommodation are observably prominent issues of this sign, especially near-sightedness. The *choroid* in the eyeball's vascular tunic appears influenced by this sign (Hill). The lower lobes of the lung (tradition). Cancer holds some relationship with the nutrient storage properties of the liver. The mucus membrane and gums are largely under the rulership of this sign and their level of moisture. Cancer and/or Virgo are stated in alternate texts to govern the pancreas and spleen. My study of pancreatic cancer and ruptured spleen cases confirms these organs are co-ruled by both signs.

The Internal Universe of Memories: Natives of this sign are memory bank dominant. The internal feelings, thought processes, and memories dominate over incoming sense data. Mental and physical response to sensory and motor data appears slowed, as if the synapses in the ascending sensory tract are deficient. This sign is opposite in nature to the previous sign Gemini. Later, we will discuss the relationship of this sign to the *amygdala* and *hypothalamus*.

Conversely, this is the best sign for intense focus within a small area, such as studying cells in a petri dish. This penchant for the local environment contributes to the Cancer native's love of cherished collections, such as buttons, books, stamps, dolls, photographs, or records.

Cancer appears to govern personal memories with its natives renowned for never forgetting either a kindness or an insult! For example, select memories of childhood, parents, and distant past life recall issues are perhaps more dominant in the health portrait than for most other signs. In some afflictions, the recent or current time memory suffers; for example, "where are my glasses?" when they are sitting atop their head. Memory issues often involve this sign, or its opposite, Capricorn, or afflicted Moon and Mercury to Neptune, Nodes, or Saturn.

The internal, *personal* emotional world predominates, whereas, for fellow Water sign Pisces, it is the *universal* emotional world. Cancer is preoccupied with their own emotional connections: "My children, my feelings, my memories, my past." Memory types vary. The Cancer native can't get over what their father once said to them, whereas Gemini recalls the latest game, and Taurus that delicious pasta. The health practitioner must take the memory type firmly into account when evaluating Cancer health issues.

MPD: The Cancer native experiences their memories as overwhelming. Rather than Post Traumatic Stress Disorder (PTSD), let us call it "MPD," my acronym for *Memory Preoccupation Disorder*, and all the grief, depression, regret, and fear this engenders.

For natives of this sign, stored data is more influential than incoming data. Grief, love, regret cannot readily be surmounted. I recall one Cancer native who stayed home in her twenties, blinds drawn, watching movies all day. One double Cancer I knew well, when grievously preoccupied, went to the wrong house and tried to get in the front door, thinking she was home. Such observations are not uncommon in the more extreme type. Flower essences are perfect for MPD!

Functions under consideration for Cancer's rulership

Stored memory and memory storage: The sign Cancer has everything to do with personal memory, past recall of personal events, and sentiment. We must look to the brain centers and glands most active in the process of storing the more emotionally invested and long-term feeling memories. Observation suggests that these functions of the brain (and soul) are somehow more active at this stage in the yearly cycle.

Cancer natives reliably experience strong memory recall, often suffering from distant memory related feelings that impinge on their current incoming sensory reality. Cancers are also noted for outstanding melody and word recall. Many are excellent poets, actors, folk singers, and historians. The *hippocampus* and *cerebral cortex* both play prominent roles in the process of long-term memory storage, as discussed below.

This sign is also habitual in its nature. The "Law of Habit" works strongest in these natives, supporting my assignment of personal memory storage processes as being governed by this sign. The *basal ganglia* of the brain play a key role in emotional development, pattern recognition, memories, and the construction of habitual behavior.

Feeling: Cancer governs the distinctly *receptive* feelings and the subsequent response to these feelings (think of an oyster opening and closing to the tides.) This is quite a different matter from the passionate expression of feeling we witness in Leo! Phobias are common to Cancer. One also notes the tense diaphragm, so often a product of subconscious or conscious fear. It is obvious that brain centers relating to stored memories and fear reactions are heightened in this birth month. Cornell assigns the diaphragm to Cancer and Virgo. However, both in zone and function, it clearly errs to Cancer.

In Cancer, the fear-defense mechanism far outweighs either the attacking response or immediate logical assessments. Hence, the Crab's shell. It needs it.

Nurturing: Maternal instinct is decidedly under this sign. It has been proven that what we perceive as "aw, so cute...", is an inherent response. This is the instinctually recognized response that awakens the gushing heart, when confronted with a tiny round face with large forehead, large wide eyes, tiny nose, no chin, and protruding ears. We automatically find irresistibly adorable any baby or animal with this appearance. Hence, the popularity of the Teddy Bear, Troll Dolls, Kewpie Dolls, and French Bulldogs.

The pleasure experienced in nurturing and feeding the family is attributed to this sign. The Moon governs all things motherly. Traditionally, Cancer is the sign of mothers and motherhood. Therefore, physically, we must consider some of the glands and hormones involved, as discussed below. Cancer natives are famous for intense devotion to family and are nurturing to their children, elders, and animals (who are often perceived as equal family members).

The Waters Within: Neither ancient physicians nor modern medical astrologers comprehend the lymphatic system. In the chapter on Pisces, we discuss the rulerships of the lymphatic system in greater depth. With respect to Cancer, obviously the thoracic duct and lymph nodes of the armpit are powerfully influenced by Pisces' fellow water sign Cancer.

Under Pisces, we discuss how that sign most likely governs the extracellular matrix and the interstitial fluids (outside the cells). The ECM engages 26% of our body's water. It is my conjecture that the intracellular fluids (inside the cell) and cell membranes are under Cancer's auspices, as this sign pertains to hollow containers, cottages, protective walls, shells, wells, and enclosed spaces. Why then wouldn't Cancer rule the cellular walls and their contained water within? Intracellular fluid is clearly a water sign domain as 67% of our bodily water is contained within the cells!

Possible Rulerships and Influences

The Posterior Pituitary: The great doctor Davidson assigned the *posterior pituitary* to Cancer's rulership, (the anterior pituitary is assigned to Capricorn). Edgar Cayce gives the gland to Jupiter, the planet that is exalted in Cancer. When looking at cases of pituitary disturbance, both rulerships bear out well in practice. The first four degrees of Cardinal signs accent this gland, especially 0° Aries-Libra, and 3-5° Cancer-Capricorn. The pituitary gland produces several hormones including *prolactin*, the precursor to breast milk (Cancer rules the breast), and *oxytocin*, a chemical messenger that acts on the breast and uterine contraction. Clearly, some Cancer and Scorpio connections here.

The Anterior Hypothalamus: This organ in the Aries-Taurus border zone strongly influences our visceral response to emotional stimuli and feelings of satiety after eating. The *anterior hypothalamus* assists *homeostasis* by regulating our challenges to wellbeing through feeling. Cancer is the sign where we become aware of what we are feeling! Early astrologers knew nothing of this organ.

Hypothalamus and Estrogen: The hypothalamus also *reads the estrogen level* in the bloodstream, a function directly correlated to the production of this hormone in the ovaries and adrenals. Estrogen plays a large role in female reproductive development (Moon, Venus), plus other functions. This is too involved to discuss here. I found this convoluted statement on Google. "Estrogen targets all of the major hypothalamic neuroendocrine and automatic cellular groups to activate multiple signaling pathways..." Obviously, there is a Lunar or Lunar-Venusian link to this connection. Cancer natives are noted for all manner of issues connected with female hormone fluctuation, such as early or late menarche, early or late menopause, sore or swollen breasts, fluidic retention, and ovarian cysts.

Hypothalamus and Temperature Regulation: Cancer natives evince more sensitivity to temperature than any other zodiac sign. The anterior hypothalamus regulates temperature. When sensing excessive heat, it signals your sudoriferous glands to produce cooling sweat. It senses cold and tells your muscles to create warmth by shivering. If one judges an organ's sign rulership by the behavior of people, then Cancer's hypersensitivity to temperature must relate this sign to the temperature regulation function of the hypothalamus. My observations are empirically backed by decades of watching Cancer people frequently changing clothes or complaining of the heat or cold. We also think of how quickly water changes temperature. Cancer is a Water sign.

The Pineal Gland: The ruler of this gland is given to Mercury (Cayce), Neptune (Cornell, Nauman). However, it is believed that this gland has much to do with our innate responses to diurnal/nocturnal cycles. This is because the moon rules Cancer. Cyclic responses are distinctly lunarian. Natives of Moon-ruled Cancer are "cycle sensitive" and may respond more profoundly to this gland than do most other signs. The pineal produces melatonin, a hormone influencing sleep. It is called "the hormone of darkness" because it increases during night hours. These are all distinctly lunar functions.

In my extreme youth I worked briefly as a daytime telephone operator on emergency lines. This job was so chaotic that very few could stick. Most of the crew were Gemini, with a few Libras (all Air folks). I couldn't stand it and switched over to the graveyard shift. Here, we read books, napped, and waited for the occasional call. Again, I took a sign poll (not including myself as the "scientist"). The entire crew were Water signs! Cancer was a favorite. Many Cancer-born prefer the cool night hours. *One looks for these behavioral correlations to identify glands and brain centers that are dominant in certain zodiac sign natives.*

Hippocampus: This structure influences many functions including the storage of long-term memories and resistance to their forgetting. This later process is Cancerian in essence. The hippocampus is also involved in spatial processing and navigation. These functions are notoriously weak in many Cancer natives (!), but quite strong in Aries and Taurus, signs that correlate directly to this structure's body zone location.

Amygdala: This brain region is believed to be the central processor for fearful and threatening stimuli, including threat detection and inciting behaviors responsive to threat and danger. We have already explained how *fear* is a predominant emotion of the Cancer type. This is distinct from the direct and aggressive emotional responses of Aries, or Leo's displays of strength. It bears consideration that the parts of the brain related to *defensive responses* are governed by Cancer. This does not mean this organ is "ruled" by Cancer but is somehow involved specifically with more defensive responses to threat.

Light Sensitivity Accommodation: We know that the eyes and vision are of Body Zone 1, Aries. That said, there are multitudinous sub rulerships within this singular zone. In this case, Cancer natives so often suffer light sensitivity. Another problem is a slightly slowed recognition of what is seen. It is as if the current inflowing sensory data (Gemini) is not processing quickly enough, or it must somehow move through the sluggish pools of internal thought processes first. This creates a split-second delay in automatic reaction time. This curious trait may explain the reluctance of some Cancerians to drive or the hesitancy of Cancer children to engage in fast moving, physical risks.

The eyeball's second and vascular tunic includes the *choroid*, a soft, moist, spongey tissue that absorbs light and prevents it from bouncing around. As a dense network of blood vessels, it also nourishes the retina and *sclera* (whites of the eyes). This choroid layer seems Cancerian in function. In cases of extreme light sensitivity, one so often sees the sign Cancer and the Moon involved. My last severe case had Moon in Cancer conjunct Saturn on an angle, exactly square Mercury. Another case was born with South Node rising in Cancer.

Another speculation is that protective pigment, in both the iris and skin, is related to this zodiac sign. Cancer's role is exactly to protect by defensive shielding. The pigment melanin does precisely this, by shielding both the iris and skin from potential Sun damage. However, some feel melanin is ruled by Saturn. These rulerships are not solved.

Distance Accommodation: Because Cancer is the primary sign of *myopia* (near sightedness), one could proffer that the eye's distance accommodation mechanism is in some as yet undiscerned way related to this sign. I believe it was Davidson who stated that Sagittarius influenced the eye's distance accommodation.

The Stomach: Perhaps this section should have been first! We have already discussed how in this season energy moves toward the center, *centripetal* motion. The typical days and thoughts of Cancer revolve more around meals than, say, for Gemini, Sagittarius, or Aquarius. Although not all Cancers are physical endomorphs (round, non-muscular), the old "endoderm" theory of embryonic development is appealing in relationship to Cancer's stomach-centered nature. Is it possible that for Cancer natives, a greater fetal emphasis was placed on the endoderm layer of the embryo, which includes stomach and digestive organs? So goes the old theory.

Physically, this would aptly match the Cancerian "Full Moon type," discussed more fully in this author's *The Astrological Body Types*. And possibly, in reverse, this creates Cancer's "New Moon type," so slender, graceful, introverted, and frail. Never confuse this Cancer New Moon type with the Saturnian Capricorn type. Although both are emaciated, the Saturnian Capricorn has notably visible joints, and is considerably more tough, enduring, dry, and brittle.

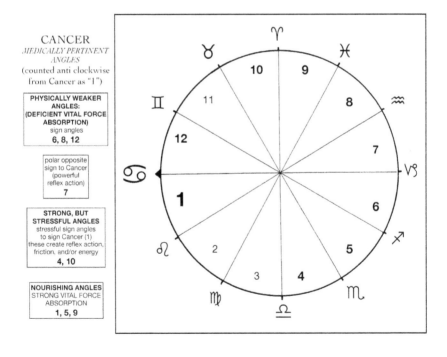

CANCER
MEDICALLY PERTINENT ANGLES
(counted anti clockwise from Cancer as "1")

PHYSICALLY WEAKER ANGLES:
(DEFICIENT VITAL FORCE ABSORPTION)
sign angles
6, 8, 12

polar opposite sign to Cancer
(powerful reflex action)
7

STRONG, BUT STRESSFUL ANGLES
stressful sign angles to sign Cancer (1)
these create reflex action, friction, and/or energy
4, 10

NOURISHING ANGLES
STRONG VITAL FORCE ABSORPTION
1, 5, 9

CANCER SYNDROME

As discussed in Chapter Two, a Zodiac Sign Syndrome is a cluster of symptoms associated with the body zones and functions of a zodiac sign and the signs positioned on the seasonal wheel opposite (180°) and quincunx (150°, 210°, 330°) the sign. Remediating and supporting these body zones and functions act to bring the body into balance, diminishing the syndrome. These symptoms may manifest when there is an emphasis in one or more of these signs. Planetary dignity plays an important role.

The Weaker Signs for the Cancer Vital Force

Quincunx Signs

Sagittarius, Aquarius, and Gemini are quincunx Cancer, as they are positioned 150°, 210° and 330° distant from this sign on the seasonal wheel. These signs represent the 6th, 8th, and 12th *averted* angles from the sign Cancer (see the illustration for this chapter). This condition makes it difficult for Cancer to absorb the cosmic rays that feed these signs. Thus, Cancer natives may have trouble absorbing the vibrational and light nutrients of these signs. Likewise, these signs may have trouble absorbing the rays from Cancer.

Sagittarius rules Body Zone 9 which includes the hips, thighs, sciatic nerve, locomotion, Central Nervous System, expiration of breath, and the arterial system. We often see a hip issue or length of leg imbalance for a Cancer Ascendant.

Aquarius rules Body Zone 11 which includes the venous circulation, lower legs, ankles, Achilles tendon, oxygenation of blood, quality of blood cells, and the electrical system of the body. Poor veinous return, lower leg fluid retention, and varicosities are common to a Cancer Ascendant.

Gemini rules Body Zone 3 which includes the upper lung, bronchial tubes, capillaries, shoulders, arms, hands, fingers, ascending sensory tracts, dendritic branching, synaptic speed, connections, and speech centers. Cancerians are noted for weak lungs and susceptibility to lung and bronchial complaints of a moist nature.

Opposite Sign, Capricorn

When the Sun is in Cancer, the opposite sign, Capricorn, "sleeps." **Capricorn rules Body Zone 10** which includes the bones, their strength and density, as well as mineral uptake, knees, skin, connective tissue, and gallbladder. Cancers and Cancer Ascendants frequently have a mineral uptake or a knee issue. A bone strengthening regime is sometimes required.

Signs Aggravating Cancer Syndrome – Squaring Signs

Libra and Aries are positioned 90° from Cancer, squaring this sign (see chapter illustration). The effect of a square is to create friction, for good or ill. Cancer can reflex with these signs, as well as its opposite sign, Capricorn.

Libra rules Body Zone 7 which includes the kidneys, salt and water balance, hormonal balances, and physical balance. Cancer is famous for fluidic bloating, water retention, and all manner of hormonal imbalances with consequent moods.

Aries rules Body Zone 1 which includes the eyes, brain, motor center commands, and the "attack" part of adrenal response, as opposed to Cancer which defends or barricades in response to adrenalin. Aries takes the offense, and Cancer the defense - hence the resultant conflict. Cancer shares rulership of the posterior pituitary with Jupiter and Aries Zone 1. Light sensitivity, night blindness, poor vision, and short sightedness are maladies common to Cancer.

How Planetary Dignity Contributes to Cancer Syndrome
Strongest Planets

The strongest planets for Cancer are the **Moon** (ruler), **Jupiter** (exalted), and Venus which is also very strong in this sign. Cancer natives may suffer excess or disturbance of these color rays. The traditional Jyotish assign the orange color ray to the Moon, blue to Jupiter, and indigo to Venus.

Cancer, as a sign, is very strong on these three traditionally moist planets. All three are productive of female hormones (Jupiter co-rules the pituitary gland). All three are emotional, sociable, protective, and somewhat relaxing. Jupiter relaxes through joyful expansion, while Moon and Venus are mutually soft and tender.

Weakest Planet

Saturn is the weakest planet as it rules the opposing sign, Capricorn. Cancer needs this planet's color rays and qualities (violet)! Saturn governs mineralization, bones, and structural form. This planet provides emotional control, self-discipline and constancy. Saturn is astringent, tonifying and drying. He brings strength, integrity and endurance, inside and out. Cancer types sometimes lack minerals and consequent skeletal strength.

Planetary and House Positions that Enhance Cancer Syndrome

(1) **Sun, Moon, or Ascendant sign in Cancer**

(2) A weakness in a body zone governed by the signs opposite or quincunx Cancer on the seasonal wheel, as discussed above under *The Weaker Signs for the Cancer Vital Force.*

(3) The Sun, Moon, Ascendant, Saturn, Jupiter, Venus, Mars, South Node, or North Node is in Cancer in the native's birth chart. This is compounded by the testimonies below:

- Cancer inhabits the 1st, 6th, 8th, or 12th houses (see discussion in Chapter Two on Weak Houses).
- Saturn or Jupiter square, opposed, or conjunct a Cancer Sun or Moon.
- Saturn and Mars conjunct in Cancer.
- South or North Node rising in Cancer, or conjunct Sun, Mars, or Moon in Cancer. This aspect brings out the light, sound, and memory related sensitivities of this sign.
- Night birth (sect), with Moon, Venus, or Jupiter above the horizon in a Water or Earth signs (strongest in Water).
- A very cold Saturn (under the horizon in a female sign), strongest in the night sect.
- Waxing Moon phase for the phlegmatic symptoms. Waning Moon for the mental-emotional issues, emotional withdrawal, or depressions.
- Jupiter in Cancer or Pisces enhance the phlegmatic potential of this sign.

SYMPTOMS OF CANCER SYNDROME

Please note that I am not discussing "Cancer people" per se, but those born with prominences in this sign that actually do suffer the syndrome. These symptoms are not listed in any order, but simply as a list of collected observations common to natives of Cancer. Please be sure to balance with Cancer's Superpowers. As with any sign, there are just as many positives!

Some items of this symptom set can occur for Cancer Moon natives, especially those related to light sensitivity, feeling-memory issues, fluidic changes, or hormones.

Should a great many of these symptoms be present, remedies are determined from the remedials and activities of Saturn, Mars, Sun, and Jupiter.

- noise or sound sensitivity
- light sensitivity
- temperature sensitivity, too hot or cold, changes frequently, on-off-on with jackets or shoes, typically cold (or hot) when others are not.
- delicate, sensitive skin
- extreme reactions to bug bites, needles, intrusion
- extreme fluidic changes at menses
- water retention
- sore or sensitive breasts (cyclic)
- life revolves around food
- stomach issues (bloat, ulcer, appetite swings, food addictions, overeating, under eating, food fears, et al)
- anorexia, bulimia, orthorexia
- mother issues
- father issues
- safety and security concerns
- fear, or when extreme, various paranoias, phobias, walling off self, pouting, retreating, going silent, refusing contact
- storing food or survival items
- storing anything, hoarding, the proverbial pack rat
- receding, weak or sore gums
- weak knees
- osteoporosis
- loss of strength in shoulders, arms, hands, hips, or thighs
- hip problems
- sluggish venous circulation
- lymphatic sluggishness
- breast and ovarian cysts
- cyst or tumor building conditions, trapped fluids
- agoraphobia
- allergies
- constant reference to self in conversation; or talking about self, own pet, child, family, or personal concerns.
- talking to oneself
- slower large motor skills in children
- myopia (near-sightedness) and light-sensitive eyes

- weak or gentle voice
- frail, delicate, and asthenic, sometimes flat chested (New Moon Type)
- large breasts and puts on water weight easily (Full Moon Type)
- cannot build muscle easily (New and Full Moon Types)
- internal feelings and memories dominate over incoming data
- fixated on the past, including world history (personal genealogy) or favorite era
- clinging to past, parents or place of birth
- needs a pet, or something to love
- compulsive melodies going through the mind
- phlegmatic damp lungs, some weakness in lungs, weak expectoration of lungs, congestion, extreme mucous production with colds or flu
- pale, damp tongue, sometimes with white coat
- prefers night hours
- poor or weak teeth
- sunlight exhausts
- prolonged hot tubs attenuate or bring nausea.
- blood cell issues
- marrow related issues
- fatigue with depression
- cell changes (cancers, benign tumors)
- blood sugar swings
- hypoglycemia and the need for frequent meals
- cyclic mood swings (toward petulance, depression, withdrawal or neediness)
- emotional dependency
- emotional withdrawal, walling off
- difficulty forgetting or releasing received insults or wrongs
- intense dislike or terror of chaos, random noise, firecrackers, and the like
- hyper defensive
- specific phobias
- terror of needles, surgery, dentistry

- tension or spasm of diaphragm
- tension in solar plexus
- shallow breathing
- trouble thinking quickly and calmly in emergency situations
- glycogen release or storage issues
- sensitive pancreas
- trouble assessing approaching or departing objects in motion (a driving skill)
- difficulty assessing spatial relations of objects in motion
- dislike of driving; may prefer walking, bicycling, feeling more in control

- fear of flying (or driving, or biking, etc.) fast motion related fears
- overly attached to either parents or children (positively, intensely devoted to family)
- highly fertile
- restricted ribcage
- very small or very large ribcage
- slow convalescence
- shyness
- tunnel vision, blindness (rare)
- mutism (rare)
- inward turning feet; or pigeon toes (rare)

Memory Preoccupation Disorder (MPD): Absorption, obsession, constant discussion of, or overwhelm from one's own memories of childhood, past relationships, one's parents, wrongs endured, grief, abandonment, lost love, and the like. It is difficult to "just let go" of insults received. Memories may consume to the point of walling off the sufferer from current reality or alienating friends. Preoccupied or hugely affected by memories as well as attachment and bonding disorders. This usually manifests as excessive bonding, but it can reverse, and you have the person who walls others out, often suddenly and without explanation.

REMEDIATION TIPS

Please note that these remedial tips are for interest only. The author is not suggesting that any person use these without the evaluation and consent of their personal healthcare practitioner.

The following is a short list of herbs that possess properties that are potentially remediative to one or more of the classic symptoms discussed above:

- **Chamomile**, *Matricaria chamomilla*, gentles the stomach, calms peevish emotions.
- **Angelica**, *Angelica archangelica*, warming hormonal regulator
- **Red Clover**, *Trifolium pratense*, hormonal regulator, famous for removal, and walling off of breast cysts, anti-carcinogenic.
- **Red Root**, *Ceanothus americanus*, traditional specific for splenic issues.
- **Sweet Violet,** *Viola Odorata,* traditional specific for the upper lymphatic system, breast clearance.
- **Dandelion Root**, *Taraxacum officinale,* specific for the cleansing of breast tissue and assists liver cleansing.
- **Bilberry**, *Vaccinium myrtillus*, improves night vision.
- **Horseradish**, *Armoracia rusticana,* a superior lymphatic stimulant, antibacterial, antimicrobial properties. Useful for lymph stagnation, lung ailments, and UTI. A perfect fit for many cold, stagnant water sign issues.

- **Cabbage juice:** lovely for stomach ulcers - proven in many cases to arrest the Helicobacter pylori bacterium responsible.

For a handy reference to herbs potentially useful for all twelve sign syndromes, see Chapter 15, *The Twelve Zodiac Sign Syndromes and their Relevant Herbs.*

Chapter Seven:
LEO SYNDROME

Regard the heart, and keep that upon its wheels
For the Sun is the fountain of Life
- Nicholas Culpeper (1616-1654)

Life of the Party

Most astrologically aware readers know Leo's reputation as the "life of the party"; happy to command the bar, lead the band, or perhaps head up the local astrological organization! But why should this be so? And how does Leo's noted playful, commanding, and affectionate nature reflect upon the very real phenomenon of *Leo Syndrome?*

Sun-ruled Leo rules the heart, the very center of life in the view of Renaissance physicians. A weakness of the Sun in a Leo's birth chart will also explain the reverse phenomenon: the occasional shy, intensely self-conscious Leo! As we shall see, Leo's traditional character intrinsically mirrors the heart's function.

Fundamentals Refresher

Leo Syndrome is a set of collaborative symptoms, consistently appearing together, which are typical for natives of the sign Leo. The symptoms associated with Leo Syndrome can be experienced by people with other sun signs when there is a particular emphasis in this sign. Zodiac sign syndromes can occur in seriatim, first one symptom, then another, weeks, months or years later. Few experience all symptoms. However, two or more of these symptoms are frequently observed clustered together at the same time.

A Leo native may have few if any of the symptoms associated with Leo Syndrome. Indeed, many Leos are specimens of perfect health. However, this symptom set often, but not always, evinces itself when a native's Sun, Moon, or Ascendant tenants Leo and displays certain astrological conditions which are discussed at length in this chapter.

This chapter describes the astrological conditions that may aggravate the syndrome. With this knowledge, practitioners can explore the underlying condition when symptoms consistent with the syndrome present themselves in a patient. Understanding the energetic cause is the first step in remediation.

THE SIGN LEO

In Classical Western Astrology, with use of the Tropical Zodiac, "a Leo" is someone born between 120 to 149 longitudinal degrees (or days) following the spring equinox.

As with all other signs, we cannot think of Leo as an isolated single entity or a static constant. "Leo" is a gestalt of strengths and weaknesses based on its angular relationship to the other signs of the interconnected solar cycle. In turn, each of the twelve phases of this cycle is influenced by the unique planetary configurations at birth and throughout the life. Leo is a unique phase-state, with its interactions peculiar to the fifth stage of the twelve-fold cyclical process.

Element and Mode: Leo is of the element Fire. Leo is the mid-summer sign and, therefore, is of the *Fixed* quadruplicity of signs. The effects of *Fixed Fire* will be discussed at length below.

Life Cycle Phase: The sign Leo represents the fifth stage of the twelve-fold human life cycle. The infant born (Aries), has fed (Taurus), was next the babbling tot (Gemini), and then becomes aware of its place in the home and tribe (Cancer). Now in Leo, the creative "I am" ego awakens, capable of physical-emotional creativity. This is the sign of flowering, of adolescence. The heart awakes to romance, self-display, and the sheer pleasure of living! Leo brings the soul experience of self-glory and power.

It is then of no surprise that Leo governs acting, sport, dancing, and the theatre. In my statistical study of jazz musicians, sampled by musical instrument, a full 60% of famous jazz bands leaders were Leos!

Understanding Leo through Sign Polarity

We can further understand Leo by its relationship to opposite sign Aquarius. Aquarius, the Water Bearer (or angel), symbolizes mental creativity, vision, imagination, and philanthropy. Whereas Leo, the Lion, symbolizes willpower and the power and glory of physical forms of creativity.

The opposite sign Aquarius aligns the self with a universal will or a higher plan for humanity. It is notoriously low on "self-push." Conversely, Leo is the ruler, the king. It is amazing how many politicians and self-producers have aspects in both signs! Barack Obama, a Leo with Aquarius Ascendant, is a good example. Mae West and Lucille Ball were both Leos and the first two women to direct, produce, and act in their own films.

Opposite signs are but opposite ends of a single pole! In this case, it is the active creativity of the Monad (individual soul) which is *physically and emotionally* expressed in Leo and mentally expressed in the creative genius and philanthropy of Aquarius.

Leo's Superpowers

Lion Power: The lion presents displays of *strength, creative will, courage, and power!* How do these qualities relate to health? A Leo Sun and ascendant so often possess both physical strength and power of the Vital Force. A strong Vital Force is essential to good health and recovery from illness. Leo Sun and Ascendant children are often remarkably energetic, athletic, and healthy. I have observed that most young Leos recover quickly from wounds and, in general, are rarely sick - unless they booze their heart, liver or gallbladder into trouble. It is all too common for older Leos to suffer the unwanted rewards of a meaty, alcohol drenched diet.

Life Loving: Leo's innate enjoyment of life assists health on all levels. They don't sweat the small stuff and prefer to be the boss and not the secretary. Neither do Leos need nagging to get some exercise, because they enjoy hiking, dancing, sport, and adventure. Few Leos accept a lifetime of hard physical labor. If at all possible, they will aspire to management or successful business ownership, providing themselves the wealth and leisure they love.

Three Fire Signs - Three Flows and Locations of Heat

What is the difference between Leo and fellow hot, dry Fire signs Aries and Sagittarius?

Aries, Cardinal Fire: Aries produces suddenly igniting heat, largely centered in the head, eyes, motor centers, and brain, that rushes quickly *outward and upward,* out of the body.

Leo, Fixed Fire: The oven. Leo produces a great, slow building and concentration of heat in the heart, aorta, liver, and gallbladder, and possibly the spleen. Leo holds heat in place, like an oven. Envision a large, brick kiln, or perhaps a pizzeria's oven. When enraged, or under physical or astrological stress, this fire force can either suddenly explode or internally corrode. Perhaps Leo, and especially its ruler the Sun, symbolize the spark of life itself, concentrated in the center of each atom. The Sun's symbol is a circle with a "dot" in the middle, an apt depiction this principle!

As a fire sign, *Leo influences the fuel burning mechanism* and the digestive enzymes that break down food products. Fire signs are catabolic in nature. However, *Leo possesses the slowest metabolism of the Fire Triplicity.*

Sagittarius, Mutable (Wild) Fire: Sagittarius is cooler and moister than Aries and Leo, but not always. The moving, or mutable, Fire energy rushes through the spinal nerves, the sciatic nerve, down the hips and thighs, and through the voluntary musculature of the limbs. This sign also brings heat to the mind, creating all manner of fiery mental states! Think of wildfire.

Fire and the Demise of Leo

The concentrated Fire element of Leo dispels damp, cold conditions with ease! However, the excessive heat, so typical of this sign, if pushed to extremes, can prove fatal.

Cornell noted that "Saturn rising in Leo" indicated exceedingly strong men. I can attest to his observation by witnessing one sixty-year-old native of precisely such a nativity. He confounded two male teenagers by solitarily lifting a huge, oak cabinet, carrying it out the door and up the street, and proceeding to load it himself on to a flatbed truck. Together, the two young men couldn't lift it off the ground! Stunned and embarrassed, they quickly fled the scene.

Strangely, when denied life's pleasures, Leo's surplus allotment of Vital Force fails them. In one statistical study I saw many years ago, the sign natives that died first from AIDS were Leos! I cannot recall the author. Neither have I seen Leo at the top of anybody's list of longest-lived signs. Perhaps their superpowers are equally their proverbial Achilles heel.

A loss of strength due to age or accident is psychologically unbearable to classic Leos! I believe that when faced with inevitable decline, the life-loving Leo type prefers to leave before the party is over. This, in essence, is a form of personal power retention.

Slow decline and dependency are just not Leo's cup of tea. Leo's 'quincunx' relationship to Pisces offers an explanation (this quincunx is explored in the Weak Signs section below). Curiously, delicate Pisces was statistically the *last* to succumb to AIDS!

Physical Appearance

Chest and shoulder weight, small hips (unbalanced upper and lower body). Often the upper body is large or hulking, and the lower body narrow or slender. Many Leos have very few fat cells on their thighs and carry their weight above the belt. This is a handsome sign, having earned the award of astrology's three traditional "signs of pulchritude" (beauty).

Exhaustive detail with illustrations is provided in this author's *The Astrological Body Types*.

FIXED FIRE AND THE VITAL FORCE

The Sun is the great generator of what has been called the "Vital Force." There are many recognized perturbations of this solar generated Vital Force that we experience in the Four Elements, three modes, twelve Signs, and planets. Consider from Source one great stream of solar cosmic life energy moving through a prism and refracting into diverse colors, tones, and rates of motion.

The three modes (Cardinal, Fixed, Mutable) describe the *rate of motion* of this Vital Force, as it moves through each element. In fixed signs, the seasonal energy concentrates, moving slowly or not at all. *When in the presence of many Leos, one so often feels a sensation of condensed power.* They seem to bask in themselves. Fine examples are Leo actors May West, Madonna, and Arnold Schwarzenegger.

Fire is the first thrust of the life force, closest to the original source, or first creative impulse. We see in the Kabbalah that the element Fire is listed first in the order of descent into matter from the world of pure energy, creation. The fourth, final level is Earth, the dense chemical-molecular plane. Thus, we see a densification of matter and planes, escalating downward from Source, through the four Elements in this traditional order: Fire, Air, Water, Earth (with Air representing the mental plane and Water the astral world just before the Earth plane.)

In his great work, *The Reflexive Universe*, great physicist Arthur Young correlated the photon, an elementary light particle, with the first of four levels of descent from Source, towards the state of dense matter. (I have no idea if Young was familiar with the similar Kabbalistic idea). He explained how the photon enjoyed the greatest amount of freedom, far greater than that afforded the molecule or, at extremity, a rock. One notes the adventuresome and freedom delighting nature of fire sign people.

It seems apt to correlate the photon with Fire signs. In Leo, the fire element is at its most condensed, full of potential creative force. Perhaps *Leo symbolizes, in part, the energy stored, or "fixed" in the center of atoms, and tiny sub-atomic particles.*

Consider the symbol of Leo's ruler the Sun, a circle with a dot in the middle. The dot in the circle also symbolizes the Monad, the individual being, or *jiva*. In Leo arrives the awareness of self as an individual being, capable of creativity, a veritable little God. In a similar vein, this dot can also describe the enormous force locked within the atom's center.

The Danger of Fixed Fire

To reiterate, *the element Fire brings the first, most direct current of solar Vital Force, life itself.* It is my conjecture that the sign Leo and its ruler, the Sun, represent the life force itself, and the enormous power stored in the core of the atom as *Fixed* Fire. We witness this latent force displayed in some Leo natives when angered! Although warm and big hearted, this affectionate sign is famous for temper tantrums and violent displays of force.

A strong Vital Force of the Fire type is necessary for good metabolism, energy, and health. We note that Leo natives commonly have good appetites, burn calories well in youth, love life, and rarely know constipation. The classic Leo type is handsome, broad shouldered, vividly romantic, sportive, and muscular. In age, they run from quite lean to paunchy… a huge beer gut is not uncommon in older males (though some maintain their gorgeous physiques into advanced age).

It is also possible to possess an excess of this hot, dry, solar force. One sees this in the athlete who without warning suffers a violent stroke. Heart attack, aneurysm, aortic dissection, or hot seizure are common to this type in excess, mostly in middle age. The glamorous fire sign track star phenom Flo-Jo died in this manner at thirty-eight, shocking the world.

Curiously, for all its vitality, Leo is not the longest-lived sign. The type will not suffer life in bed or thrive long when deprived of love and joy. I well recall one big, strong Leo who warned his girlfriend that if she moved away, as promised, that he would die. He carried forth his promise within days of her removal, by dropping dead of a violent stroke in a gas station. In his grief, he stopped taking his blood pressure medicine.

The healer should assess a Leo native's excess of Vital Force seriously, on both the physical and psychological levels. Physicians might diagnose high blood pressure, gallbladder disease, or tachycardia (rapid heart rate) without considering that for Leo natives, these can be physical manifestations of an excess influx of fixed solar force! Glaucoma and stroke are not uncommon in this type, if due to internal pressures generated from the heart, liver, or *excess internal heat.* In extreme cases, one sees internal corrosion in the form of stomach ulcers, pancreatitis, inflamed gall ducts, and severe dehydration. This awareness now becomes the key to healing.

LEO BODY RULERSHIPS AND FUNCTIONS

As described in Chapter One, a body zone is a general box that overlays many organs, functions, vessels and their sub-rulerships. Leo will typically be seen in natal charts, or by current transit, when one observes accidents or symptoms in this zone.

Leo, Body Zone 5

This sign governs the heart as both a physical organ and the repository (reservoir) of the Vital Force. Leo's rulerships also include the heart muscles, aorta, coronary arteries, vena cava, the spinal sheath, the dorsal spine, and the muscles of the mid-back (longissimus dorsi, transversalis, and latissimus dorsi). Cornell specifies the 2nd dorsal spine to Leo. Leo also holds a significant co-rulership over the gallbladder (with Capricorn), and the bile (with Mars). The heat of the liver, our hottest organ, is also associated with this sign. Leo co-rules the forearms and wrists with Gemini. This sign concentrates the solar Vital Force in the heart region.

Sol and the Spleen

There is a strong tradition for the spleen as a storage and distribution center for the solar Vital Force. Many sources (Cornell, Heindel) state that the spleen is Sun-ruled. The spleen is also variously listed under either Cancer or Virgo (traditional sources give Saturn).

I decided to investigate these ideas a little deeper and collected the charts of five famous people who suffered ruptured spleens. (I could find no famous cases of splenomegaly, which would perhaps have better served my cause). Each case showed a great natal dominance in Virgo, yet also, a strong Cancer component. On the day of the injury, all cases displayed a closely, and harshly afflicted Sun, and Mercury, often directed to the sign Virgo, with Cancer a close second.

My tiny research sample is hardly enough to draw firm conclusions. However, I've formed a tentative opinion that tradition is correct. Sun, Virgo and Cancer have a great deal to do with the spleen. Mercury vividly contends for co-rulership.

Question: Do Sun-ruled Leo natives suffer from an excess influx of solar force arising through the spleen center, even though the spleen's sign rulership is assigned to Virgo and Cancer?

The Gallbladder and the Liver

The gallbladder is ruled by Leo, Capricorn, and Saturn, while Mars precipitates the gall (Cornell). Virgo also holds a great influence over both organs.

In practice, I have never seen a case of gallstones or gallbladder disease without both Leo and Capricorn strongly implicated, and often Virgo too, with dominant Mars and Saturn in relation to these three signs.

The liver creates the bile that is stored in this organ. Both organs release bile. This is a very "hot" area of the body, the Liver generating a large percentage of our bodily heat! There are various good articles on the thermodynamics of the liver, and the problems generated by excessive liver heat.

Excess fixed fire can bake down the cholesterol into hard little balls called gallstones. Jupiter, Sol's great friend, rules the liver. As a sign, Virgo holds a general and easily verifiable rulership over the liver, and in observed cases, plays a strong role for the gallbladder too, with Capricorn. Dr. Cornell states that the liver is "presided over by Virgo" but has an "internal rulership of Leo," without providing further details. He also gives the upper lobes of the liver to Cancer and the lower lobes to Virgo; and involves several more signs as influential. Other moderns assign the liver to Jupiter and Virgo, sometimes with a Cancer influence for the upper lobes.

Considering all this, it's clear that the *heat concentrating function of the liver* is influenced by Leo, although both Leo and Virgo suffer "hot liver" complaints. When working with Leo patients presenting internal heat, the logical practitioner considers allaying the heat of the liver, gallbladder, heart, and spleen.

It's All About the Heart

"She's all heart." Leo is a generous, vividly expressive, and loyal sign that is all about both the proverbial heart and the physical heart. When studying heart complaints of all kinds, always look first to Leo (and ruler, Sol), then to its opposite sign Aquarius. These two signs work in tandem, governing the general circulation of blood through the body.

There are, of course, other influences. Sagittarius chimes in by governing arterial circulation, while Venus co-rules the venous system with her companion Aquarius. Capillaries are under the auspices of Gemini. Pressures from squaring signs Taurus (diet and thyroid) and Scorpio (the colon) can potentize heart diseases.

The heart (Leo and Sol) generates the largest electrical field of the body, while Aquarius rules the *distribution* of electrical conduction through the nerves and muscles. Leo governs the heart and Aquarius the circulation, specializing in the venous system. Leo pumps the blood, and Aquarius rules oxygenation and the oxygen-carbon exchange. These signs are partners!

The brain and eyesight are notably influenced by Leo, although the brain, eyes, and vision are generally under the auspices of fellow fire sign Aries.

The unchecked rising of internal heat so common to Leo natives results in all manner of migraine like symptoms, temper fits, and pressure to head or eyes. In the language of Traditional Chinese Medicine, *there is a lack of Yin for holding down the Yang*. This idea fits Leo Syndrome well. Alternatively, rising heat could just be *excess Yang!* Astrologically, we note that the *fiery trilogy of planets* (Sun, Mars, Jupiter) and the Lunar North Node *increase Yang*, especially when in fire signs. This tendency is further enhanced when the Sun, Mars, or Jupiter are above ground in a daylight nativity.

The Sun-Saturn Connection and Nutrition

Traditional planetary rulerships conceal all manner of relevant symbolism. On comparing modern scientific discoveries with our ancient planetary associations, one so often thinks "how did they know that?" Let's take a look at one such example.

The Sun rules Leo, the sign of *mid-summer*. Leo's opposite sign, Aquarius, is governed by Saturn. Aquarius is the sign of *mid-winter*. Conversely, Sol is in detriment in Aquarius, whereas Saturn's *detriment* is found in sunny Leo.

The Sun governs the light of life, while Saturn rules death. The ancients assigned Sol to the metal gold, whereas Saturn ruled lead, a metal that blocks light and radiation. The Sun is hot, Saturn is cold, and so forth. However, it is with modern nutrition that this part-nered planetary pair sees their great moment.

I have had difficulty determining exactly when the vitamins and minerals were assigned to their planets. The revered C.C. Zain (Elbert Benjamin) provides a list in 1934. Astrologers Robert Carl Jansky (1973), and Eileen Nauman (1982) seconded many of Zain's associations and depart only slightly from each other. Nauman gives the most comprehensive descriptions and usages.

All three state that the Sun governs vitamins A, D, and Paba, and minerals magnesium, manganese, and iodine. Saturn is given vitamin C, folic acid, and most obviously calcium (he rules the bones).

How is all this relevant to the partnership between Leo's ruler the Sun and Saturn the ruler of Leo's opposite sign Aquarius? After all, opposite signs are partners, as well as antagonists, much like many couples. Sol and Saturn's home signs, Leo and Aquarius, govern two ends of one pole! Although each sign independently governs several functions, one might best describe the Leo-Aquar-ius polarity as the heart and circulatory system.

Nutritionists realize that calcium (Saturn) and magnesium (the Sun) work in tandem to regulate the heartbeat. As actin (a protein in the muscle fiber) absorbs calcium around the Leo/Sun ruled heart, the heart muscle contracts. Magnesium then gives a positive charge, pulling calcium back out of the actin. This creates a second contrac-tion in a cycle that continues until our last breath.

Astrologically speaking, this is not the only pumping action of paired minerals that have coincidental assignments to planets that just happen to rule opposite signs. This is quite apt, because oppo-site signs work as balancing and antagonistic pairs, controlling one or more bodily systems. Visualize a seesaw.

There is more, and merrier. Calcium (Saturn) is best absorbed when combined with Vitamin D (Sun). Conversely, for the Sun-ruled magnesium to successfully absorb, we require an adequate availability of both calcium (Saturn) and phosphorous (Mars). Why Mars? Sol is exalted, in Aries, a Mars-governed sign! Mars and the Sun are also traditional "friends," governing signs positioned on the seasonal wheel, in natural trine to each other (Leo and Aries). The astrological symbolism perfectly depicts these nutritional links.

Now, let's check out nutritive deficiencies correlated to this Sun-Saturn partnership. Excessive calcium carbonate (an antacid) can stimulate magnesium dumping, resulting in magnesium deficiency (negative Sol).

In astro-nutrition theory, any hard aspect or quincunx between natal Sun and natal Saturn could produce deficiencies of calcium or magnesium, or any other nutrients governed by these planets. For example, one could suspect deficiencies of any solar ruled nutrient (A, D, Paba, Iodine, Manganese or Magnesium), should transiting Saturn be afflicting the natal Sun by hard aspect or quincunx.

Both a Leo or Aquarius Sun (or Ascendant) would be uniquely predisposed to nutritional deficiencies when Saturn afflicts the Sun in these signs, natally or by transit. Should symptoms present, study the birth chart of a Leo Sun or Ascendant for these possible afflictions.

Gold, Leo, and the Sun

What did the ancients know about the relationship of minerals and metals to the planets? Quite a bit! But we have time here for only a brief discussion of Leo, the Sun, and gold. See the books referenced below for more detail.

Since antiquity, *gold has belonged to Sol*. And Sol and his sign Leo govern the heart. Thus, the Sun rules both gold and the heart. See Culpeper's quote heading this Chapter.

Medical science accepts a strong medical link between gold and the heart. Gold is found in trace amounts in the body, especially in the heart. There exists a plethora of sites on the web describing the utility of gold in heart treatments.

For a personal example, my grandmother was near death of hyperthyroid. You could hear her rapid heartbeat from across the room. She was completely and permanently cured by the sipping of a gold solution. They did not remove her thyroid.

Below, for those inclined, are three books that provide significant detail on the relationship of the planets to the metals, in this case the Sun-gold connection.

- M. Uyldert, *Metal Magic: The Esoteric Properties and Uses of Metals*, Turnstone Press Limited, UK, 1980
- Alison Davison, *Metal Power, The Soul Life of the Planets*, Borderland Sciences Research Foundation, Garberville, California,1991
- Nick Kollerstrom, *The Metal Planet Relationship*, Borderland Sciences Research Foundation, Garberville, California, 1993

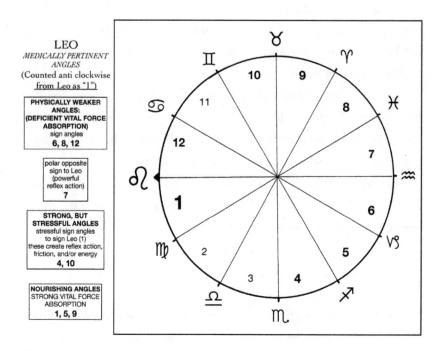

LEO
MEDICALLY PERTINENT ANGLES
(Counted anti clockwise from Leo as "1")

PHYSICALLY WEAKER ANGLES:
(DEFICIENT VITAL FORCE ABSORPTION)
sign angles
6, 8, 12

polar opposite sign to Leo
(powerful reflex action)
7

STRONG, BUT STRESSFUL ANGLES
stressful sign angles to sign Leo (1)
these create reflex action, friction, and/or energy
4, 10

NOURISHING ANGLES
STRONG VITAL FORCE ABSORPTION
1, 5, 9

LEO SYNDROME

As discussed in Chapter Two, a Zodiac Sign Syndrome is a cluster of symptoms associated with the body zones and functions of a zodiac sign and the signs positioned on the seasonal wheel opposite (180°) and quincunx (150°, 210°, 330°) the sign. Remediating and supporting these body zones and functions act to bring the body into balance, diminishing the syndrome. These symptoms may manifest when there is an emphasis in one or more of these signs. Planetary dignity plays an important role.

The Weaker Signs for the Leo Vital Force
Quincunx Signs

Capricorn, Pisces, and Cancer are positioned 150°, 210° and 330° distant from Leo on the seasonal wheel. These signs represent the 6th, 8th, and 12th *averted* angles from the sign Leo (see the illustration for this chapter). This condition makes it difficult for Leo to absorb the cosmic rays or the vibrational and light nutrients that feed these signs. Likewise, these signs may have trouble absorbing the rays from Leo.

Capricorn rules Body Zone 10 which includes the knees and skin. This sign also influences skeletal structure and co-rules the gallbladder. Leo-Capricorn involvement is a primary astrological signature for potential gallbladder issues. This quincunx also relates to possible poor calcium or mineral absorption of the spinal column, or knees, possibly producing scoliosis, lordosis, and other spinal misalignments so classic to Leo and Leo Moon. One so often sees the older Leo, Leo Ascendant or Leo Moon with the bad knee due to an early football injury, etc.

Pisces rules Body Zone 12 which includes the lymphatic system, feet, fascia (Hill), the parasympathetic system, extracellular matrix (Hill), sleep, and "reincarnation hangovers." It is not uncommon to see older Leos suffer from dropsical conditions due to heart failure or possible lymphatic stasis. Look to the feet as a possible source of Leo's renowned spinal complaints.

This quincunx has a spiritual indication. The sign Leo is uncomfortable with the classic Piscean fortes of self-reflection, sorrow, empathy, solitude, and physical delicacy. One notes in Leo a fear of frailty, anonymity, or decline. Pisces is the sign of sorrows, so comfortable in the deep caverns of the psyche and accepting of their inevitable dissolution. Conversely, Leo avoids sorrow and is uncomfortable with sticky emotional situations, grief, weeping, loss of power, and the like. Pisces natives rarely experience "power" as Leo knows it, but they could care less about that concept.

Cancer rules body zone 4 which includes the stomach and breasts. This sign also influences mucus membrane, gums, synovial and interstitial fluids (Hill), fertility, and the womb (when pregnant, otherwise Scorpio).

Leo Sun, Ascendant and Moon are common signs for sufferers of infertility. Leo natives are prone to hot stomach conditions and nausea, as Cancer's lunar moist coolness is lacking!

Cancer is the sign standing immediately behind Leo and therefore occupies the mysterious twelfth angle to it. Thus, Leo syndrome involves *fear of displaying emotional receptivity or weakness.* Thus, the emotional vulnerability so typical of Cancerians is difficult for Leo natives. The twelfth house position of Cancer to Leo may signal psychological issues behind some of the physical symptoms of Leo Syndrome. Cancer related emotional concerns include issues with parents and family of origin and deficient infant nutrition.

Opposite Sign, Aquarius

When the Sun is in Leo, the opposite sign, Aquarius, "sleeps". **Aquarius rules Body Zone 11,** which includes the shins, ankles, calves, and venous circulation; it co-rules the spinal nerves. As discussed previously in greater detail, Aquarius also influences oxygenation of the blood, oxygen-carbon exchange, electrical distribution, and the quality of the blood. *The Leo-Aquarius opposition sees all manner of circulatory and heart complaints.* High blood pressure is typical.

Signs Aggravating Leo Syndrome - Squaring Signs

The two signs squaring (positioned 90° from) Leo are Scorpio and Taurus (see chapter illustration). The effect of a square is to create friction, for good or ill. Leo can reflex with these signs, as well as its opposite sign, Aquarius.

Scorpio rules Body Zone 8 which includes the bladder, colon, genitals, nose, and sweat glands. Heart problems (Leo) can be compounded or caused by colonic stasis.

Taurus rules Body Zone 2 which includes the mouth, lower jaw and teeth, ears, tongue, throat, upper esophagus, lower rear of the brain, and cervical vertebrae; co-rules the thyroid. Heart and thyroid issues can reflex off one another. An unattended septic tooth (Taurus) can poison the heart (Leo).

Both these signs squaring Leo can indicate heart and spine conditions. Thyroid-heart (Taurus-Leo); diet-heart (Taurus-Leo); neck-spine (Taurus-Leo); colon-heart (Scorpio-Leo); pelvis-spine (Scorpio-Leo).

How Planetary Dignity Contributes to Leo Syndrome
Strongest Planets

The **Sun** governs Leo, and the **Sun** reigns supreme! So, there is no planet exalted in Leo! However, we can look to Mars and Jupiter who rule the two fellow fire signs Aries and Sagittarius. Mars stimulates dry heat (like the Sun) and moist heat. Expansion is brought by Jupiter.

Weakest Planet

Saturn, the planet of laws and karmic retribution, falls in Leo. This may be metaphoric of the Universal Law (so exalted in Libra) becoming self-governing in Leo, the sign of the king. The self is now king, and the natural authority is reversed. Spouses of Leos typically complain that their partner is "always right" or mocks counseling.

As discussed previously, Saturn in Leo has nothing to do with any lack of strength! Au contraire. If well disposed, this position produces unusual strength! However, his cooling, astringent, and "wisdom ray" are less available when tenanting this hottest of signs. Saturn in Leo contributes to anger control issues, hypertension, ego issues, and arterial sclerosis. Saturn governs the bones, so it is not surprising that scoliosis, lordosis, and other spinal misalignments are common with this placement. Older Leo, or Leo Moon types are commonly prone to osteoporosis of the spine, especially if Saturn afflicts Sun, Moon or Ascendant in Leo.

Planetary and House Positions that Contribute to Leo Syndrome

(1) **Sun, Moon, or Ascendant sign in Leo**

(2) A weakness in a body zone governed by the signs opposite or quincunx Leo on the seasonal wheel, as discussed above under *The Weaker Signs for the Leo Vital Force.*

(3) Planets in Taurus or Scorpio square planets in Leo, as discussed above.

(4) The Sun, Moon, Ascendant, Saturn, Jupiter, Mars, Venus, South or North Node is in Leo, compounded by the testimonies below:

- Leo inhabits the 1st, 6th, 8th, or 12th houses.
- Saturn, Mars, or Jupiter square, oppose, or conjoin a Leo Sun or Moon.
- North Node, and possibly Uranus, conjunct Sun or Mars.
- South or North Node rising in Leo, or conjunct a Leo Sun, Mars, or Moon.
- Day birth (sect), with Sun, Mars, or Jupiter above the horizon in a Fire sign.
- Fire sign emphasis
- Deficient Water signs.
- Saturn or Mars in Earth Signs. Saturn in Earth prevents Fire from escaping at the surface and Mars (excretions and catabolic Fire energy) is suffocated in Earth.

SYMPTOMS OF LEO SYNDROME

Please note that I am not discussing "Leo people" per se, but those born with prominences in this sign <u>that actually do suffer the syndrome.</u> These symptoms can occur in seriatim, first one symptom, then weeks, months or years later, another. However, two or more of these symptoms are frequently observed clustered together at the same time. These symptoms are not listed in any order, but simply as a list of collected observations common to natives of Leo. Please be sure to balance with *Leo's Superpowers.* As with any sign, there are just as many positives!

As a rule, Leo is a healthy, sportive sign. The chances of a young, mindful Leo suffering the more dire symptoms listed below are rare, provided that overheating and other excesses are avoided. Leo is prone to chronic issues, accrued from a *lifetime* of bad habits.

- flushed face and/or palms
- craving for meat and/or alcohol
- may love junk food
- voracious eating, overeating
- constantly sipping sweet, sugary carbonated beverages
- acidosis
- alcoholism
- meningitis
- internal corrosion due to building internal heat and dehydration; stomach ulcers, gastritis, pancreatitis, gallstones.
- internal inflammations
- internal hemorrhage
- sciatica (often with Sagittarius)
- hot rashes
- injuries from muscle building, weightlifting, or sports
- gambling or spending addiction
- compulsive gaming, sports, or partying
- anger management issues, explosive or violent rages

- manias
- high fever with "fits"
- heart disease (almost any type, but more typically hypertensive, hot)
- heart palpitations, arrhythmia (especially for Mercury, Moon, or Uranus in Leo)
- congenital heart defect (rare)
- spinal issues
- scoliosis, lordosis (especially with Leo Moon)
- osteoporosis of spine
- spinal sheath lesions
- in rare cases, diseases of the spinal cord
- outward turning feet, strident walk
- gallstones (especially with Leo Moon)
- GERD (very common with Leo Moon)
- circulatory imbalance
- gout
- sunstroke
- brain dehydration
- general dehydration
- dry, hot stomach (sometimes serious ulcers)
- infertility
- vision disturbances
- chronic eye problems
- glaucoma
- loud voice
- strongly voiced opinions, bossy
- love of weaponry
- migraines
- hot sleeper
- deficiencies of magnesium, Vitamin A, D, Paba, iodine (especially if hard aspect or quincunx to natal Sun from natal or transit Saturn)
- arterial surges
- aortic dissection (rare)
- arterial sclerosis (especially Saturn in Leo)
- intense dislike of convalescing in bed
- inexplicable buildup of heat in the chakras (especially the first through four or five)
- "choler", biliousness, hot liver
- jaundice
- knee issue, injury, or weakness

Heat in Excess

As a mid-summer, Sun-ruled sign, Leo is hot, concentrated heat. *An excess of internal heat is behind most of Leo's complaints*, ranging from gallbladder disease, GERD, hypertension, stroke, aneurism, heart issues, violent temper, arterial tension or engorgement, tachycardia, hot seizures, sunstroke, fever, and what the Renaissance physician referred to as "fits", especially in cases of fever.

REMEDIATION TIPS

Please note that these remedial tips are for interest only. The author is not suggesting that any person use these without the evaluation and consent of their personal healthcare practitioner.

Should a great many of these symptoms be present, remedies are determined from the remedials and activities of our cooling, gentling planets: Moon, Neptune, and Venus. Leo's hot dry conditions respond beautifully to the cooling, moistening and sedative herbs and other remedials.

For Leo Syndrome in persons with a prominent Leo, physicians might consider reducing heat in the liver, assisting and clearing the gallbladder, reducing acidity, and promoting alkalinity. Question eating and drinking habits, study the spine for subluxations, scoliosis, lordosis, and other spinal deformities; observe the positioning and strength of the feet and knees; assist lymphatics, balance the arterial and venous circulation, or calm the "high blood." Improve, moisten, and cool the stomach lining and skin. And, especially, treat the heart, the heart, the HEART!

The practitioner must design remedies to reduce fixed fire.

- Relaxing heart remedies, such as Linden and Hawthorn
- Circulatory balancing herbs, such as Yarrow and Rosemary. Note that Rosemary is more typical for Aquarius.

- Various cooling moistening herbs. Peach for hot stomach; fruit, cucumber, and lettuce; celery is great for Leo gout!
- Stroke preventative herbs, such as Sage, Yarrow, Melilot, and Rutin and lecithin (supplements).
- Relaxing balms are excellent, such as Lemon Balm.
- Hydration. Lemon juice with sea salt is a specific for assisting deeper hydration.

Renaissance Heart Strengthening Tip

Renaissance Physician Joseph Blagrave prescribed various natural substances to strengthen hearts in trouble. A nugget of gold, or a bag containing one, and three or five solar herbs were his recommended favorites. I've discovered that a large piece of real amber was very calming and energizing to one Leo Ascendant, born with Jupiter rising in Leo, trine his Sun.

Blagrave's gold nugget worn over the heart of one 92-year-old heart failure patient (born with Saturn and Neptune rising in Leo) was not so successful. He said it made his heart "hurt" and removed it.

Dave Roell, the late, famous astrological publisher, was himself a victim of heart failure, to which he finally succumbed. He reported to me that the nugget of gold was quite effective for him. (We can thank Dave for republishing Blagrave's classic and disinterring this easy, practical technique).

Personally, I've discovered that one, three or five large beads of blue turquoise worn directly over the heart, touching the skin, is wonderfully effective for a soft, weak pulsing heart with fatigue, especially for Air and Water ascendants.

The Need for Water

Dehydration is a real problem for many Leo natives. One notes the taste for alcohol in the classic type - due to its relaxing, wet properties. However, alcohol further dehydrates. The need for relaxing hydration should be filled with pure water or fruit juices, or perhaps Lemon Balm Tea! Also note the hydration tip above.

Typical of all Fire signs, Leo enjoys stimulation. However, coffee dehydrates this sign further. Peppermint is a traditional *cooling* stimulant that strengthens the heart, but it should not be used in gallbladder disease or problems with the stomach's pyloric valve.

For Leo, cooling is best. Despite the old idea of "fetch out fire with fire", it is rarely safe in this sign to increase the internally building liver, heart, and gallbladder heat!

Chelidonium is the time-honored favorite herb for the Gallbladder, an organ co-ruled by Leo and Capricorn. In practice, I have never seen a case of gallstones or disordered gallbladder without these two signs, and often Virgo involved, with dominant Mars and often Saturn.

See also Chapter 15, *The Twelve Zodiac Sign Syndromes and their Relevant Herbs.*

ADDENDUM

LEO, CANCER, AND THE NESTED HEART

(This addendum, lightly edited, was first posted on Judith Hill's blog in November 2022. See original blog post on judithhillastrology.com for full article with accompanying images)

The ancient Greeks discovered that our twelve zodiac signs are physically correlated to twelve horizontal body zones. However, this tradition, known as *Melothesia* may enjoy far earlier roots. Papyrus scrolls from the tomb of Ramses V (1150-45 BCE) assigned ascending constellations (by the hour) to body parts. Although not precisely the same concept as Melothesia, one can assume a strong correlation exists.

The first sign Aries corresponds to the head, whereas the last sign Pisces to the feet, completing the zodiac circle. I've written quite a bit about this in previous articles, omitting some curious anomalies. It later occurred to me that sign zones within the body trunk evince considerable interactive blending between their zones. These seeming inconsistencies within the simplistic "chocolate layer cake" body zone model, reveal that the Greek designers were indeed intentional in their anomalies. Today, we will focus on the remarkable positioning of the Cancer-Leo body zones.

Cancer correlates to Body Zone 4, supposedly positioned *directly above* Leo's Body Zone 5. Cancer rules the rib cage, breasts, sternum, lower lung, pericardium, pleura, axillae, thoracic duct, uterus (when pregnant), mucus membrane, and stomach. Leo governs the heart, aorta, spinal sheaths, gallbladder, and thoracic spine. Obviously, these two zones overlap here and there - and are even *positionally reversed* in the case of the stomach and heart! For instance, the Cancer-ruled Body Zone 4's stomach and lower lung rest lower in the body than does the Leo-ruled heart, positioned in Zone 5. Additionally, both signs, plus Virgo, strongly influence the liver. Leo (with Capricorn and Saturn) is said to govern the gallbladder, whereas Mars rules the bile.

This Cancer-Leo positional anomaly appears to be an egregious error if one does not consider how the ancients regarded the role of the two Lights of Heaven - *Luna* and *Sol*. These "Lights" (as we know them today) stood apart from the planets. Astrologically, the Sun was conceived as the source of all life and light: *The Center* itself. Sol and Luna were the sole two commanding Lights of heaven, the overlord and lady of day and night. Sol and his sign Leo always govern the heart. The Sun governs this sign, and the Moon governs the sign Cancer. Leo is the domicile of the Sun, and Cancer is the domicile of the Moon.

From this discussion, we can see that Body Zone 5 (Leo) is actually *surrounded* by Body Zone 4 (Cancer), with both zones occupying relatively the same band width! In this one case, we see two body zones occupying mostly the same space; *one internally and one externally,* as in a circle with a circle around it. They appear thus to work in a cooperative manner.

Most other body zones stack approximately one above the other. Here, it appears more as though we have one Body Zone 5, somewhat surrounded by Body Zone 4. (However, see comment on anterior/posterior, below).

How does this reflect in the body?

The Leo-ruled heart is surrounded by the Cancer-ruled pericardium. Similarly, the Leo-ruled heart is protected and enclosed by the Cancer-ruled ribcage.

The Sun-Moon dance can be either viewed frontally, or, on a horizontal slice through the body. Frontally, draw a circle around the heart region, in the center of the chest. This is *Leo-Sol.* Surrounding this, draw a larger circle, encompassing the Cancer/Moon ruled breasts and rib cage.

Internally, one can envision Leo-Sun as the physical heart center, with a horizontal circle swirling around it, representative of Cancer-Moon, extended as a thick horizontal slice through the body.

It is essential to note that signs and planets are not the same things, nor always govern the same body parts. In Leo-Sun's case, however, they both govern the heart. In Cancer-Moon's example, they both rule the breasts and stomach.

Astrologically, *Sol is the central Vital Force and Luna distributes Sol's Vital Force.* In this paradigm, these two govern the body more so than any planet. Classic medical astrology depicts this unique status and function by embedding Leo's Body Zone 5 partially within Cancer's Body Zone 4. And, in practice, it works!

To reiterate, the Leo-ruled heart is encircled by the Cancer-ruled pericardium and ribs. Body Zones 4 and 5 are best envisioned as nested circles, more so than as stacked layers. *There is one exception.* The thoracic spine and upper back are under Leo, on the body's exterior *posterior*; whereas and the Cancer ruled sternum is on the body's exterior *anterior*. Here, we note an interesting posterior/anterior effect.

Leo's *internal* organs (heart, aorta,) lie fully within the thoracic cavity, with only one outlier: the Leo-ruled gall-bladder lands in the abdominal cavity. However, this is less remarkable as Leo shares rulership of this organ with Virgo, Capricorn, and Saturn. Conversely, only some of Cancer's interior organs share thoracic space with Leo (lower lung). Many Cancer-ruled organs are located lower down, in the upper abdominal cavity (stomach, spleen, pancreas). This reverses normal melothesian body zone order, by placing some organs of zone 4 beneath zone 5, rather than above! Thus, the body zones and organs of the only two Sun and Moon-ruled zodiac signs are observed to intermingle, invert zones, and share zone. *This mirrors the complex monthly Sun-Moon dance of the heavens.*

Cancer is also held to govern the diaphragm, that flexible, membranous structure that separates these two great cavities of the body.

Two other sign groups enjoy posterior-anterior effects. These are Libra-Scorpio and Sagittarius-Scorpio.

Zodiacal Man's nested circle zones and his anterior/posterior shared co-zones are adequately depicted and described on my *Medical Astrology Wall Charts.*

Zodiac signs also rule *functions*, as well as body *zones*. Their functional rulerships are apt to be found anywhere in the body, regardless of their positionally associated body zones. For instance, the Pisces-ruled lymphatic *function* roams throughout all twelve body zones, whereas Pisces governs Body Zone 12, the feet.

Functional rulership explains why, for instance, the liver, while residing in the shared Cancer-Leo region, appears to be influenced so strongly by Virgo. The liver's role partakes of much of Virgo's discernment and selection function. When confronted by a tiny food molecule, the liver asks, "What have we here?" So, we say that Virgo rules the discerning functions of the liver. We also know Virgo is strongly associated with the liver because we can repeatedly verify a Virgo emphasis in multiple cases of liver disease.

Leo, as the hottest sign of the pantheon, *concentrates heat*. Thus, Leo governs the heat of the liver. This is no small matter because the liver supplies about 30% of the body's heat! Intense, concentrating heat can relate to Leo when found anywhere in the body! Similarly, we know that Cancer's medical function is to protect, nourish, store and hoard. The liver's glycogen storage might well be considered a Cancer function. Cornell assigns the liver's upper lobes to Cancer, and lower lobes to Virgo, probably due to their body zone influence. I can see no other reason for him to do so because no known difference in liver lobe function pertains.

Chapter Eight:

VIRGO SYNDROME

The Greeks tell us that the goddess Virgo,
in distress at the end of the Golden Age,
left humankind forever and returned to the heavens.

\- Bernadette Brady, Brady's Book of Fixed Stars

Take-Home Boxes

I always puzzled at the reason behind why my Virgo dining companions will invariably take half of their dinner home in a box. Or, why my Virgo neighbors abhor a wide selection of neighborly odors. And again, why so many born of this sign enter helping professions, or are keenly aware of nutrition, and, curiously, clothes. Delving deeply into the organ rulerships and physical functions of this amazing sign explains why! This proverbial "sign of health" governs many of our essential digestive organs. A thorough comprehension of discerning Virgo benefits any cosmos-aware medical practitioner or lay person!

Fundamentals Refresher

Virgo Syndrome is a set of collaborative symptoms, consistently appearing together, which are typical for natives of the sign Virgo. The symptoms associated with Virgo Syndrome can be experienced by people with other sun signs when there is a particular emphasis in this sign. Zodiac sign syndromes can occur in seriatim, first one symptom, then another, weeks, months or years later. Few experience all symptoms. However, two or more of these symptoms are frequently observed clustered together at the same time.

A Virgo native may have few if any of the symptoms associated with Virgo Syndrome. Indeed, many Virgos are specimens of perfect health. However, this symptom set often, but not always, evinces itself when a native's Sun, Moon, or Ascendant tenants Virgo and displays certain astrological conditions which are discussed at length in this chapter.

This chapter describes the astrological conditions that may aggravate the syndrome. With this knowledge, practitioners can explore the underlying condition when symptoms consistent with the syndrome present themselves in a patient. Understanding the energetic cause is the first step in remediation.

THE SIGN VIRGO

In Classical Western Astrology, with use of the Tropical Zodiac, "a Virgo" is someone born between 150 to 179 longitudinal degrees following the spring equinox.

As with all other signs, we cannot think of Virgo as an isolated single entity or a static constant. "Virgo" is a gestalt of strengths and weaknesses based on its angular relationship to the other signs of the interconnected solar cycle. In turn, each of the twelve phases of this cycle is influenced by the unique planetary configurations at birth and throughout the life. Virgo is a unique phase-state, with its interactions peculiar to the sixth stage of the twelve-fold cyclical process.

Element and Mode: Virgo is of the element Earth. This is the late summer sign positioned at the gradual change from summer to autumn, hence, our second member of the *mutable* quadruplicity of signs.

Life Cycle Phase: Virgo represents the sixth stage of the twelve-fold human life cycle. The infant born (Aries), nurses (Taurus), becomes the curious toddler (Gemini), and then attains awareness of its place in the home and tribe (Cancer). In the previous chapter, we saw that the sunny, carefree adolescent basks in the pleasurable glory of a creative "I am" ego (Leo). Not anymore. Come Virgo, playtime is over and it's time to get to work! Virgo adjusts to a work ethic. The harvest is in, and all efforts are "grist for the mill". So much to do now, to polish and shine, and so little time!

This is the sign of the active maintenance, improvement, and perfection of the *physical body and material world.* The Virgo life stage represents *discernment* and, thus, *the making of boundaries.* This boundary making is not the shell-making we observe in Cancer. Boundaries, in this case, are flexible barriers at the behest of cognitive (or intestinal) discernment. As we shall see, this function is complementary to the entropic function of Virgo's opposite sign, Pisces, which dissolves boundaries and returns matter to universal source. Similarly, Virgo, the sign of earthly labor, stands opposite to Pisces, the sign of sleep and convalescence.

Virgo Superpowers
Alertness, acuity, usefulness

Virgo natives are smart, quick and have good hand skills and acuity. They are the most *flexible and fast* of the Earth signs, combining the toughness of Earth with the speed of Mercury. This is the limber gymnast or wiry mechanic. Virgo is also good at living on very little food, so useful in famine. Virgo on a mission can endure a significant amount of deprivation without complaint and not be the worst for it. Virgo is the sign of the industrious ant colony, beehive, or marching army, all fine examples of useful co-working units.

No sign is more capable of physical hardship, or discipline. This is the sign of the dutiful, tough foot soldier or nurse. I recall the awe felt watching my nimble forty-year-old Virgo landlord scamper up and down ninety steep concrete steps, twelve times per day, in maintenance of her girlish figure. The superpowers of this sign include nearly endless stamina and self-adjustment under stress. As the 1960's expression advised, they "keep on truckin'."

Natural nutritionists, Virgo natives are typically interested in their healthy nutrition (and yours too). The only problem is that they can overdo it, with sometimes the cure being worse than the disease! A keen interest in health, combined with their love for serving, brings many Virgos to the health, mental health, and social service fields. Good with numbers, many are excellent astrologers too! Virgos make excellent nurses, herbalists, nutritionists, psychologists, veterinarians, chiropractors, and others in the healing professions. The Virgo Sun or Moon native, happily serving or devoted to a useful team effort, appears unconcerned with self. Helping *others* to heal is perhaps their other superpower! They also often make happy farmers.

The native Virgoan efficiency of the intestine and liver provides its Virgo's natives the magic power to live off restricted food resources for extended periods in relatively good shape. This is a monk's sign!

The efficiency of their immune system, if not self-attacking, allows for fast wound healing and speedy recovery from colds and flus.

Physical Appearance

Exhaustive detail with illustrations is provided in this author's *The Astrological Body Types*.

VIRGO'S BODY RULERSHIPS AND FUNCTIONS

As described in Chapter One, a body zone is a general box that overlays many organs, functions, vessels and their sub-rulerships. Virgo will typically be seen in natal charts, or by current transit, when one observes accidents or symptoms in this zone.

Virgo, Zone 6

Virgo rules the duodenum, small and large intestines; pylorus and pancreas (with Cancer); jejunum, and ileum. It also rules the liver's parceling functions - "this-not that". Cornell gives the lower lobes to Virgo. This sign is almost always indicated in liver troubles (with Cancer); spleen and pancreas (with Cancer); and the immune system (with Pisces, Cancer, and Mars). The appendix seems to be Virgo affair, although some say Scorpio. For clarification, Scorpio rules lower colon, rectum and anus.

In my experience, appendicitis appears to be influenced by planetary obstructions indicated close to the 16°-18° of any earth or water sign.

Virgo probably governs the identification of alien bacterial and viral intruders, the lower dorsal nerves, the abdomen; the mesenteric glands (with Pisces), and the portal veins (with Aquarius and Venus as the general rulers of all veins). We will break this down later with a tour through the various species of immune cells and their roles. Cornell feels that the uterus, normally under Scorpio and Cancer (when pregnant), is shared with Virgo. As the quintessential sign of labor, Virgo governs the birth labor prior to parturition, but one might assume too, that Scorpio is involved with both labor and parturition.

Cornell also assigns the fingers and nails to Virgo. However, the hand is also strongly under a combined Gemini and Mercury's governance, and nails share Saturn. The pinkie finger is particularly Virgo, Mercury, and Gemini. The few hand injuries I have studied do not definitively show Virgo, but almost always Mercury and/or Gemini, and Mars for the thumb.

Cornell gives the umbilicus to Virgo, but I say Cancer. This is verified by the magnificent proving of a large, benign, umbilical tumor for a client born in Cancer with Jupiter closely rising in that sign. The belly button connects us to our mother, and she to her mother... back to the end of time and "first mother". No concept is more Cancerian!

The gallbladder is governed by Saturn, Capricorn, and Leo, with Mars precipitating the gall. However, in my experience, Virgo is equally represented in gallbladder problems!

Traditionally, Virgo "rules the gut", but what does this really imply? We know from experience that Zone 6 is certainly dominant and/or afflicted in most maladies of the upper intestinal organs. Yet, common sense asserts that some specific functions of these organs are shared with many of the planets and some other signs. Although this is true for all body zones, it is especially cogent here. Most essentially, we cannot consider Virgo, without including its constant polarity with opposite sign Pisces. For instance, Davidson says the duodenum and cecum are strongly influenced by Pisces.

Cornell assigns the mesentery and peritoneum to Virgo. What about the omentum? Observing the fatty nature of this large protective "apron", plus one case of its regretful surgical removal, informs me of a strong Pisces-Jupiter element. Here again we see the Virgo-

Pisces polarity at work in Virgo's body zone 6. Cornell agrees that the serum of the peritoneum is Piscean in nature.

The Liver and Gallbladder

We have already mentioned that the liver is primarily governed by Virgo, Body Zone 6, and the gallbladder by Leo, Capricorn, and Saturn. Virgo's governance of some specific liver functions is discussed above in the section on *discernment*. The liver makes the bile, distributes some directly to the blood, and stores the greater portion in the gallbladder for immediate release under immediate demand. Obviously, the two are closely associated. The liver's splitting up and sorting function is certainly Virgo, whereas its glycogen and nutrient storage function would appear more aligned to the sign Cancer's nature. Davidson states this.

In my experience, gallstones are often associated with natal Mars (in particular), Saturn, or some other afflicted planet in the sign Virgo and is usually coincident with planets in Leo and Capricorn. To reiterate, Cornell gives the liver's lower lobes to Virgo, without explanation, other than the upper lobes hedge into the Cancer body Zone.

The Spleen

There is a strong tradition for the spleen as a storage and distribution center for the solar Vital Force. Modern sources (Cornell, Heindel) state that the spleen is Sun-ruled, but variously under Cancer or Virgo for sign rulership. Traditional sources give the spleen to Saturn (although this may vary in the Jyotish tradition which allots the Sun-ruled 5th house to the spleen). I decided to investigate these variances a little deeper and collected five charts of famous people who suffered ruptured spleens. I just now received my first case of splenomegaly, which perhaps better serves my cause.

Each rupture case presents a great natal dominance in Virgo, and a strong Cancer component. On the day of the injury, all cases showed a closely, and harshly afflicted Sun and Mercury, often in or afflicting the signs Virgo and / or Cancer. The singular splenomegaly (engorged spleen) case featured exactly what one would expect: Jupiter, Pluto, and South Node in Virgo; Mars afflicting the splenic signs Virgo and Cancer, and Sun in Taurus opposed by Neptune, plus other supportive features.

This is a tiny group, hardly enough to draw firm conclusions. However, I have formed a tentative opinion that tradition is correct. Sun, Virgo and Cancer, all three, have a great deal to do with the spleen. Additionally, my research sample adds one new rulership for consideration: Virgo's ruler, Mercury.

Through the traditional Solar rulership of the spleen as a vital force distribution nexus, we find a Leo association. Question: *Do Leo's suffer from excess influx of solar force through the spleen center?* I have not encountered this, but it is worth checking into.

The Pancreas

The pancreas is listed by various sources under the rule of either Virgo or Cancer. My collection of pancreatic cases indicates both signs as equally indicated with a slight edge to Virgo. This is interesting as the pancreas straddles both Cancer and Virgo body regions, lying near the stomach and tucking its head up against the Virgo-governed duodenum. The pancreas also has multiple functions. First, it releases digestive enzymes for breaking down food particles. We have already seen the correlation of digestive enzymes to Mars and Virgo.

Additionally, the pancreas has a great deal to do with the body's regulation of sugar. Is this a Virgo function or the province of some other sign? Three types of pancreatic cells are involved. *Beta* cells secrete insulin, to assist the cells of the body to absorb and utilize needed sugar. When blood glucose swings too low, the *Alpha* cells secrete glucagon, preventing insulin from dropping too low and stimulating the release of stored glycogen in the liver. The *Delta* cells release the hormone somatostatin, an insulin and glucagon *inhibitor*! We can simplify this into "discernment then release, discernment then stop, discernment then go." A delicate balance.

Virgo is recognized as one of two natural "inhibiting" signs, hence the virgin mascot. However, Matthew Wood opined that the pancreatic blood sugar weighing and balancing dance is quintessentially Libran. Curiously, Libra is one of the three signs most typical for diabetes. The other signs are Virgo and Libra's opposite sign, Aries.

In medical astrology, we certainly see secondary participation from sign rulers operational within the overarching territory of another sign's body zone. In the case of the pancreas, we discover a Libra sub function operating within Body Zone 6 (Virgo). Diabetes is an overwhelmingly Virgo-Libra disease, though also often seen in Aries. What does the adrenal axis (Libra-Aries-Mars), have to do with diabetes? In diabetics, one so often sees the Virgo-Aries quincunx, with planets in Virgo, Libra, and Aries. (See an explanation in the chapter on Aries).

Pancreatic enzymes break down sugar, fats, and starches. Curiously, Virgo natives, as do Capricorns, thrive on low calories and simple, seemingly insufficient diets. One would think this was because of excellent pancreatic enzymes at the top of the digestive chain, combined with fastidious gut absorption. Yet why is Virgo internally and externally dry? I blame this on a slow hepatic system, cholesterol underproduction, poor bile, and insufficient gut mucus. This in turn may cause low bowel lubrication and the poor lipid distribution so often seen in this sign. Remember, Jupiter rules fat, and his detriment is in Virgo for a reason.

Fats

Jupiter is in detriment in Virgo. This implies that fats, ruled by Jupiter, are a problem for this sign. Virgos are often lean, though not always. Personally, I have met few obese Virgos. Conversely, I have met many Virgos so emaciated and that one wonders how they thrive at all. Of course, one does occasionally encounter the obese Virgo, but this is usually reflected by other factors in the horoscope.

Three Virgo clients immediately spring to mind. All three are bone thin and unable to maintain weight. Two have Saturn plus Sun and Mercury in Virgo. A fourth case, refusing fats in his diet, now has a body that's become an unhappy mass of emaciated tension. He was born with retrograde Saturn and South Lunar Node rising in Virgo.

The key issue here is insufficient fat or caloric utilization, or deficient cholesterol and bile. Poor lipid distribution is often evident in dry flakey skin, jittery nerves, dandruff, etc. See insights above, in the section on the pancreas. Of course, anorexia, orthorexia, and "tiny eating" appear to play a part as well.

Jupiter also governs the liver, our cholesterol factory. Virgo is the overarching ruler of this organ. Yet Jupiter is compromised in Virgo, being in its traditional detriment. It is amazing how often Jupiter in Virgo correlates to a *slow or toxic liver*. However, this position, well aspected, could also indicate a fastidious liver, one doing an exceptional job detecting poisons and selecting out the nutrients. (Allergies are already discussed above).

Virgo Body Functions

As a principal, Virgo governs identification, and sorting of data, or units. Below, let's itemize Virgo functions in order to distinguish them from Pisces, Scorpio and Cancer, which are relevant to the discussion.

Separation of wholes into parts: In this case, we focus on food particles. Virgo, with Mars, specializes in stomach, pancreatic, and duodenal enzymes, plus the bile created in the liver. All these secretions work to break down specific types of nutrient particles.

This quintessential Virgo function varies from the breakdown, recombining, and *eliminative* function of Scorpio or the *incendiary* quality of Mars. However, Mars certainly plays a big part in digestive enzymes and bile.

Nutrient break-down varies between Virgo and Scorpio: This is an important distinction. Virgo divides food particles, a *catabolic* function, on the *in-cycle*. A process dedicated to supply the building up of the body, *anabolism. We thus see a catabolic function in service to an anabolic function!* Earth signs build form.

Conversely, Scorpio's catabolysis is directed toward the ejection of waste *out* of the body, thus ruling the bladder, nose, sweat glands and colon!

Both signs are notably interested in purification themes, though again, in separate arenas. The Virgo type errs toward hygiene, whereas the Scorpio prefers emotional and colonic purging. Curiously, one so often finds Scorpio natives engaged in truly dangerous or filthy work or happily assisting at the local hospice. As a longtime vocational astrologer, I can well attest to this. Virgo, on the other hand, is preoccupied with cleanliness, nutrition, and the preservation of life. Study their glyphs! Virgo's glyph resembles the intestines of the nutrient "in cycle", whereas Scorpio's symbol reflects the lower intestines of the "out cycle" (waste excretion)! More detail on this discovery below.

Identification: Encountering fats, the gut says, "what do have we here?" The enteroendocrine cells in the intestine sense specific nutrients and enable conditions for their absorption by releasing what is required from a palette of about twenty peptides. These cells also recognize pathogens and supply hormones and cytokines to the immune cells.

Sorting data or particles: An identified particle (or fact) is placed with others of the same type in the correct box and tagged as "good, bad, reject, keep, or useful." Thus, Virgo natives are often great file or data entry clerks! In the same way, Virgo's immune roles act to identify the "useful" cell or nutrient and to spot the menacing antigen.

Particle sorting is one of the many functions of the Virgo ruled liver, that great bodily factory specializing in receiving, identifying, and storing nutrients; breaking down toxic substances; repackaging molecules, and distributing nutrients.

Discernment: The gut must say "yes", or "no". We let this particle in or disallow another. This Virgo function is obvious in the liver. However, we see this function too, within the villi of the small intestine, its covering mucus layer, and the interaction with the lacteals, the lymphatic vessels of the villi.

The Virgin of the zodiac also symbolizes the discrimination function of our thinking (as much as that of our bowels) and the sorting of data (and food particles) into categories. Virgo is the file clerk of the zodiac, both physically and *mentally*! When someone lacks discernment, they often lack Virgo! Poor discernment in the gut can lead to maladies associated to Virgo's opposite sign, Pisces, such as leaky gut, excessive production of cholesterol, low immunity, and psychic porousness.

Hyper discernment: Encountering a host of elevated immune responses and food intolerances can result from the Virgo function of discernment, but in over-drive.

Mucus: This is not a Virgo thing, but more specifically ruled by Pisces. It is also ruled by that sugary planet Venus, as mucus is demulcent, moist, and composed of glycoproteins and proteoglycans, amongst other items. As described below, here in the gut mucosa, we observe the Pisces-Virgo sign polarity at its finest!

Goblet cells in the intestine produce mucus. This layer of mucus slathers the villi in the small intestine and is charged with defense molecules similar in action to an electrical fence! Here we see a Pisces function, mucus, conflating with Virgo's boundary making function. Here we see opposite signs Pisces and Virgo working in partnership. Researchers once considered the gut mucus as a lubricating, passive defense barrier existing between the host and antigens. However, they have now discovered an intricate relationship between the mucus layer and the microbiota.

The mucosa is not a completely closed affair (typical of Pisces, the sign that can't say "no"). There are intentional loopholes extant in this layer, located just above the Peyer' Patches. M-cells in this region are specific to the sampling of the gut's diverse and varying bacterial colony, the microbiome. *Sampling* is a Virgo function along with discernment and sorting.

Traditionally, Pisces is said to govern the lymphatic system, and Virgo the immune system. Obviously, these too basic, if not crude assignments, require more work. There are specific lymphatic structures (lacteals) in the villi, and lymphatic ducts around the abdominal aorta and inferior vena cava of the abdomen. Thus, we have a Pisces system (lymphatics) encased within the Virgo body zone (gut)! We can safely consider the lymphatic system of the gut, and the lacteals, under the Pisces-Virgo polarity. The lacteals drain the villi and the connecting submucosal network. The lymphatics drain the intestinal muscle layer within Virgo's zone.

Boundary Making: A *boundary* is a different concept than a *barrier*, in that a boundary marks a *division* between compartments whilst a barrier walls something completely out. Boundary making is a distinctly Virgo function - note the symbol, a Virgin. In contrast,

Virgo's fellow female sign, Cancer the crab, symbolizes defense barriers: the creation of shells, houses, storage tanks, cell walls, and the like. *Cancer works with distinct, typically circular and/or inward spiraling units, whereas our zodiac's best critic, Virgo, draws a line, and then, decides what particles (or facts, people, etc.) will pass in, pass out, be utilized, or rejected. Virgo is more about utility to the whole and less about protection, which is more Cancer's domain.*

Virgo's boundary function is essentially changeable, impermanent and flexible (mutable!). I prefer to symbolize Virgo as a beehive, which seems a more apt depiction of Virgo functions than a virgin.

Note that we see this boundary making process throughout the digestion process, but particularly in the mucus-gut wall relationship, and the absorption process that goes on through the lining of the gut wall and lacteals.

Processing: In the processing of nutrients, we see *all four primary Virgo functions: separation, sorting, the making of boundaries, and discernment.* These functions are all partial to the Virgo ruled organs and contribute to a greater cycle called nutrient processing. The latter stages of processing include the recombining of molecules, and waste removal. These two functions are attributed to Scorpio. Processing includes the combining and repackaging of nutrient molecules and the creation of proteins, hormones, useful fats, and more for assimilation. Next comes the elimination of rejected or toxic matter through defecation and urination.

Virgo vs Scorpio Digestive Processing Functions: In astrological thinking, processing functions are assigned to both Virgo and Scorpio. Scorpio specializes in cycling systems, such as the continuous recycling of used bile salts back into the bile. Scorpio is also preoccupied with waste removal, especially feces, urine, and sweat. On the other hand, *Virgo is dedicated to the sorting of useful nutrients.* Thirdly, Scorpio, that great chemist of the zodiac, is operative everywhere we see the combining of different components to create something new. This occurs in the liver in the construction of proteins and bile. I do not see this as a Virgo function, but more descriptive of Scorpio, the sign of transformation. However, traditionally, there are no correlations of the liver with Scorpio and more work is needed.

Comparing the Virgo and Scorpio Symbols: These well-established glyphs supposedly originated in the Medieval Byzantine period and were more firmly adopted during the European Renaissance.

Some zodiacal glyphs are obvious, such as Taurus which clearly resembles a bull. However, it's difficult to uncover the true meanings of the Virgo and Scorpio emblems, *sister signs* that hold two of the three malefic angles of the natural zodiac. Some opine that the "M" in Virgo is a conflation of the first three letters of the Greek word for "virgin," with a curious cross at its base that is included for any number of possible reasons. The same source describes the "M" in Scorpio, with the stinger attached, as merely symbolizing a scorpion's tail!

Take a closer look, keeping in mind the close historical relationship of medicine and astrology. The Virgo symbol resembles an intestine more than that of any other sign. This is interesting because Virgo does rule the upper intestines, cecum, and influences the ascending colon. The curious "cross" at the symbol's base, *is curving backward and inward upon itself.* This aptly represents the curve of the cecum and ascending colon. Also, as discussed above, Virgo represents the digestive process on its way *inward,* and liver bound, for the purpose of bodily uptake.

Now, compare Virgo's symbol with Scorpio's. Here we have a plausible depiction of an intestine, ending in an *outward moving arrow.* Here, in the descending colon, rectum, anus, bladder and sweat glands, we see the *expulsion* of feces, urine, sweat and mucus from various dedicated orifices. We know that waste outlets are all traditionally governed by Scorpio! *Could it be that the original zodiacal glyph designers were familiar with both zodiacal man and basic intestinal anatomy?* Some Renaissance doctors certainly were.

VIRGO AND THE IMMUNE SYSTEM
Healing Strength

It has been my limited experience that both Virgo and Aries natives heal quickly from wounds and recover swiftly from flus and colds (Virgo being more frequently ill than Aries). This is the good side of an impressive immune response! Scorpio, however, is the sign of the proverbial "cat's nine lives," renowned for overcoming the most mortal of illnesses.

Conversely, natives of the opposite sign Pisces tend to heal slowly from colds and flus, requiring twice the recovery time of their Virgo friends and relatives. This adds evidence that the defensive cells of the immune system are hyper alert and efficient in Virgo, but also a plausible source of their autoimmune issues!

The sign Cancer is noted for weak recovery and long convalescence, oddly coupled with an impressive allergic response!

Traditional Rulerships

Traditionally, Virgo governs the immune system and co-rules (with Cancer) the spleen, an organ intimately involved with immune defense by housing a supply of white cells. Yet the opposite sign Pisces is held to rule over the lymphatic system, home of the immune response. The simplicity of these traditional rulerships is confusing, and frankly, silly, considering the hyper complexity of both systems.

Certainly, there is more to the immune system than just Virgo type functions, and far more sign involvement within the lymphatics than only Pisces. We must excuse the ancients for what they couldn't yet know!

Let's dissect the components of these systems to assist the reader in sorting this out for themselves. My brief effort here might also serve to demonstrate a process that can assist other neglected areas of Medical Astrology, such as the rulership assignment of individual hormones, or perhaps the brain's many components.

The fluid lymph and overall lymphatic systems working through the body is indeed a *Pisces* affair. However, the thoracic duct is under *Cancer*, as are the lymph nodes of the breast and axilla. *Virgo*, governing the identification and boundary making functions of the body, must govern specific immune responses. *The immune cells that recognize antigens must have a strong Virgo function.*

Identification is only one part of this process. I have noticed that immune responses are fast and strong in most Virgo people. Allergies, cytokine storms, dangerous reactions to pollen, bee stings, and the like are not untypical. Intolerance to foods, mold, chemicals, and smells are very common in Virgo types, or those with planets afflicted in this sign, especially Moon or Saturn. Some immune cells are designed to wall off antigens, others attach and dismantle, still other cells devour them. It appears that the body uses all possible wartime tactics to outwit antigens. However, I do not see Virgo functions in these last described antigen disabling tactics. It is *antigen discernment cells that are clearly Virgoan* in function. They ring the bell and call out the troops!

Possible Rulerships

The distinctive parts, functions, and cells of the human immune system are many, and remain largely unassigned to signs and planets. Let's take an incomplete and simplistic stab at this, leaving further research to another day.

Before segregating cells and chemicals, let's first consider some plausible zodiac sign and planet rulerships for the attack and defense functions or strategies utilized by various immune cells.

- *Recognize and Memorize:* Cancer, Taurus, Moon, Water Signs
- *Sound alarms, incite riot (inflammation):* Mars, Aries
- *Phagocytosis (eat your enemy!):* Scorpio, Taurus
- *Attach to and explode the cellular membrane:* Scorpio
- *Poison with secreted chemicals:* Scorpio
- *Bind and Disable:* Saturn, Capricorn, and possibly Mars
- *Imprison (build a wall around):* Saturn, Capricorn

Divisions of the Immune System

The immune system is divided into two primary divisions: the *innate* and the *adaptive*. Let's review the possible astrological rulerships of their components. Most essentially, the immune system has three basic processes: *Recognition, mobilization, and attack*.

The faculty of memory, and thus "recognition," would fit best under Luna, Cancer, Taurus, and the Water signs as a group (see explanation below).

The faculty of "mobilization" has many candidate rulers. Mars and Aries functions ring the bell and incite inflammation. Whereas in a traditional army situation, Aries-Sagittarius is associated with alarms and the recruiting and guidance of the troops to the site of an invasion. Virgo governs the army itself on a mission (see more on this below), with of course Mars, the God of War, at the helm.

The final defensive function of "attack" is primarily the province of Mars and his signs Aries and Scorpio. However, the most *defensive* signs of all are Cancer, Scorpio, and Capricorn - so we would expect an immune association with these signs too.

The many styles of attack are listed below, with suggested ruler-ships. Importantly, Scorpio governs *strategy*. This sign is clearly linked to a variety of inventive attack-and-defense strategies observed for a diverse variety of immune cells.

The Innate Immune System
Recognition

Discerning "self" from "other" is the first step of the immune response: Invader (antigen) recognition. We see this function in both the innate and adaptive systems. However, the more primitive innate immune system initiates a general response to all invaders and remains basic to all people.

The discernment of "this, not that," "me, you," is a quintessential Virgo function! This sign governs boundary making, file clerks, and all manner of sorting processes. Virgo also governs the organization of impersonal ground troops - we see this influence in bee-hives and ant colonies. *In this manner, Virgo is the general overlord of the immune response*, as millions of lymphocytes organize their actions - as does any other type of army on a defensive mission.

However, a house has many rooms! As we shall see, the immune system has diverse protective schemes and living components. To date, these have no astrological assignments, other than that they all live happily together under the general auspices of Virgo, the landlord.

The innate immune defense comprises the first and most primitive immune response associated with barriers, skin defense, and inflammation (Virgo, Aries); creating protective shields (Cancer); protecting the boundary from "other" (Virgo); fast attack, inflammation, fever (Aries, Mars), and Cytokines (Aries, Mars).

Corroborative evidence for these tentative assignments was received just hours after completing this paragraph! A friend called me, having just returned from an all-nighter at the local hospital with her feverish toddler, whose raging temperature hit 105°. The tot is the ultimate Martian type, even having a notable "widow's peak." She was born with both Lights in Mars-ruled Scorpio, and precisely when Mars was positioned in its other home sign Aries (within a wide orb of her Ascendant).

Following a fast, dangerously high fever, she recovered completely by morning, soon to be running about, squealing happily, and demanding chocolates. Transit Mars was in Virgo at the time the fever struck, exactly quincunxing the child's natal Mars in Aries. Supportive transits were also involved, but too many to list here. This incident demonstrates the very essence of a strong Mars, and Aries, and their mutual involvement with the 'Innate Immune System'. Similarly, I have witnessed other people with natal Mars in fire signs cope with cytokine storms and hyper immune responses.

Primary Innate Immune System, Selected Cells

Macrophages and Monocytes: When Macrophages migrate into tissues of the body, they are called Monocytes.

These cells confer innate immunity, engulfing and digesting microorganisms, clearing debris and dead cells, and activating other immune functions. Could this be Taurus-Scorpio ruled function? Taurus loves food, and Scorpio is the primary sign of waste excretion. However, Macrophages go a step further by cleverly displaying the invading antigens on their outer membrane, presenting them to a B cell and helper T cell. This display and presentation appears intelligently cooperative, but what sign best describes this function? Libra?

Neutrophils: These innate immune cells kill and ingest bacteria (sounds like Scorpio!). Antibodies also are good candidates for Scorpio assignment. These proteins attach to invading organisms and then attach to receptors on the neutrophils. However, antibodies are a component of the more evolved adaptive immune system.

Eosinophils: They attack parasites and cancer cells through both phagocytosis (engulf and consume) and the secreting of toxic chemicals (poison your enemy). These strategies fit Scorpio.

Basophils: These cells drive allergic reactions (like that runny nose!).

Inflammation Response: In response to injury or antigens, inflammation is provoked in the innate immune system by pattern recognition receptors (PRRs) on cell surfaces and in the cytoplasm. Inflammation is an outstandingly a Mars attribution, and secondly, Aries. Pluto is involved in sepsis.

The Adaptive Immune System

The Adaptive Immune System targets specific disease antigens and varies per person (as per disease memory, cell ratio, etc.). This process largely involves the white blood cells and their many strategies, as discussed below.

White Blood Cells: In his book *Holistic Medicine and the Extracellular Matrix*, Matthew Wood discussed the enormous numbers of white cells produced, which at death feed the matrix with their bodies. This sacrifice and composting function holds Scorpio-Pisces implications. The primary white cells of the *adaptive* immune system include: *B-cells, helper T cells*, and *cytotoxic T cells*. However, neutrophils, monocytes, eosinophils, and basophils comprise the white cells of the *innate* immune system.

B cells: These lymphocytes start life in the bone marrow. They must pass their nursery "exams" prior to being acceptable for release into the blood stream and lymphoid follicles - where their job is to recognize antigens ("evil" organisms). Recognition of invaders triggers multiplication of B cells, which differentiate into plasma cells that secrete antibodies that "capture" antigens by binding them, thus preventing their devious designs.

Personal memory is a faculty of the Moon and the sign Cancer. Bone marrow is traditionally thought to be governed by Cancer and sometimes Mars. However, "binding" is a Saturn-Capricorn function.

Plasma Cells: These make *antibodies* to fight bacteria, viruses, infection, and disease. This sounds like Virgo-Scorpio-Aries. Virgo governs conveyor belts, factory workers, and skilled craftsmanship. Scorpio is best at strategic defense. Aries is our sign of urgent attack.

Helper T-cells: We might think of these cells as the "muscle" of the adaptive system because they are needed for almost all adaptive immune responses. They help the B cells create antibodies and macrophages to destroy ingested microbes. Helper Ts also activate cytotoxic T cells to kill infected target cells.

T-cells (and macrophages) produce cytokines which stimulate immune responses (fever, aches, inflammation etc.). This is the province of Mars and Aries. Cytokines help regulate both the innate and adaptive immune systems. T cells diversify into cytotoxic, memory Ts, and helper Ts.

Memory T-cells: After exposure to an antigen, the "naive" T cells become "memory T cells", or "helper Ts". Memory imprinting is a lunar function, governed by the Moon's sign Cancer, and, to some extent, all three water signs (Cancer and Scorpio never forget an insult!), plus Taurus (the exaltation of the Moon is in Taurus). Memory T-cells have extremely long lives, a noted tendency of female sign Taurus. The thymus gland is the destination of maturing T cells arriving from their bone marrow nursery. This gland is in the Taurus body zone. We must allow both Cancer and Taurean influence to memory T cells.

Cytotoxic or Killer T-cells: These "killer" cells are obviously related to attacking Mars, and possibly Aries (the sign of frontal attack). These T-cells directly attack infected cells by means of a pro-tein "missile" called a *lymphokine*. Directly launched attacks are Mars and Aries by nature.

The war planet Mars rules both Aries and Scorpio. The fighting strategies of these two signs are quite different - hence my varied assignments. Aries flies to battle without a shield; whereas Scorpio plans a strategy, quietly awaiting the perfect moment to strike (think of trap door spiders).

Furthermore, killer T cells secrete *interferon*, which acts as a beacon to guide neutrophils to the body site of the invading antigen, to attract and "recruit" an army of immune cells. This function is Aries-Sagittarius in essence. Aries governs leadership whereas fellow fire sign Sagittarius is the guide and zealot of the zodiac.

Although the immune response is very Martian, or fiery, all groups of selfless individual soldiers (such as white cells!) working collectively together as a unit (such as in ant colonies and beehives) are Virgo in nature. Virgo governs teamwork and, conversely, teams of workers!

Histamine: This chemical is released by both innate and adap-tive immune cells. It initiates the body's inflammatory response, inclusive of cytokine secretion. Sounds like Aries and Mars to me! Indeed, anaphylaxis and cytokine storms are often observed in people with excessive Mars in their horoscopes.

Cytokines: chemical produced by many of the body's cells, including skin cells (keratinocytes), although are predominantly secreted by helper T cells and macrophages. Their function appears largely Martian (inflammatory).

The Lymphatic System and Extracellular Matrix

Astrological sub-rulerships for these systems are postulated in the Pisces chapter, with additional commentary in the *Cancer* chapter.

VIRGO AND THE NERVOUS SYSTEM
The Autonomic Nervous System

The nervous system is extremely complex, with many primary and sub-rulerships. That said, the *mutable cross* largely governs the two primary nervous systems (voluntary and autonomic) and the two subdivisions of each. We discussed the *voluntary nervous system* under Gemini-Sagittarius. At hard right angles to these signs stand Virgo and Pisces governing the *autonomic* (or *vegetative*) nervous system. There is no doubt that sleepy Pisces governs the parasympathetic function of the autonomic. Virgo, as Pisces' opposite sign partner, must therefore have a strong link to the *sympathetic* division of the autonomic.

How does this work? The entire upper digestive zone, except for the stomach, is largely under Virgo's auspices. Whereas the relaxing, digesting, parasympathetic functions are under opposite sign Pisces. How can we see this in real people and cases?

Virgo cases present anxious stress, poor appetite, slow liver, intestinal dryness, dry head and scalp (poor lipids), laconic tendencies, shyness, digestive disruptions, and insomnia. Immune functions are heightened, largely in the gut, including food allergies. The Virgo type is alert, awake, dry, and in extreme cases neurotic, or excessively fastidious. All too often, Virgo Sun or Moon natives suffer various digestive troubles, often diagnosed as stress. I prefer to sort it out astrologically. Mars, Mercury, Saturn, and Uranus in Virgo can evince similar tendencies.

Autonomic Pathways

Virgo's impressive fight-or-flight mechanism varies considerably from our other sympathetic regulator, Aries. In Aries, a Mars-ruled sign, the sympathetic influence is distinctly muscular and arterial.

Let's compare types. The classic Aries enjoys a good fight, or competition - joyously springing to action. Classic Aries types are irritable, athletic but cheery, and not anxious as are Virgos, their fellow sympathetics. The Aries appetite and thirst is hearty. They laugh loudly. Compare this with the Virgo native, pushing her food around on the plate and never finishing the meal.

Aries is prone to *inflammatory response*, but largely of the muscles, heart, eyes, and brain. Virgo inflammation attacks the digestive organs and colon. In Virgo, the immune attack turns inward, upon itself (note the inward turning glyph). Virgo turns up in all manner of autoimmune problems. (The motor centers and voluntary muscular functions also have at least a partial governance in Aries-Sagittarius).

In meditation upon the variations observed between the fight-flight response of Virgo versus Aries natives, it dawned on me that *different nerve pathways of the autonomic dominate these two signs*. In Aries, the adrenal gland is activated, heart rate increases, pupils dilate, and more blood and sugar are released to the *muscles*. For Virgo, the sympathetic-enteric "gut-brain" system is activated. These differences are readily observable in samples of Aries and Virgo subjects!

Virgo issues and behavior typically errs towards the *sympathetic-enteric* (gut-brain) activation, whereas Aries embraces the *sympathetic-adrenal* network. Virgo gets anxious, sometimes panicked, shutting down digestion and sleep; or inflaming the intestinal organs. Whereas Aries type rushes red faced and muscles bulging into battle, eyes flashing (dilated). Aries shouts out loud and vigorously gesticulates in full arm (or leg) displays. Conversely, Virgo is famously contrite, modest, and self-possessed, specializing in small muscle movement. Virgo natives often make excellent skaters, yogis, and gymnasts.

The map of autonomic pathways reveals how *the singular pre-ganglionic nerve of the system serves the adrenal glands* (Aries-Libra-Mars). This is a very immediate circuit. Conversely, all the intestinal autonomic nerves are post-ganglionic.

It follows that Virgo and Mercury govern the enteric-sympathetic network. Conversely, Aries, Libra, and Mars dominate the adrenal axis. More work is needed.

The hormone adrenalin is clearly Mars-Aries. As a glandular extension of the sympathetic division of the autonomic nervous system, the adrenal medulla releases the two substances norepinephrine and epinephrine into the blood stream. This process occurs in response to threats, and its action is clearly governed by the Aries-Libra axis, plus Mars.

To know what nerves and hormones are most active in various signs, just observe their natives.

Fight, Flight, Freeze

Medicine identifies three responses to threats and stress: *Fight, Flight or Freeze.* We know Aries is *fight* (adrenals), Sagittarius, the running horse, is obviously *flight!* In fact, Sagittarius is the traditional sign of flight, separations, sudden departures, and exiles. Then Virgo, governing the sympathetic nervous system, must be *freeze* (shut it down)! What is going on here?

Sagittarius governs the arterial system and the large muscles of the hips and thighs, so necessary to fleeing. Aries reigns over the motor center of the brain, whereas Sagittarius enjoys the greatest command of any sign over the voluntary muscles. We know that one tactic of the autonomic's threat response is to shunt more blood from the body's interior to the arteries and muscles! This is precisely what is observed in your classic Sagittarius native. Why do we need to know this to understand Virgo?

Virgo exists in a stressful ninety-degree (square) angle with Sagittarius. I have observed that stressful configurations between these two signs repetitively produce panic attacks, hyperactivity, hyperthyroid, restlessness and/or insomnia.

VIRGO SYNDROME

As discussed in Chapter Two, a Zodiac Sign Syndrome is a cluster of symptoms associated with the body zones and functions of a zodiac sign and the signs positioned on the seasonal wheel opposite (180°) and quincunx (150°, 210°, 330°) the sign. Remediating and supporting these body zones and functions act to bring the body into balance, diminishing the syndrome. These symptoms may manifest when there is an emphasis in one or more of these signs. Planetary dignity plays an important role.

The Weaker Signs for the Virgo Vital Force
Quincunx Signs

Aquarius, Aries, and Leo are quincunx Virgo, as they are positioned 150°, 210° and 330° distant from this sign on the seasonal wheel. These signs represent the 6th, 8th, and 12th *averted* angles from the sign Virgo (see the illustration for this chapter). This condition makes it difficult for Virgo to absorb the cosmic rays that feed these signs. Thus, Virgo natives may have trouble absorbing the vibrational and light nutrients of these signs. Likewise, these signs may have trouble absorbing the rays from Virgo.

Aquarius rules Body Zone 11 which includes the venous circulation, oxygenation, oxygen-carbon exchange, electrical conduction of nerves (with Uranus, Mercury, Gemini, and Sagittarius), and the entire lower leg and ankle. This quincunx appears to produce stagnation in the portal circulation.

Aries rules Body Zone 1 which includes the motor centers of the brain and, essential to our observations, the adrenal-pituitary axis (with Libra). Excessive adrenal response releases glucocorticoids into the bloodstream. More glucose is released from the liver. This process can over time produce insulin intolerance. Virgo co-governs the pancreas, whose specialized cells in the islets of Langerhans produce insulin. This axis is one signature for diabetes.

Virgo dominates the sympathetic nerves and governs the general processes of the digestive organs. It is possible that Virgo hyperstresses under adrenalin release, as if allergic to their own adrenalin. Virgo natives so often suffer panic attacks, insomnia, and anxiety especially, when afflicted out of Aries or Sagittarius. The same quincunx produces a remarkably different effect in Aries natives who are not so strong on sympathetic nerve responses.

Leo rules Body Zone 5, which includes the heart, gallbladder, and spinal sheaths. This sign seems to compound or cause an excess of internal heat for both Leo and Virgo natives! Hidden heart quirks or gallbladder issues may lurk unnoticed behind other conditions.

Opposite Sign, Pisces

When the Sun is in Virgo, the opposite sign, Pisces, "sleeps." **Pisces rules Body Zone 12**, which includes the parasympathetic system, sleep, the fluid matrix, the lymphatic system, and the feet. Virgos are weak on sleep, possibly because their end of the year specializes in the sympathetic nerves and is weak on the parasympathetic response. With few exceptions, Pisces natives eat excessively, with gusto and sleep it off. Conversely, Virgo natives eat slowly and cautiously, and then suffer insomnia, or just naturally don't need much sleep. Leaky gut syndrome, or conversely, failure to absorb enough nutrients through the intestinal wall are both conditions assigned to the Virgo-Pisces axis. Poor, or conversely, excess intestinal mucus is also attributed to the Pisces-Virgo interaction in concert with various planet combinations.

Signs Aggravating Virgo Syndrome – Squaring Signs

Gemini and Sagittarius are positioned 90° from Virgo, squaring this sign (see chapter illustration). The effect of a square is to create friction, for good or ill. Virgo can reflex with these signs, as well as its opposite sign, Pisces.

The Gemini-Virgo square speeds the synapses, sense receptors, and afferent peripheral nerves. This is a mind activating combination, excellent for small muscle sports, (gymnastics et al), but a combination ripe for insomnia. Both signs are governed by nerve-activating Mercury. This enables hyperactive senses and a fast, alert mind!

The Sagittarius-Virgo square is an insomnia combination which might be mitigated by aerobic movement. Thus, the need for hard work plus muscular exertion. This square is common in panic, anxiety, hyperthyroid, Graves' disease, and excessive exercise. Many great weavers and compulsive knitters have this square, though I'm not sure why! Perhaps Sagittarius loves to coordinate, bringing the threads together, whereas Virgo enjoys minutiae.

How Planetary Dignity Contributes to Virgo Syndrome
Strongest Planet, Mercury

Virgo's ruling planet is Mercury. Also, the Jyotish assign the exaltation of Mercury to Virgo. This speedy planet governs the peripheral nerves in Gemini, Mercury's second domicile. In Virgo, it governs digestive signaling and the autonomic nervous system (see discussion above). Mercury appears to have a great deal of co-governance over the liver (with Jupiter, Virgo, Cancer, and Leo), pancreas (with Virgo and Cancer), spleen (Virgo and Cancer), and upper intestines (Virgo). *Mercury is almost always afflicted* in charts of persons suffering the maladies of these organs.

Weakest Planet, Jupiter

Jupiter is in detriment in Virgo, as it rules the opposing sign. The Jupiter-ruled liver is notoriously slow, fussy, or impaired in this sign. Jupiter also rules fat. In Virgo, his role in the digestion and absorption of lipids is often deficient, which can manifest as dry hair and skin, emaciation, delicate appetites, fat avoidance, eating disorders, and insufficient bile. So many Virgo maladies appear to stem from the hyper fastidiousness of the liver. Poor lipid distribution would manifest as the dry hair and skin so typical of this sign. Although there certainly are overweight Virgo types, (and I've known a few), this sign appears less inclined than many to overweight - especially so, the Virgo Moon. Underweight appears more common. At best, you see the lean, well knit, agile form.

Venus "Falls" in Virgo

Venus governs copper, sugar, estrogen, and mucus. Although Venus bequeaths a love of service to Virgo natives, "she" generally lower mucus, copper and female hormone levels for this sign - contributing to blood sugar issues, dryness, premature greying, etc. These tendencies are common to Virgo natives and/or those with a strong emphasis in this sign. Conversely, when Venus' *transits through Virgo* she can soothe and moisten a dry intestinal tract because she herself is a moist and demulcent planet. See chapter on Venus in the book *Medical Astrology in Action*.

Astrological Conditions that Enhance Virgo Syndrome
(1) **Sun, Moon, or Ascendant sign in Virgo**

(2) A weakness in a body zone governed by the signs opposite or quincunx Virgo on the seasonal wheel, as discussed above under *The Weaker Signs for the Virgo Vital Force.*

(3) The Virgo symptom cluster is accentuated when one or more of the Sun, Moon, Ascendant, Mars, Mercury, Saturn, Jupiter, Venus and the South or North Node is in Virgo in the native's birth chart. This is compounded by the testimonies below:

- Virgo inhabits the 1st, 6th, 8th, or 12th houses.
- Saturn in a hard angle to Jupiter.
- Any planet that opposes or conjoins a Virgo Sun, Moon, Mars, or Mercury.
- Any planet conjunct either Node in Virgo.
- Night birth (sect), with Saturn in a female sign, especially below the horizon.
- A malefic, Mercury, or a Node in any sign in the 6th, or 8th house.
- Uranus, Neptune, or Pluto afflicted in Virgo, or in the 6th house.
- Capricorn, Taurus or Leo emphasis (with Virgo)

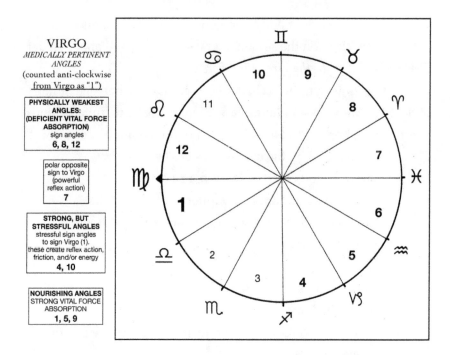

VIRGO
MEDICALLY PERTINENT ANGLES
(counted anti-clockwise from Virgo as "1")

PHYSICALLY WEAKEST ANGLES:
(DEFICIENT VITAL FORCE ABSORPTION)
sign angles
6, 8, 12

polar opposite sign to Virgo (powerful reflex action)
7

STRONG, BUT STRESSFUL ANGLES
stressful sign angles to sign Virgo (1). these create reflex action, friction, and/or energy
4, 10

NOURISHING ANGLES
STRONG VITAL FORCE ABSORPTION
1, 5, 9

SYMPTOMS OF VIRGO SYNDROME

Please note that I am not discussing "Virgo people" per se, but those born with prominences in this sign <u>that actually do suffer the syndrome.</u> These symptoms are not listed in any order, but simply as a list of collected observations common to natives of Virgo. Please be sure to balance with *Virgo's Superpowers.* As with any sign, there are just as many positives!

- poor collagen
- premature greying or facial lining
- affectless facial expressions
- extreme shyness (especially in males)
- inadequate lipid absorption
- fear of fats in diet
- insomnia
- anxiety
- panic attacks

- marijuana addictions for relaxation
- workaholic
- lack of leisure, mental pleasure
- lack of imagination (Aquarius deficient)
- GERD (also Leo), especially with Mars in Virgo
- internal bleeding
- diverticulitis, especially with Mars in Virgo
- duodenal ulcer
- pancreatitis
- pancreatic tumor
- liver problems of all types, especially with Jupiter or Saturn in Virgo
- ruptured or enlarged spleen
- dehydration
- dry, hot stomach
- infertility
- vision disturbances
- deficiency of Vitamin B1, B6, and Niacin
- heart defect
- obsession with body form perfection
- embarrassment about some aspect of one's body or appearance
- cosmetic surgery addiction
- dandruff or premature grey
- intense sense of smell
- intense odor repulsions
- does not understand concept of motiveless leisure and play (always have to be useful or working)
- eating disorders (anorexia, orthorexia and bulimia)
- food intolerances
- emaciation, or trouble gaining weight (often just not enough fats or calories)
- extreme diets
- allergies
- choler, biliousness, hot liver
- jaundice
- diabetes
- hypoglycemia
- low female hormones
- OCD
- germ and cleanliness phobias

- difficulty relaxing, or just having fun for no reason (not work or business related)
- sexual inhibition
- sexual fastidiousness ("they never smell right", or "the color of his socks turns me off")
- sexual disinterest, or good libido but a purely mechanical-technical approach to intimacy
- fear of emotional intimacy
- liver cirrhosis
- gallstones, gallbladder problems
- sluggish portal circulation
- slow or toxic liver
- poor appetite
- oversensitivity to smell (often disabling)
- extreme skin sensitivities (cannot stand certain fabrics)
- eczema, psoriasis, dry or flaking skin
- autoimmune diseases (especially of the digestive organs)
- colitis, Crohn's disease
- entomophobia
- dislike OR craving for water and swimming
- adrenal exhaustion
- neurological problems due to constant stress, deficient sleep, and poor nerve sheath protection
- thin or deficient intestinal mucus
- poor absorption of nutrients through the intestinal wall, or conversely, leaky gut syndrome (more typically the former)
- obsessed with clothing or fashion

REMEDIATION TIPS

Please note that these remedial tips are for interest only. The author is not suggesting that any person use these without the evaluation and consent of their personal healthcare practitioner.

Should a great many of the above symptoms be present, remedies are often determined from the remedials and activities of our relaxing and sleep-inducing planets: the Moon, Neptune, and Venus.

- **Lipid Distribution:** The Burdock root and seed's ability to open the lipid pathways may be beneficial. (Wood)
- **Anxiety:** Agrimony for the tense, anxious person with intestinal issues.
- **Gallbladder:** Chelidonium for gallbladder. (Wood)
- **GERD:** Chamomile (avoid if Ragweed allergy), Chelidonium, Ginger (avoid Peppermint)
- **Liver:** For assisting and moving the bile, Centaury (cold), Barberry (warming), and Olive Oil
- **Spleen:** Red Root (*Ceanothus americanus*), Elecampane (*Inula helenium*)
- **Sleep:** There are many choices of sedative herbs for sleep, including Passionflower, Milky Oats, Hops, Lemon Balm, and Skullcap. (Valerian is too stinky for Virgo's sensitive nose). The best are herbs that relax the sympathetic nerves and turn on the parasympathetic.
- **Digestion:** Carminative Mercurial herbs such as Fennel Seed and Caraway
- **Internal Heat:** Heat relieving herbs, such as Dandelion Root (Wood)
- **Bowel Demulcents:** Linseed Tea, Marshmallow Root (short-term use as it can inhibit nutrient absorption in the

gut), Fenugreek (Dry roughage e.g., bran is not recommended for dry bowels).

- **Inflammatory Bowel:** Yellow Dock (*Rumex crispus*)
- **Dry, thin hair:** Fenugreek, Sesame Seed Oil, and Olive Oil, and possibly Saw Palmetto.
- **Low Estrogen:** Black Clover, Don Quai, and Black Cohosh, and Wild Yam (debated).
- **Dry, hot skin conditions:** Chickweed, Aloe Vera gel juice, water
- **Hay Fever:** Freeze Dried Nettles
- **Emaciation, muscle atrophy:** Nettles

The Need for Water, Sleep, and Relaxation

Dehydration is a problem for many Virgo natives. However, we do not observe in Virgo natives the taste for alcohol that is so typical of the dehydrated Fire signs Leo, Aries, and Sagittarius. Perhaps Virgo's liver is just too alert and sensitive to tolerate excessive drinking. However, Virgo may incline to marijuana addiction, which is a constitutionally drying herb that can contribute to dehydration. The two most extreme pot addicts I have known were both born in this sign. This is not enough to draw conclusions, but I believe they felt a need to turn on a reluctant parasympathetic system and relax. They shared as much.

See also Chapter 15, *The Twelve Zodiac Sign Syndromes and their Relevant Herbs.*

Chapter Nine:
LIBRA SYNDROME

Who does not love a tranquil heart,
a sweet tempered, balanced life?

- James Allen, *As a Man Thinketh*

Dining with Libra

I often experience that a Libra native peruses the menu a few rounds, then requests wine (while I sit there, starving). Next begins the discussion regarding the merits of the offered wine selections. Now commences the ordering ordeal. "Should we have hors d'oeuvres?" Another fifteen minutes goes by. Finally, a substantial consultation with the waiter over the finer points of each entry. Throughout the meal, I endure astute commentary on the appropriate etiquette of eating our spaghetti; and requests that I put down my fork in mid-flight so we may rest our palates and engage in polite conversation.

This style of dining etiquette perfectly demonstrates the very essence of Libra: balance, reason, pause before action - as in between two breaths. Libra is, after all, the pause point of the zodiac, positioned exactly halfway through the yearly zodiacal wheel.

As discussed in depth in this chapter, these characteristics reflect the Libra-ruled kidney's many balancing roles in the body, and why all Libra balancing functions combine in *Libra Syndrome*. To the keen observer it is readily apparent how the famous outward personality quirks of zodiac signs precisely reflect their assigned physical functions and organs!

Fundamentals Refresher

Libra Syndrome is a set of collaborative symptoms, consistently appearing together, which are typical for natives of the sign Libra. The symptoms associated with Libra Syndrome can be experienced by people with other sun signs when there is a particular emphasis in this sign. Zodiac sign syndromes can occur in seriatim, first one symptom, then another, weeks, months or years later. Few experience all symptoms. However, two or more of these symptoms are frequently observed clustered together at the same time.

A Libra native may have few if any of the symptoms associated with Libra Syndrome. Indeed, many Libras are specimens of perfect health. However, this symptom set often evinces itself when a native's Sun, Moon, or Ascendant tenants Libra and displays certain astrological conditions which are discussed at length in this chapter.

This chapter describes the astrological conditions that may aggravate the syndrome. With this knowledge, practitioners can explore the underlying condition when symptoms consistent with the syndrome present themselves in a patient. Understanding the energetic cause is the first step in remediation.

THE SIGN LIBRA

In Classical Western Astrology, with use of the Tropical Zodiac, a Libra is someone born between 180 to 209 longitudinal degrees following the spring equinox, or though the 30 days following the autumn equinox.

As with all other signs, we cannot think of Libra as an isolated single entity or a static constant. "Libra" is a gestalt of strengths and weaknesses based on its angular relationship to the other signs of the interconnected solar cycle. In turn, each of the twelve phases of this cycle is influenced by the unique planetary configurations at birth and throughout the life. Libra is a unique phase-state, with its interactions peculiar to the seventh stage of the twelve-fold cyclical process.

Element and Mode: Libra is of the element Air. As the initiating sign of the autumn season, it belongs to the *Cardinal* quadruplicity of signs.

Life Cycle Phase: Libra represents the seventh stage of the twelve-fold human life cycle. The infant born (Aries), feeds (Taurus), becomes the babbling tot (Gemini), attains awareness of its place in the tribe (Cancer), then basks in the glory of adolescence (Leo). Come Virgo, we perfect the body, sharpen our skills, serve, discern, and labor hard to maintain the physical world. Come Libra, we are halfway through the zodiac, where we take pause. Remember how each sign is wholly different in nature than the sign preceding it?

The Pause Point of the Zodiac

In Arthur Young's demonstration of the Measure Formulae (The Geometry of Meaning), he breaks circle-cycles down into twelve components, which also applies to the to-and-fro swing of a pendulum. These twelve steps are easily conflated to the twelve-fold cycle-circle of the twelve zodiac signs. Libra is stationed at the pause point of a pendulum's swing.

In this way, Libra stands halfway through the cycle of the year, begun at the opposite sign, Aries. Here, the swing of the pendulum reaches halfway on the circle at 180 degrees, and stops, pauses, looking back at the Aries starting point. All Libra lessons and character traits are related to pausing, considering, observing. As discussed later in this chapter, its very symbol reflects its unique status as a pause point between any two cycles. Libra is thus described by some writers as a "lazy" sign. Artist Howard M. Duff allegorically portrayed Libra reclining in a chair, feet up, sampling chocolate!

Libra is indeed the great pause point of the zodiacal cycle; the great celestial rest stop of the ecliptic. Every cycle has a pause point between two beats. One might envision Libra as the cyclic pause point between two heart beats or two breaths. Perhaps it rules those spaces! Curiously, our culture has few terms to describe this pause. I tried in many ways googling the medical terms for the space between two breaths and two heartbeats. It wasn't easy to find!

Similarly, Libra and the 7th house symbolize the return karma generated from action performed at first cause, Aries. Aries throws the ball against the wall, and in Libra it bounces back! Here again, we see the initial swing of the pendulum pausing before returning to home base.

The Balance Point of the Zodiac

Libra symbolizes halfway between day and night, youth and age, Spring/Summer and Fall/Winter. Similarly, the upper and lower body are divided at the Libra-governed waist. Curiously, one often notes a considerable disparity between the weight of the upper and lower bodies in Libra females.

Libra's symbol is very close to our symbol for equal (=). Libra represents the balance of body and mind as well as spirit and body. Libra symbolizes the neutralization of positive and negative charges, and the opposition or combining of male and female gender (more on all these later).

Libra rules balance (with Taurus) and poise. Libra plays a role in all balances: hormonal, electrolyte, sodium-potassium, blood pressure, and mental. This last is so essential that we devote a section of this chapter to mental balance.

Libra Superpowers

As a rule, Libra dislikes stress and avoids it, abhorring hard or dirty labor. Typically, some would rather attend their minds to entertaining, cultural, or intellectual pursuits. Unlike some other signs, Libras rarely brew over past wrongs. Instead, find them bird watching, studying law, or art, or snuggled up with a partner watching a sitcom. Neither are they particularly concerned with health. However, they make excellent consultants, psychologists, and counsellors.

I always say that Libra would be one of healthiest signs if it cared to be. This curious lack of adrenal response lowers stress and allows thought to intervene action. Libra often has excellent natural health, beauty, and grace. All too often, over decades, they squander their health through excess sugar, wine, and romance (results show after fifty and hit like a sack of beans).

Diplomacy, wisdom, and charm are Libra's superpowers. My favorite quote of Libra native Eleanor Roosevelt is, "To handle yourself, use your head; to handle others, use your heart." This exact approach lowers health-disturbing stress that might otherwise be due to social conflict and poor social skills. Libra natives are popular with everyone, so good at pleasing others while still getting their own way. They display poise, but can be argumentative if Aries, Leo, or Cancer dominate the birth chart. This tendency is also especially common in Libra moon.

Wisdom is the gift of the pause point in the pendulum's swing. Libra is the great observer of the zodiac, the most objective of all signs, save perhaps fellow air sign Aquarius.

Physical Appearance

Exhaustive detail with illustrations is provided in this author's *The Astrological Body Types.*

LIBRA BODY RULERSHIPS AND FUNCTIONS

As described in Chapter One, a body zone is a general box that overlays many organs, functions, vessels and their sub-rulerships. Libra will typically be seen in natal charts, or by current transit, when one observes accidents or symptoms in this zone.

Libra, Body Zone 7

This is a general area that overlays the waist, the dividing point between above and below. Body Zone 7 includes the waist, kidneys; ovaries (with Venus, Moon, and Scorpio), filtration of blood, distillation of urine, ureters (with influence from both Scorpio and Gemini; and with Scorpio governing urine).

Body Zone 7 also includes the lower back, lumbar region, and co-rules the buttocks with Scorpio and Sagittarius. Cornell opines that Libra governs the "rump" and gives the sides of hips to Sagittarius. Not all writers agree, because the buttocks are firmly within the shared Scorpio and Sagittarius region and are largely fat and muscle (Sagittarius) and shield the anus (Scorpio).

Note that Libra does not rule the neural origins and ganglia that innervate the kidneys but are situated outside of the Libra zone. They are instead ruled by the zone of their origin point.

Libra Functions
Distillation of the Urine

The distillation of urine and filtering of the bloodstream are mainly governed by Libra. The distillation process returns water, vitamins, electrolytes, hormones to the blood stream, while expressing water, urea, and excess electrolytes and wastes. Solids and water are separated, another function of this "weigh station" of the zodiac.

How does this filtration process differ from Virgo's intestinal discernment, or Scorpio's waste excretion? Every aspect of the distillation of urine involves weighing, balancing, deciding, *returning* constituents to the system, and selecting others for excretion. Do we have too much water in the blood stream, or too little? Is salt in excess or deficient? Is the blood pressure too high or too low? Decisions are made according to the volume of these constituents *already* existing in the blood. Libra's function is, as retired US President George Bush once said of himself, "The Decider". Libra, the scales, carries out this selective balancing act. Secondly, the Libra governed kidneys decide what and how much to reabsorb of salt, water, and various other constituents. The reabsorption is for later use. Conversely, our Virgo ruled intestines absorb select nutrients and shuffle the remaining effluvia down the intestinal track, colon, and rectum for final exit at Scorpio.

Libra governs distillation but does not govern either urine itself, or the process of urination. These are ruled by the following sign Scorpio. Urine is held in the Scorpio-ruled bladder, awaiting the first discreet opportunity for release. It is expressed through the ureters, which appear to share their rulership between Libra and Scorpio, with

Gemini likely playing a part because it influences tubes. Two case horoscopes of sufferers of serious ureter maladies bear this out, although more studies are needed.

Kidney and bladder cases almost invariably have an emphasis in both Libra and Scorpio. These two signs are closely aligned in the urinary process.

Maintaining pH Balance

The kidneys maintain the acid-base balance of the blood in two primary ways. Kidney cells reabsorb bicarbonate HCO3 from the urine back into the bloodstream, and they secrete hydrogen H+ ions into the outgoing urine. This adjustment balances the blood's pH.

Hormonal Balancing

Libra's role in balancing hormones is *underrated* and little understood. This needs more work. The kidneys, and the adrenals atop them, produce several significant hormones. The kidneys are also receiving signals from the pituitary gland. I will briefly address this complexity.

Note how Libra stands halfway, in a stressful "square" formation to the two signs governing the pituitary gland: Cancer (posterior pituitary), and Capricorn (anterior). Jupiter also governs this gland. In passing, I've noted that a natal Jupiter positioned in the first 5 degrees of Libra, Aries, Capricorn, or Cancer is prevalent in expressed pituitary disturbances.

The Adrenal Axis

The adrenals perch atop the kidneys, one per each. These glands secrete many different hormones and are largely ruled by fighting Mars and the Libra-Aries axis. Their associated degree is 0° Aries-Libra (the two equinoctial points). However, the entire two signs, plus Mars, influence these essential glands, with the critical 26th degree especially active. There is a close relationship by square to the rulers of the pituitary gland, whose locus is 0-5° Cancer-Capricorn, also with influence throughout those signs.

The main hormones secreted by the adrenal cortex include cortisol, aldosterone, DHEA, adrenaline, androgenic steroids, and noradrenaline.

Aldosterone balances sodium and potassium in your blood. Too much of this hormone causes a loss of potassium and a retention of sodium. This, in turn, influences how much water is reabsorbed from the blood stream. This process attempts to maintain homeostasis of the blood's pH level.

Cortisol and adrenalin serve many functions. The fight-or-flight hormone adrenalin is a very Mars-Aries substance and, amongst other actions, *increases the kidney's production of urine.*

Mineralocorticoids are mediated by messages triggered by the kidneys. The hypothalamus produces corticotrophin-releasing hormone (CRH), thus stimulating the pituitary gland to produce and secrete adrenocorticotropic hormone (ACTH). This hormone stimulates the production of cortisol. Cortisol is a steroid hormone made by the adrenal glands that is important for regulating glucose, protein, and lipid metabolism, suppressing the immune system's response, and helping to maintain blood pressure. Libra natives appear more prone to cortisol sensitivity than to adrenalin responsiveness. One often sees fat storage in the upper body and slim lower body. Note how Libra's opposite sign Aries is the "adrenalin" sign!

Blood Circulation and Blood Pressure (Air Triplicity)

What is Libra's hitherto unwritten role in the blood's circulation and pressure? We know that Aquarius and Venus govern the *venous* circulation, while Sagittarius and Jupiter govern the arterial circulation. Gemini and Mercury influence the capillaries. Libra is an air sign, as are Gemini and Aquarius, and must have some oxygenating function. What part does Libra play in this circulatory scheme?

Most obviously, Libra's salt-potassium balancing function helps monitor, maintain, and raise/lower the blood pressure. Certainly, this is a significant role in the circulation.

New studies are revealing that the hormone *erythropoietin* influences blood pressure. This hormone is created in the Libra-ruled kidneys, with a small amount in the liver.

Oxygenation: We know that oxygen intake occurs at inspiration within the alveoli of the bronchial tree and the tissues of the lung (Gemini). Next, the oxygenation of the blood is governed by Aquarius. It is my belief that it is really the oxygen-carbon exchange within the cells that Aquarius controls. Factually, Aquarians typically suffer sub oxygenation (or too much carbon?). However, our discussion here is regarding Libra, and its influence upon this process of oxygen uptake.

Libra's Role in Breathing: *Inspiration* is relegated to Gemini, the zodiac's first air sign. Aquarius, the zodiac's last air sign, appears to influence the cellular uptake of oxygen, and the oxygen-carbon exchange within the cells. But what role does the central Air Sign, Libra play in breathing? This seems undiscussed in previous texts. Gemini's opposite sign, Sagittarius, governs the *expiration*. So that's not it! However, what governs the *space between two breaths?* As discussed previously, pausing is a Libra function! And the breathing cycle is a cycle-circle too. Inspiration-Pause-Expiration-Pause-Inspiration. We therefore postulate that this pause point in the breathing cycle is ideally related to Libra! We further suggest that Libra governs the space between the *diastolic* and *systolic* heart beats.

Blood Pressure Maintenance: The kidneys (Libra) can indirectly report blood volume as a tissue oxygen signal. In response, the kidney produced hormone erythropoietin calls on the bone marrow to produce more oxygen carrying red blood cells. These cells carry oxygen from the lungs (Gemini) to the rest of the body.

Note: Here we have the Libra-Cancer square connection. Kidneys (Libra) and bone marrow (Cancer).

We can therefore postulate that Libra has a great deal to do with the maintenance of blood pressure homeostasis. Sagittarius (arteries), Aquarius (veins), and Leo (heart, aorta) are also strongly involved.

Comparing the Libra and Scorpio Symbols, *Libra's* symbol, (a set of scales), accurately shows, in part, the multi-faceted balancing function of the kidneys (hormonal, electrolyte, water, and blood pressure).

Scorpio's symbol aptly describes the process of urination, including distillation, ureters, and exit. Scorpio may play a role in the distillation process, especially removal. Scorpio is the zodiac's master chemist. This sign is implicated equally with Libra in all manner of urinary and bladder complaints. Certainly, Libra and Scorpio are closely joined functions in the urinary process.

Air Sign Glyphs

There is an obvious similarity in the three glyphs that humans have created to signify the three zodiacal Air signs. All three are composed of two adjacent lines. This is contrary to all other signs which involve animals, except Virgo whose planet ruler Mercury co-rules an air sign.

What could this mean? One can only extrapolate a guess from the fact that air signs collectively govern neural transmission, oxygenation, and venous circulation. In old times, before the nervous system was known to exist, Air signs were thought to rule "the blood." That assignment requires a revisitation because the blood is approximately 80% water! However, the circulation of the blood (a vital function!) is influenced by air signs, as discussed elsewhere.

Could the two adjacent lines seen in the glyphs for Gemini, Libra and Aquarius represent the arterial and venous system running alongside each other, the way they do? Or could they represent the bilaterality of the body? (Gemini rules the hands, and individual coordination.) Or something else? Do these glyphs suggest the dual process of neural conduction? Signals running from the body to the CNS and brain, and conversely, from the brain and CNS outward to the body? The airy power to observe the self?

Neural Conduction

Air signs *as a team* have not been well assessed as to their role in neural conduction. This below is my personal view, open to discussion.

Gemini and Mercury govern the peripheral afferent nerves, their receiving of incoming data, the branching of dendrites, and the creation of new synaptic networks.

Aquarius and Uranus certainly govern electricity and sodium, both essential to *neural transmission*. Aquarius is the established ruler of the homeopath's Nat Mur (sodium), so essential in the process of signal conduction through the neural network. Neurons carry messages in the form of electrical signals, known as *nerve impulses*. The neurons are excited in several ways (light, touch, sound), but are especially activated through chemicals released by other neurons.

Now we have a nerve "wire" (Gemini), conducting electrical signals via sodium ions (Aquarius). However, we need a chemical "talent agent" to open the door for the signal to jump between neurons!

Nerve impulses are electrical charges that rush along a neural membrane. Sodium ions flow in, precipitating the *action* potential, and then, potassium ions flow out to reset the *resting* potential. If sodium is aligned to Aquarius, is potassium of Libra? (Nauman and Jansky assign potassium to the Moon, offering us no sign). After all, Libra is the scales, and the pause point in any pendulum's swing. Is Libra related to the *Neural resting potential?* But we have another step in this neurotransmission cycle that can be attributed to this sign.

In vocational astrology, Libra governs all agents who work to introduce and connect two entities desiring connection. For instance, Libra rules matchmakers (I fondly recall a beloved native of Libra, Barbara Walters, a world-renowned interviewer)! *Could Libra govern those chemical messengers that open a neuron's doors to receive electrical messages?*

For example, news of a pricked finger swiftly arrives at the brain by means of generated electrical signals swiftly traveling up the chain of neurons. With each neuron encountered, the message "ouch" is introduced to the next neuron, all heading towards their brainy destination. Enter *neurotransmitters.*

Neurotransmitters are chemical messengers required by the molecules of the nervous system to transmit messages between neurons and from neurons to muscles. Neurotransmitters can be amino acids, neuropeptides, or small amine molecules.

In other chapters, we see how the ANS and CNS are largely influenced by the mutable cross of Gemini (peripheral afferent), Virgo (sympathetic), Sagittarius (CNS, motor), and Pisces (parasympathetic), with input on the adrenal axis of the parasympathetic from Aries. All of this is new research that necessitates a great deal more work.

A possible way to view the collective function of air signs in neurotransmission is summarized below. However, I am not yet completely satisfied with Libra's role in this picture:

- **Gemini:** the nerves, dendrites, network creation
- **Libra:** neurotransmitters, potassium, neural resting potential
- **Aquarius:** electricity, sodium, the flow of electricity through the body

Mental Balance/Imbalance

This book is about the physical implications of the twelve Sun Signs. However, the importance of Libra's role in mental balance cannot be overestimated. Situated at "pause" on the yearly swing of the sun's cycle, Libra emphasizes observation and objectivity *over action.*

Being the quintessential sign of balance, Libras are purported to be calm, reasonable, and just. However, when the sign is afflicted, balance can all too easily flip to mental and emotional imbalance. All we need is this or that hormone to run amok. Any failure in balancing out just the right amount of hormones, sugar, or electrolytes can result in spectacular mental-emotional and behavioral changes. Many normally tranquil Libras are indeed prone to surprise others with an "out of the sheer blue" tantrum or irrational argument (typically denied later). This appears to be a balancing mechanism with their opposite sign, the feisty Aries.

Another of Libra's more annoying habits is the tendency to compulsively present opposite opinions. You say green, they must say red. Or, failing to side with you, just when you expect them to. After all, they must be *just.* As I wrote this, a small, classically Libra-type boy trotted up to me inquiring about why I was carrying an umbrella. *"It's going to rain,"* said I. *"No it's not!"* he shot back. *"Yes, look at the sky,"* said I, pointing upward to the heavy, dark, impending clouds. *"No, it's not going to rain!"* he retorted. The conversation continued along this vein. Upon departing I regretted not asking him his birthday!

Mental balance is ever important to natives of this sign. Balance, grace, and poise are their essential gifts. *Lack of balance becomes their proverbial Achilles heel.* For Libran health, we must attend to balance in all things: diet; work vs play; mental vs physical exertion; sleep vs waking. Too often, they don't maintain balance. Few signs are less concerned with rigorous health regimens.

Libra natives are often champions of truth and justice. Heroic social justice workers, and vociferous truth tellers, are often natives of this sign, case examples being Eleanor Roosevelt, Jimmy Carter,

John Lennon, and the venerable Mahatma Gandhi. Typically, many Libras are devoted and faithful spouses until death do us part. However, tradition holds that this sign is occasionally prone to deceit, especially in marriage. Strangely, the two most compulsive marital liars I ever knew, were both natives of this sign. Curious about this phenomenon, I inquired of my Libra friend Ray, just why this might be so. He happily offered that Libra strives for balance in all things, and thus *"halfway between the truth, and what you want to hear, is a lie"*. Touché! On balance, I have known several Libra natives who were obsessed with truth and honesty. "Truth," as both a concept and reality, seems to be a Libra issue, either way. This must be understood in a health context because a Libran can become tensely overwrought over issues of familial, spousal, or social truth.

Gender

In discussing astrological gender, we are adhering to traditional designations because the train of discussion necessitates this. I refer to "male" and "female" signs as more pertaining to electrical and magnetic current. See the illustration in Chapter 1: "Electrical and Magnetic Exchange Through the Twelve Zodiac Signs".

In the matter of electric-magnetic exchange, Libra holds a unique position among all signs except for Scorpio. In Libra, we find Venus, a quintessentially female planet, governing a traditionally male sign. There is no other sign with this specific honor. Conversely for Scorpio, a traditionally male planet, Mars, rules a magnetic female sign. However, this anomaly is not as strong as for Venus in Libra because Mars holds a traditional rulership of the feminine Water Triplicity too. Venus has no such honor within the Air Triplicity. There must be something unique in how Libra influences gender, electric-magnetic charges, marriage, and conception!

(Note that some argue that Saturn is given by some to female gender, and rules Air sign Aquarius, a male sign. Not all agree with the former. Neither is Saturn a quintessentially female or male planet and is prominent in the horoscopes of asexuals and celibates.

Libra is situated perfectly halfway through the zodiac. Similarly, this sign symbolizes the mid-point between age-youth, mind-body, two halves of the year, and day-night. In the same way, Libra symbolizes the *midway point between the genders, as well as the meeting point of the genders (marriage).*

It is obvious that Libra's scale glyph resembles our equal sign (=). *Libra represents where positive and negative charges first meet.* At Libra, the electrical and magnetic forces either join, cancel, or neutralize. Three choices! (See Illustration). If the marriage is successful (Libra governs marriage), these opposite charges move to *consummate at Scorpio!*

In Libra, the sexes meet, combine, or reject. Traditional astrology states that Libra and its natural house (the seventh house) govern two distinctly polarized concepts: partners, contracts, marriages - and - competitors, open enemies, conflict.

Like everyone else, Libra natives will follow the normal population statistics. However, all Air signs, in concert with multiple planetary signatures, are evidenced in charts related to homosexuality, bi-sexuality androgyny, and gender dysphoria. Related to this spectrum, let's underline *"in concert with multiple planetary signatures".* All twelve signs are involved in the human gender spectrum in certain, specific planet and house combinations. If a native is other than heterosexual, look for a strong Air sign component (Gemini, Libra, and Aquarius), especially near the 15th degree. You may find something there, or not. These three signs represent androgyny as a concept, and only sometimes as an experience. As said, most Air sign natives will follow the normal population graph and identify as heterosexual. As an aside, I knew one fashionably inventive Libra woman (with a Gemini moon), who wore frilly, feminine clothes waist up, and classic male attire (i.e., striped men's pants and combat boots) waist down! Balance.

The consciousness of gender equality is under the auspices of the Air Triplicity, far more than for any other element. This is so, because Air signs (most especially Aquarius) represent a consciousness of the mind and eternal spirit first, wherein gender, age, and other social labels are not high on the value list.

Over the decades, I have noticed two Libra styles of mating behavior. The many Libra people I have known are either devoted to their spouse (around whose affairs their own life revolves), or, conversely, are compulsively or serially partnering. (See comments on hormonal partnering between *Libra-Capricorn* and *Libra-Cancer* squares, below.)

LIBRA SYNDROME

As discussed in Chapter Two, a Zodiac Sign Syndrome is a cluster of symptoms associated with the body zones and functions of a zodiac sign and the signs positioned on the seasonal wheel opposite (180°) and quincunx (150°, 210°, 330°) the sign. Remediating and supporting these body zones and functions act to bring the body into balance, diminishing the syndrome. These symptoms may manifest when there is an emphasis in one or more of these signs. Planetary dignity plays an important role.

The Weaker Signs for the Libra Vital Force
Quincunx Signs

Pisces, Taurus, and Virgo are positioned 150°, 210° and 330° distant from Libra on the seasonal wheel. These signs represent the 6th, 8th, and 12th *averted* angles from the sign Libra (see the illustration for this chapter). This condition makes it difficult for Libra to absorb the cosmic rays or the vibrational and light nutrients that feed these signs. Likewise, these signs may have trouble absorbing the rays from Libra.

Virgo rules Body Zone 6 which includes the pancreas, liver, spleen, small intestines, ascending colon, digestion, sympathetic nerves, gut efficiency, and immune system (with Pisces, Mars).

Libra natives love sweets. Based on my observations, this is one of the three signs traditionally most prone to diabetes. The Libra-ruled kidneys role in diabetes is unknown, despite this disease being as common to Libra as to Virgo. I can offer two plausible explanations.

First is the position of the pancreatic sign Virgo on the 12th angle to Libra. This can indicate some weakness in one of the digestive organs, possibly the pancreas. The delta cells of the pancreas excrete somatostatin, a hormone that blocks as needed the release of both glucose and insulin. The pancreatic alpha and beta cells (located in the islets of Langerhans) produce glucagon for the conversion of liver-stored glycogen into glucose (alpha cells), whereas insulin, expressed by the beta cells, is required for glucose uptake. The delta cells "judge" whether to lower insulin or block glucose. This wise weighing and balancing act is essentially Libran in nature!

The second explanation involves the adrenal axis, governed by Aries, Mars, and Libra. See the section below on *Opposite Sign, Aries.*

Pisces rules Body Zone 12 which includes the feet, fluidic matrix, lymphatic system, and possibly the fascia (Hill). One would think that an inefficient lymphatic system would contribute to kidney filtration overload, or the reverse. Does the lymphatic system take up the slack of sluggish kidney filtration? Both signs process fluids, but for different reasons. The Pisces-Virgo axis cleans the extracellular fluid of the matrix, while Libra (kidneys) filters the arterial blood stream. Can a sluggish ECM lurk behind some kidney complaints?

Taurus rules Body Zone 2 which includes the mouth, tongue, throat, thyroid, neck, ears, lower, back brain, and trapezius. Libra is prone to sugar and wine addiction. Taurus obviously influences balance and poise, ruling both the region's balance-controlling organs - the brain's cerebellum and semi-circular canals of the ear. The thyroid, while not exclusively under Taurus, is certainly housed in this sign's body zone. It would be interesting to discover if natives with a Sun or ascendant in Libra suffer a heightened tendency toward thyroid complaints.

We also see the Taurus-Libra connection in calcium balance. When blood calcium levels are too high, the Taurus-zoned thyroid produces the hormone calcitonin, signaling the Libra-ruled kidneys to excrete more calcium and block the reabsorption of bone calcium from the bones. When blood calcium falls too low, the Taurus-zoned parathyroids secrete parathyroid hormone, which instructs the kidneys to retain calcium, and the bones to release calcium. For more about Libra's connection to the bones, see the section below on the Libra-Capricorn square. Tonsilitis (Taurus) has been linked to kidney complaints (Libra). This is an example of the remote causation of which quincunxes disclose.

Opposite Sign, Aries

When the Sun is in Libra, the opposite sign, Aries, "sleeps." Aries rules Body Zone 1, which includes the head, upper and frontal brain, eyes, adrenal gland, motor nerves of brain, and some cranial nerves.

Interestingly, Dr. Davidson said that headaches (Aries) are frequently caused by Saturn in Libra, due to an accrual of gravel in the tiny kidney tubules. Libra is thus hypothetically prone to all manner of problems caused by hyper or hypo states of various adrenal hormones such as Cushing's syndrome and Addison's disease.

Continuing the discussion on diabetes under the Virgo section, above, Aries and Mars appear to govern the adrenal glands, and certainly adrenalin. They are stationed like tiny hats atop the kidneys in Libra's Body Zone 7. The Aries adrenal type possesses active and constant adrenal response, directing the muscles to increase sugar uptake for immediate fight or flight needs. More sugar is demanded, and therefore more insulin. This process can lead to insulin insensitivity, hypoglycemia, or excess blood sugar. This can sometimes contribute to hyperglycemia and eventual diabetes.

Signs Aggravating Libra Syndrome - Squaring Signs

Capricorn and Cancer are positioned 90° from Libra squaring this sign (see chapter illustration. The effect of a square is to create friction, for good or ill. Libra can reflex with these signs, as well as its opposite sign, Aries.

The Libra-Capricorn Square. Calcitonin, a thyroid produced hormone, decreases the renal tubular reabsorption of sodium, phosphate, and calcium. According to a 1975 article by Raymond Ardaillou, *"Renal receptors for calcitonin have been demonstrated in the membranes of rat tubular cells."* Capricorn has a great deal to do with bones. However, see the Taurus-Libra quincunx section above for more detail.

We also note the kidney's role in converting Vitamin D to its useful form, so necessary in the absorption of calcium into the bones. Should Libra be afflicted in the horoscope, could we foresee a heightened tendency toward osteoporosis?

Capricorn and Jupiter co-govern the anterior pituitary, whereas Libra governs balances of all kinds. We also would search for interactions between the kidneys and/or adrenal hormones and the pituitary gland. Clearly, Libra plays a role in sex hormone balance and puberty (Libra and Scorpio co-governs the ovaries, and possibly the testes).

The Libra-Cancer Square. This one puzzles me. The water sign Cancer governs in part, the thoracic duct, lactation, breasts, stomach, mucus membranes, and interstitial fluids. Cancer is Moon-ruled. The Moon plays a role in Libra and Venus ruled female hormone production. One often notes excessive breast tissue growth in female Librans. I have noticed that Cancer natives with Libra Moons are extremely moody. The moods swing up and down, depending on the weather, time of day, menstrual cycle, and other factors. Cancer is prone to water bloating, especially during menses.

The Libra-Cancer Square reflects the water volume adjusting powers of Libra. As one of our three water signs, Cancer and its ruler, the Moon, together govern all daily and monthly tidal rhythms. Libra attempts to balance these out. Water volume rises and falls, and Libra must weigh and adjust this volume! *In astrology, water and moods are related.*

Cancer, Capricorn (Cornell, Nauman, Davidson, Hill) and Jupiter (Cayce, verified by Hill) govern the Pituitary gland. Interestingly, Capricorn and Cancer both square Libra, the scales. What is Libra's pituitary hormone balancing role?

Cancer and Jupiter co-govern the posterior pituitary, whereas Libra governs balances of all kinds. We also could search for interactions between the kidneys and/or adrenal hormones and the pituitary gland. Unbalanced progesterone, excessive bloating and swelling is common to Libra Moon or for biological females with Libra-Cancer squares.

We also find another connection. The bone marrow as a blood cell nursery is thought to be governed by Mars (red blood cells) and the sign Cancer (that great nurse maid of the zodiac). The kidneys request more red blood cells from the Cancer-ruled bone marrow by sending their messenger erythropoietin. This hormone, produced mostly in the interstitial kidney cells, prevents the destruction of red blood cells, while simultaneously stimulating an increase in their formation within the bone marrow. The whole scheme helps the body receive more oxygen (Libra is, after all, an air sign!).

How Planetary Dignity Contributes to Libra Syndrome
Strongest Planets

Ruling Planet, Venus. This temperate, moist, relaxing planet influences copper, the veins (with Aquarius), and ovaries (with Libra). It is both anodyne and alkaline.

Exalted Planet, Saturn. This planet does well in Libra because the *Law of God*, or karma, works best in the sign of justice. Hence, the scales are the traditional symbol of Libra, also representing the function of the Libra-ruled kidneys (weighing and balancing water and electrolytes, and so forth). Libra's calcium regulation role is strongly expressed here. Saturn rules bones and Libra responds to calcitonin and parathyroid hormone to assist in regulation blood calcium levels. Saturn emphasizes reason and delayed response over action - Libra's forte.

Weakest Planet

Mars: The ruler of Libra's opposing sign, Aries, exemplifies action on behalf of self or towards a goal or objective. Conversely, Libra works in partnership and is ever focused on "the other". Mars is fight, immediacy, and action, while Libra governs dispassion, diplomacy, non-action, and delayed judgement and response.

We can now understand why Libra changes Mars' natural impulse, but also tempers him. This can be helpful, but sometimes it is not. For instance, Mars in Libra can cause excessive dumping of sodium, or water, by overstimulating the Libra-ruled kidneys. Also, because Mars is our prime excreter of the planetary pantheon, his natural diuretic powers may weaken, resulting in poorly filtered blood, toxemia, over acidity, and acne.

We could postulate a tendency for deficient or, conversely, excessive androgens, adrenalin, or iron in the blood. However, Libra would theoretically trend low and Scorpio high!

Mars also rules the red blood cells that are both stimulated and protected by the kidney hormone erythropoietin. However, Mars is in detriment in this sign! Could this Mars-Libra link reflect in either lower or higher than normal red blood cells in Libra natives; or those with malefics in Libra?

The Sun: The ego, willpower, purpose, and self-consciousness "fall" in the sign of partnership and marriage. The focus is more often on the partner (or partnering) than the self.

The Vital Force of Librans can lack stamina, but not invariably so. The Vital Force will be quite high if the Sun is well placed and simultaneously well supported by Venus, Mars, Jupiter, or fire signs!

Planetary and House Positions that Contribute to Libra Syndrome

(1) **Sun, Moon, or Ascendant sign in Libra**

(2) A weakness in a body zone governed by the signs opposite or quincunx Libra on the seasonal wheel (Aries, Virgo, Pisces, and Taurus), as discussed above under *The Weaker Signs for the Libra Vital Force.*

(3) <u>Any</u> natal planet, luminary, or lunar node in Libra, compounded by the testimonies below:

- Libra inhabits the 1st, 6th, 8th, or 12th houses of the natal chart.
- <u>Sun, Moon, or Venus in Libra</u>, afflicted by Mars or Saturn, or closely conjunct a lunar node.
- Any planet opposing or conjunct a Libran Sun, Moon, Mars, Mercury, or lunar node.
- Saturn in hard angle to Venus, Libra's ruler.

- Natal Venus in its detriment or fall (Aries, Virgo, Scorpio), especially if situated in the 1st, 6th, 7th, 8th, or 12th houses, or any house if seriously afflicted by a malefic, especially Saturn.
- Venus is conjunct, trine, or square Jupiter or Neptune, with Sun, Moon, or Ascendant in Libra.
- Saturn in the 7th or 8th house, or in Libra, or in a cardinal sign.
- Mars in cardinal signs, especially when conjunct the South Node, or in Libra.

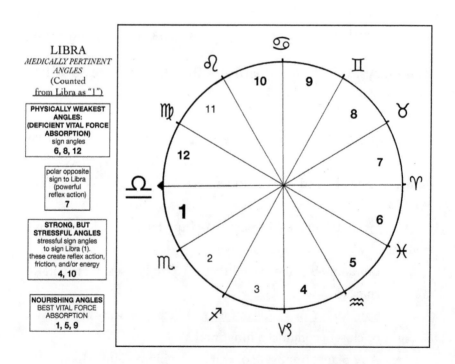

LIBRA
MEDICALLY PERTINENT ANGLES
(Counted from Libra as "1")

PHYSICALLY WEAKEST ANGLES:
(DEFICIENT VITAL FORCE ABSORPTION)
sign angles
6, 8, 12

polar opposite sign to Libra (powerful reflex action)
7

STRONG, BUT STRESSFUL ANGLES
stressful sign angles to sign Libra (1).
these create reflex action, friction, and/or energy
4, 10

NOURISHING ANGLES
BEST VITAL FORCE ABSORPTION
1, 5, 9

SYMPTOMS OF LIBRA SYNDROME

Please note that I am not discussing "Libra people" per se, but those born with prominences in this sign that actually do suffer the syndrome. These symptoms can occur in seriatim, first one symptom, then weeks, months or years later, another. However, two or more of these symptoms are frequently observed clustered together at the same time. These symptoms are not listed in any order, but simply as a list of collected observations common to natives of Libra. Please be sure to balance with *Libra's Superpowers*. As with any sign, there are just as many positives!

- sugar, wine, or soft drink addiction
- excesses or deficiencies of any of the kidney or adrenal hormones and their associated maladies
- kidney diseases
- alcoholism (wine preferred)
- enuresis
- polyuria
- acne due to poor kidney filtration (or conversely, beautiful, velvety skin)
- hyponatremia (low sodium and water in the blood stream)
- ovarian cysts or other ovarian problems
- osteoporosis/osteopenia (especially lumbar)
- bloating and water retention (square Cancer, quincunx Pisces and Scorpio)
- copper-iron imbalance
- alkaline-acid imbalance
- salt-potassium imbalance
- migraines, headaches
- diabetes
- hormonal imbalances of sex hormones
- hypoglycemia
- chronic indecision
- compulsive argument (providing the opposite argument or point of view to any statement or

opinion regardless of one's true opinion)

- entertainment addiction (need for visual stimulation, excitement)
- pornography addiction
- sex and love addiction
- low motivation, except if strong fire component in chart
- excessive breast growth
- two body types in one body (stout above, skinny below; large breasts, flat gluteals; etc.)
- poor lymphatic filtration
- poorly filtered blood - resulting in all manner of blood chemistry imbalances, and acid-alkaline imbalance.
- pancreatic weakness
- weak feet, swollen feet, foot fatigue, foot issues

- thyroid imbalance
- osteoporosis (may relate to low production of the kidney produced hormone erythropoietin)
- kidney stones or gravel especially with Saturn in Libra or Aries (Davidson) or lunar nodes in these signs (Hill)
- ureter issues or blockages
- kidney malfunction or failure
- bladder apex issues
- vertigo and sensitivity to spinning
- edema
- sedentary lifestyle
- mental imbalances, often due to hormone imbalances
- baldness

REMEDIATION TIPS

Please note that these remedial tips are for interest only. The author is not suggesting that any person use these without the evaluation and consent of their personal healthcare practitioner.

The following is a short list of herbs possessing properties that are *potentially* remediative to one or more of the classic symptoms discussed above.

- *Goldenrod*, a favorite warming kidney herb.
- *Parsley*, a specific for enuresis. Dorothy Hall warns against use for kidney stones.
- *Osmunda*, Royal Fern, specific for lower back pain (Wood).
- *Alfalfa*, excessive acidity (Hall).
- *Nettles*, iron rich, blood cleansing.
- *Nettle Seed*, specific for kidney disease.
- *Celery*, helps process uric acid.
- *Black Cherry Juice*, an Edgar Cayce specific for the kidneys.
- *Collinsonia* (Stoneroot), *Gravel Root* for Saturn or North Node in Libra.
- *Poke Root*, Dorothy Hall's pick for the hormonally imbalanced Libran. A "handle with care" herb.
- *Dandelion Leaf*, good, mineralizing diuretic, and cooling.
- *Watermelon Seeds*, very strong, cold, diuretic. Good only for hot Libra conditions.
- *Black Walnut*, considered a specific for relief in some edema cases.
- *Corn Silk and Marshmallow*, excellent urinary demulcents.
- *Sarsaparilla*, hormonal balancer and alterative.
- *Saw Palmetto, Fenugreek, and Borage*, all possible hair thickening herbs, but not necessarily together.

See also Chapter 15, *The Twelve Zodiac Sign Syndromes and their Relevant Herbs.*

Chapter Ten:

SCORPIO SYNDROME

Energy and persistence conquer all things.

\- Benjamin Franklin

Intense Tastes

For years, I wondered why my many Scorpio friends typically prefer intensely flavored treats and potent taste sensations - kumquats, raw garlic, chili peppers, kimchi, or that 98% cacao chocolate bar! While tidying up this book for publication, the reason dawned upon me. Intense flavors speed metabolism, excite secretions, and so often discourage antigens. Governing the excretory system, Scorpio's waste dumping excesses may require a little extra help. Furthermore, this sign's native tendency for yeast, bacterial and parasitical infection is addressed by many potently tasting, anti-parasitical, and antibiotic herbs and spices. The classically intense Scorpio native never balks at horseradish! This is a good example of how sign natives so often seek foods that most resemble themselves! We will learn more about that in this chapter.

Fundamentals Refresher

Scorpio Syndrome is a set of collaborative symptoms, consistently appearing together, which are typical for natives of the sign Scorpio. The symptoms associated with Scorpio Syndrome can be experienced by people with other sun signs when there is a particular emphasis in this sign. Zodiac sign syndromes can occur in seriatim, first one symptom, then another, weeks, months or years later. Few experience all symptoms. However, two or more of these symptoms are frequently observed clustered together at the same time.

A Scorpio native may have few if any of the symptoms associated with Scorpio Syndrome. Indeed, many Scorpios are specimens of perfect health. However, this symptom set often, but not always, evinces itself when the native's Sun, Moon, or Ascendant tenants Scorpio and displays certain astrological conditions which are discussed at length in this chapter.

This chapter describes the astrological conditions that may aggravate the syndrome. With this knowledge, practitioners can explore the underlying condition when symptoms consistent with the syndrome present themselves in a patient. Understanding the energetic cause is the first step in remediation.

THE SIGN SCORPIO

In Classical Western Astrology, with use of the Tropical Zodiac, a Scorpio is someone born between 210-239 longitudinal degrees after the spring equinox.

As with all other signs, we cannot think of Scorpio as an isolated single entity or a static constant. "Scorpio" is a gestalt of strengths and weaknesses based on its angular relationship to the other signs of the interconnected solar cycle. In turn, each of the twelve phases of this cycle is influenced by the unique planetary configurations at birth and throughout the life. Scorpio is a unique phase-state, with its interactions peculiar to the eighth stage of the twelve-fold cyclical process.

Element and Mode: Scorpio is of the element Water and belongs to the Fixed quadruplicity of signs.

Life Cycle Phase: Scorpio represents the eighth stage of the twelve-fold human life cycle. The infant born (Aries), feeds (Taurus), babbles and toddles (Gemini), emotionally bonds with tribe, emotionally sensitizes, (Cancer), glories in nubile adolescence (Leo), perfects work skills and discernment (Virgo), and takes pause (Libra).

We now arrive at 210° on the cycle, Scorpio. Here, the wheel either falls backward from its own weight or, *from past momentum,* moves ahead. This is a deeply karmic sign! A Scorpio lifetime is rarely an easy affair. Rather, this birth season demands grit, overcoming, self-transformation, seriousness, and courage. I considered replacing the introductory quote with *"endurance and resourcefulness makes lemonade from lemons".*

Notice the sigil for number 8 is the classic eternity symbol. Scorpio must purify itself of accumulated dross, both spiritually and physically. Bravely arising from the ashes of its own transformative processes, Scorpio and its ruler Mars govern all excretory functions of the body!

Scorpio also governs sex. But this is not the latent sex force of Taurus, nor Libra's attraction and/or repulsion of opposites, nor sexual pleasure - that being the province of Pisces. Scorpio governs both the transformative and destructive forces of sex, and the attendant arousal of associated instincts (desire, jealousy, revenge, obsession, intense love or hate). A Scorpio life experience wallows in and/or wrestles with these deep, intense, emotional waters. These natives gain wisdom regarding the human condition!

Scorpio is our singular 'Fixed Water' sign. Water governs retentive feeling, memory, love, and deep instinct. All Water signs are depicted as creatures of pure instinct (crab, scorpion, fish). Fixed Water indicates a condensed state of the element, such as ice or toxic ponds. Thus, the most extreme and concentrated emotions are found in this sign, allowing its natives a significant power for good or ill, depending on their druthers. We also find those willing to kill or die for a beloved. Many of our greatest healers, surgeons, psychologists, and hypnotists are Scorpio, blessed with a curiosity about all hidden workings of the body and mind.

Fixed Water equals ice and all its powers. Ice forgets nothing, preserving mastodons for millennia. Neither does Scorpio forget a kindness - or a wrong! Fixed Water also symbolizes brewing, stagnant, ponds of both emotion and bodily fluids. Considering this fact allows a window into Scorpio health idiosyncrasies and their treatment.

In Scorpio, we have the potential for transformation of toxic and stagnant emotional states. This overcoming is the key to Scorpio health. James Allen reminds us that: *"If you would perfect your body, guard your mind. If you would renew your body, beautify your mind. Thoughts of malice, envy, disappointment, despondency, rob the body of its health and grace."*

Scorpio Superpowers

The great superpower of Scorpio is the **Phoenix**, the power to rise again. Scorpio is the cat with nine lives. Curiously, this sign is known to attract mortal diseases unto itself, and then overthrow them, confounding their doctors. One triple Scorpio I know has outlived three mortal diseases. Scorpio is the most resilient of signs!

My Scorpio-cusp father told me that he instructed his dentist to provide no anesthetic for his root canal, because he "found pain interesting." A second Scorpio friend had a dental crown installed sans pain medication because "it saved money, so why not?" I have seen a cancer diagnosed Scorpio native, given "three months, and no hope", beat the statistics and flummox her physician. How did she do it? She focused intense thought in daily healing visualizations, imagining her white blood cells in the guise of white knights on horseback attacking her cancer.

It benefits the healer to recognize this Scorpio Phoenix Power. One must never underestimate the overthrowing powers of the Scorpio native suffering a so-called "mortal" diagnosis.

Physical Appearance

Exhaustive detail with illustrations is provided in this author's *The Astrological Body Types*.

SCORPIO BODY RULERSHIPS AND FUNCTIONS

As described in Chapter One, a body zone is a general box that overlays many organs, functions, vessels and their sub-rulerships. Scorpio will typically be seen in natal charts, or by current transit, when one observes accidents or symptoms in this zone.

Scorpio, Body Zone 8

This zone includes the colon, rectum, anus, bladder, urethra, and co-rules the ureters (with Libra and Gemini); genitals, nose, sweat glands, urine, the expulsion of urine and feces, and peristalsis. Scorpio maintains a close reflex with the throat, as it is governed by opposite sign Taurus. Scorpio also holds rulership over the uterus (with the Moon and with Cancer when pregnant). Scorpio shares governance of the ovaries with Libra and Venus; and co-rules the buttocks, sacrum, and coccyx with Sagittarius.

Scorpio Body Functions
Distillation of the Urine (Libra/Scorpio)

Libra governs distillation, but it does not govern either urine itself or the process of urination. The distillation and micturition (process of expelling urine from the body) include and blend both Libra and Scorpio functions. Libra weighs, contemplates, decides. Scorpio acts, expels, transforms, and recycles. Scorpio is the great chemist of the zodiac (incidentally, this sign is often seen in charts of herbalists, chemists and waste recyclers).

Libra governs the "top" and Scorpio the "bottom" of the urinary process. Libra weighs and balances the constituents and water in the blood. Next, decisions must be made: too much this, too little that. Should we maintain the calcium or pee out the salt?

The act of urination is decisively Scorpionic (look at its symbol!) However, although usually given to Libra, it is my opinion that the reabsorption of water into the blood (recycling) is quintessentially Scorpio.

The linkage of these two signs in the urinary process is borne out empirically, *as kidney and bladder cases almost invariably have an emphasis in both Libra and Scorpio.*

It is of significant interest to note that Libra and Scorpio were originally conceived as a *single, joined constellation,* with Libra being the Scorpion's claws. Then the Romans decided that there should be twelve constellations instead of eleven.

Hormonal Balances

Scorpio's hormonal role is little understood. It is my observation that Scorpio is uniquely prone to severe and disfiguring acne, sometimes paired with strong body odor. Scorpio governs the sudorific (sweat) glands. "Dirty blood" is associated with this sign too. Does Scorpio's legendary tendency to dump excess metabolic wastes, hormones, and yeasts into the blood lie behind many of their maladies? As a water sign, we know too, that lymphatic clearance issues must be involved.

Scorpio is one of our notable *hirsute* signs, stimulating growth of unwanted hair, especially for females, and heavy, dense beards for males. This observation leads me to consider if this birth season is a strong androgen producer. One double Scorpio client born with Mars, Moon, Sun, and Ascendant all in Scorpio, suffered from excessive testosterone. Let's exam why this might be so.

Venus, the quintessentially female planet, is curiously in detriment in this female sign, while the quintessentially male planet Mars rules it. This hints at some sort of hormonal reversal, particularly seen in those biologically female gendered Scorpio natives who are gifted with powerful libidos and disproportionately experiencing unwanted body hair, deep voices, or other secondary masculine characteristics.

We can conclude that as a sign, Scorpio favors the production of testosterone and other androgens over estrogens. Scorpio natives of all genders might be prone to higher male and lower female hormones. Naturally, this is more noticeable in the biological female of the species.

Adrenaline and Testosterone

Because of Mars' dominance of this sign, we observe a strongly functioning adrenal gland in the natives of this sign. However, its channel of operation appears quite different than that of fellow Mars-ruled sign, Aries.

Aries' adrenal response is fast and short lived. Anger or fight explode off the top. The native with Sun, Moon or Mars in Aries rarely conceals their rage! Aries seeks immediate resolve and hates to sit long on a grudge. Those reactions are the opposite of Scorpio, the king of disgruntlement. I've known several Scorpio friends who (metaphorically) maintain emotional barbecue spits in their backyard, upon which rotate their enemies, basted weekly. However, once a Scorpio settles the score, they are sated. Naturally, it's this tendency of "brewing and stewing" that can generate a host of chronic health complaints.

Scorpio's symbol aptly describes the processes of urination, defecation, and ejaculation. This glyph is composed of squiggly lines (tubes) that outlets in the Scorpion's "stinger". Thus, Scorpio's symbol resembles a distillation process, ureters, and exit; also, the process of seminal release through seminal vesicles, vas deferens, penis and urethra (the latter is governed by 0-1°of Scorpio).

Gender and Sex

For the gender conscious, we will state at this juncture that Venus, Mars, the zodiac signs, and elemental energies, do not belong to any gender, being intrinsic to all beings, in various degrees and balances.

In discussing astrological gender, we are adhering to traditional designations because the train of discussion necessitates this. As seen in our Libra chapter, I refer to traditional sign designations "male" and "female" as more pertaining to *electrical and magnetic current*. Those that prefer can instead conceive of "electrical" and "magnetic" signs. This concept is a work in progress. See the illustration of "Electric and Magnetic Current Through the Twelve Zodiac Signs" through the zodiac signs in Chapter 1: Melothesia.

Astrological gender is a traditional practitioner's index for specific behaviors, preferences, character, and, for our purposes here - health tendencies. It is readily observable that people born with Sun, Moon, and Ascendant in "female" signs, with a strong natal Moon and Venus, will behave in a socially classic feminine way. Whereas those born with the Sun, Moon, and Ascendant in "masculine" signs, with a prominent natal Mars, Sun, or Jupiter, will err towards socially classic masculine tendencies.

In the matter of electric-magnetic exchange, Scorpio holds a unique position among all signs *except for Libra*. In Libra, we find Venus, a *quintessentially* female planet, governing a traditionally male sign. Venus, amongst all planets, is quintessentially female because "she" governs female genitals. Libra is the only male (electrical) sign with the honor of hosting a quintessentially female planet. Clues as to why this must be so can be found in the chapter on Libra Syndrome.

Conversely for Scorpio, the traditionally male planet, Mars, rules this traditionally female (magnetic) sign. Mars is *quintessentially* male because he governs male genitals. However, in Scorpio, "he" governs a female sign. This anomaly is not as striking as the reverse condition, because Mars holds a traditional rulership of the entire "feminine" Water Triplicity. Truly, Venus-in-Libra wins the crown as our most gender anomalous planetary-sign assignment. *The upshot here is that there must be something unique in how both Libra and Scorpio influence gender, electric-magnetic charges, marriage, and conception! These signs work as a duo, one following the other in the cycle-circle of life.*

As with urination, Scorpio and Libra together govern the continuum of the sexual act. Let's explain further.

Situated perfectly halfway through the zodiac, Libra symbolizes the midway point between the genders and the meeting point of the genders (marriage). The attraction and meeting of opposites or lovers occurs in Libra. This explains why Libra governs marriage.

It is obvious that Libra's scale glyph resembles our equal sign (=). *Libra represents where positive and negative charges first meet.* The lovers meet, court, and spark in Libra. Or they can repulse.

At Scorpio, sexual congress consummates in what was known as the "little death," orgasm. It is no accident that the 8th house governs both the exchange of genetic matter, and death. Throughout the animal kingdom, genetic material is exchanged, driven by nature's prompt to seed the next generation. The mated pair signal their readiness for eventual if not the immediate death. Some insects and fish do in fact die soon after mating (or, as in some hapless insects, are devoured by their mate).

The connection between death and the outflow of genetic material, causes humans to devise various practices to inhibit the exit of generative fluids. The object is to recycle these same forces towards the extension of bodily youth and longevity. Some practitioners assert that immortality itself, or at least, the attainment of several centuries of healthy life is possible by means of this conservation and recycling of the sexual forces and fluids. Because female generative fluids held little status, these traditional practices were largely confined to the male person, though not in all cases.

Sexual consummation is represented by the 8th position in the twelve spoked zodiacal cycle. Notice, once again, how the symbol for the number 8 is also the eternity symbol. Scorpio is the 8th sign, and the natural ruler of the 8th house. The 8th house also governs death!

Although Scorpio governs genitalia, you may be surprised to learn that the Jyotish tradition assigns sexual pleasure to fellow water sign, Pisces. My years of observation and readings for natives with the Sun, or Moon in Pisces lead me to strongly agree.

In truth, Scorpio types often go celibate for long periods, providing the number one sign for monks (an observation gleaned from one study I heard about but cannot verify). Most Scorpio natives I've known swing from sexual extremes to long celibate periods. This is especially true of the Scorpio female. I fondly remember a Scorpio acquaintance, who while a successful and talented nurse, left her stable position to try her hand in the sex industry, "to see what it was like." The one, true, triple Scorpio woman I've known has been celibate for forty years. Another 8th house born Scorpio woman I knew closely, was celibate most of her life. Conversely, three others were madams in the sex industry! I could go on, but I've always observed some extreme.

Death

Scorpio governs death, but similar to sex, this is far too simplistic! The end of the life cycle is Pisces, wherein the spirit departs the body, returning to its "heavenly home" in the astral world (not all persons or religions accept this ideology). The body breaks down, returning to the earth. The grave is allotted to Cancer, and the decaying process is clearly Piscean. So, why then, does Scorpio govern the house of death?

Your guess is probably as good as mine. But let's give it a try. Scorpio is primarily interested in recombining, recycling, chemistry, and the joining of *two forms into one for a new purpose.* Scorpio governs all symbiotic and parasitic partnerships. Scorpio is the master chemist, hypnotist, surgeon, psychologist, and magician. *Scorpio has power and knowledge over the physical, chemical-molecular world.*

Scorpio governs the life stage positioned at 210° on the zodiacal wheel where we experience a necessary cleansing, so that the wheel of life can continue. Scorpio rules the colon! If prevented from waste release, we die.

Not everyone dies a natural death at a ripe old age. Diseases can intervene before we get there. The 8th phase of the cycle, or "Scorpio," provides our chance to turn our health around. Hence arrives is the sign phase of vigorous cleansing and catharsis.

The 8th stage of life, Scorpio, offers a time to transform self and body. Perhaps this is why Scorpios are so blunt and to the point. Why waste time at this crucial opportunity on the life cycle? Here, we must release, cut out, and purify those things that would threaten our emotional, spiritual, and physical health. In Scorpio, we also find those chemical processes of the body that turn waste into useful material. Hence, Scorpio's partnership with Libra in the distillation of urine. Scorpio governs the useful compost heap. Hence the ouroboros symbol of a snake biting its own tail precisely resembles the symbol for number 8. Scorpio, our 8th sign, governs not death per se, but rather, death and rebirth! We could argue that Scorpio is the true sign of the Phoenix.

Recycling

Per the above, *Scorpio is in the recycling business.* One prominent Scorpio city council member I know is admittedly obsessed with both wastewater and sewage treatment strategies, as well as her own bowel function. The body has some interesting waste recycling systems. One example would be the mineral salts recycled in bile. Approximately 95% of bile salts are recycled in the terminal ileum, the last section of the small intestine just at the border to the Scorpio-ruled colon.

Scavenger cells called macrophages destroy red blood cells that have completed their usefulness. However, the iron and heme components within them are recycled to form new red blood cells. *Heme* is the essential component that contains iron, so necessary to oxygenation. Iron and heme bind oxygen. True to any Scorpio theme, heme is highly toxic and can cause severe tissue damage and even death if it isn't recycled properly. Interestingly, both Scorpio and hemoglobin are governed by Mars.

Certainly, many constituents, plus water, are returned to the body for further use in the process of urination governed by a cooperation of Libra and Scorpio.

Symbiosis

Scorpio governs symbiosis, which is the intense interaction of two organisms living in close physical association, hopefully to the advantage of both. Does this explain why this sign is so terribly prone to bacterial infections, viruses, fungus issues, candida, or parasite infestation? Blood transfusion, organ transplants, fecal transplants, and the like are under the province of this sign.

The Veil

A thin psychic veil, while not a medical issue, can certainly become one! The season of Pisces shows this same predilection, though offering far less resistance to ghostly intrusion than does fellow 'spooky' sign Scorpio. Delicate Pisces requires considerable psychic protection, whereas tough Scorpio makes the best exorcist! I personally know one fearless lady who performs them. She is born with the Sun, Moon and Ascendant in Scorpio, and Mars rising.

SCORPIO SYNDROME

As discussed in Chapter Two, a Zodiac Sign Syndrome is a cluster of symptoms associated with the body zones and functions of a zodiac sign and the signs positioned on the seasonal wheel opposite (180°) and quincunx (150°, 210°, 330°) the sign. Remediating and supporting these body zones and functions act to bring the body into balance, diminishing the syndrome. These symptoms may manifest when there is an emphasis in one or more of these signs. Planetary dignity plays an important role.

The Weaker Signs for the Scorpio Vital Force
Quincunx Signs

Aries, Gemini, and Libra are positioned 150°, 210° and 330° distant from Scorpio on the seasonal wheel. These signs represent the *averted* 6th, 8th, and 12th angles from the sign Scorpio (see the illustration for this chapter). This condition makes it difficult for Scorpio to absorb the cosmic rays or the vibrational and light nutrients that feed these signs. Likewise, these signs may have trouble absorbing the rays from Scorpio.

Aries rules Body Zone 1 which includes the head, brain, eyes, and adrenal axis (fight channels). Quincunxes between Aries and Scorpio are noted in adrenalin and testosterone extremes. Both signs

are governed by Mars! I have also noted smell and taste disturbances.

Gemini rules Body Zone 3 which includes oxygen inspiration,
upper lungs and bronchial tubes, capillaries, peripheral afferent
nerves, hands, arms, shoulders, fingers, and speech. Frequently,
colon maladies coincide with bronchitis or asthma. Ureter and fallopian tube complaints are cited for Gemini-Scorpio quincunxes
because Gemini influences all tubes and Scorpio-Libra govern the
zones wherein these tubes are situated (Body Zones 7 and 8).

Scorpios often evince a lack of the light approach common to
Gemini. Scorpio is the exposé journalist, whereas Gemini is the
gossip columnist or short story writer.

Do Scorpio's proverbial nasal problems create limitations of
inspiration (Gemini)? Conversely, does bronchial stress lead to nasal
drainage issues? Additionally, Scorpio's tendency to smoke may
relate to this quincunx.

Libra rules Body Zone 7 which includes the waist area, kidneys,
lower back, lumbar, ovaries, and the filtration of blood and distillation
of urine. The kidney function appears weak in Scorpio. Urinary complaints are equally popular in both signs, with a bladder and ureter-
urethra accent in Scorpio. When encountering a Scorpio with chronic
urinary, bladder, or genital complaints, always consider the kidneys.

Opposite Sign, Taurus

When the Sun is in Scorpio, the opposite sign, Taurus, "sleeps."
Taurus rules Body Zone 2 which includes the ear, throat, lower
teeth, gullet, jaw, tongue, vocal cords, neck, trapezius muscles, and
brain stem. Taurus influences the nose (with Scorpio) and the salivary, thyroid, and parathyroid glands (these also have planetary
rulerships).

Taurus and Scorpio work closely together, reflexing each other. Frequent ear or throat infections (Taurus) often signal a stuffy colon! The vocal cords are located in the Taurus Zone. A weak or gravelly voice can indicate a failing libido or difficulty with the recycling of generative prana.

Taurus is the top of the food cycle, governing the mouth and throat. Scorpio governs the exit point of the digestive cycle, the colon, and anus. In reflex to gustatorial Taurus, Scorpios are frequently addicted to intense substances, producing an acid condition of the blood. Often observed is the Scorpio native snacking upon intense foods such as kimchi, sauerkraut, designer chocolate, sweet liqueurs, smelly cheeses, truffles, hot peppers, straight liquor, or kumquats! Craving intense sensate experiences, the way they do, one wonders if Scorpio is one of our more addiction prone signs.

We also note ***thyroid problems*** *along the entire fixed sign axis*, with a prominence along the Taurus-Aquarius square and Taurus-Scorpio sign opposition. This is especially true in hypothyroid. Conversely, hyperthyroid is more common with a Virgo-Sagittarius square tossed into the mix, involving Jupiter, Mars, Sun, Mercury, or Uranus.

Signs Aggravating Scorpio Syndrome – Squaring Signs

Leo and **Aquarius** are the two signs positioned 90° from Scorpio (see chapter illustration). These squares create friction, good or bad. For example, colon issues (Scorpio) can influence the function of the heart (Leo) and circulatory balances (Aquarius). Of interest is Edgar Cayce's emphasis on sluggish excretory function (Scorpio) as one possible cause for varicose veins of the legs (Aquarius).

How Planetary Dignity Contributes to Scorpio Syndrome
Strongest Planet, Mars

Mars is the ruling planet of Scorpio. This hot dry planet is oddly governing this traditionally cold, moist, water sign - in truth, Scorpio is the singularly warm water sign (Hill). Mars in Scorpio can produce hot, wet states, rather than hot, dry for his other domicile Aries. Therefore, Scorpio is, by far, the warmest and most assertive of the watery trio. Mars governs bodily excretion and Scorpio governs organs of the same. Mars is quite at home here, being his *night house* (his day house is Aries). Mars joins Scorpio in holding a significant rulership over the genitals, nose, and all other of Scorpio's favored parts. This brings a strong libido and a hound dog sense of smell. No planets are traditionally exalted in Scorpio.

Weakest Planets

Venus in detriment: In Scorpio, Venus is in the sign opposite her domicile, or, in the thinking of the ancients, "in exile." The calm serenity, and romantic delicacy of Venus are not so at home in the sign of instinct, desire, and sex. However, Venus' placement in these woods actually enhances these very matters, increasing sexual interest and pleasure!

This placement typically increases the propensity for candida, yeast infection, prolapsus of uterus or bladder, STDs, UTIs, endometriosis, and all manner of uterine and genital complaints. Also, one might postulate lower copper, low estrogen, or conversely excessive estrogen - just because Scorpio does everything too much.

The Moon in its fall: The psychological implications best describe the Moon's fall in Scorpio. Whereas Scorpio's opposite sign Taurus provides the Moon her seat of happy exaltation, the Scorpio Moon type is often discontent. Why is this so? Taurus provides life's comforts and nourishes sensual gratification. The Taurus Moon native is often (but not always!) blessed with food, sex, comfort, and pleasure. Conversely, the Scorpio Moon provides experiences of emotional intensity. The native wrestles with emotional extremes of all kinds. Overcoming bitter moods and scathing memories is so often the lot of a Scorpio Moon child, with an option to channel such intensity into any number of creative and transformative purposes. Their healing abilities are legendary.

The Moon's moistening and watery qualities tenant water sign Scorpio. This position is "dribbly." Scorpio rules the uterus, bladder and colon. Water is downward flowing. This position can produce excessive or toxic watery excretions, enuresis (bedwetting), nocturnal emissions, vaginal secretions, menorrhagia, endometriosis and runny nose. Moon in Scorpio may also be prone to uterine, bladder, and colon prolapses. Although Scorpio is traditionally a fertile sign, such qualities might promote miscarriage. One notes a tendency for candida, UTIs, and as they say in Southern Folk Medicine "bad blood". This is a valuable key to the acne sufferer born with a Scorpio Moon.

Planetary and House Positions that Contribute to Scorpio Syndrome

(1) **Sun, Moon, or Ascendant sign in Scorpio**

(2) A weakness in a body zone governed by the signs opposite or quincunx Scorpio on the seasonal wheel (Gemini, Aries, Libra, Taurus). See discussion above under *The Weaker Signs for the Scorpio Vital Force.*

(3) <u>Any</u> natal planet, luminary, or lunar node in Scorpio, especially the Sun, Moon, Mars or Lunar Nodes. This is compounded by the testimonies below:

- Scorpio inhabits the 1st, 6th, 8th, or 12th houses of the natal chart.
- Saturn in hard angle to Mars, Scorpio's ruler.
- Any planet opposing or conjoining a Scorpio Sun, Moon, Mars, Mercury, Pluto, or either Node.

- Natal Mars in its detriment or fall (Libra, Taurus, Cancer), especially if situated in the 1st, 6th, 7th, 8th, or 12th houses. Any house will do, if seriously afflicted by a malefic, especially Saturn or the South Node.
- Saturn, Uranus, Neptune, Pluto in any of the four fixed signs, Taurus, Leo, Scorpio, Aquarius.
- Pluto in any sign conjunct or in an exact hard aspect to Mars, generally within 1° (the closer the stronger).
- Pluto conjunct or in an exact hard aspect (generally within 1°) to a Scorpio Sun or Moon.
- Pluto in any sign closely conjunct the Ascendant or either Lunar Node.
- Being a troublesome sign, any planet in Scorpio might reflect a serious malady. For instance, Mercury in Scorpio is famous for bladder control issues, as is Venus in Scorpio for candida. Both the Moon and Venus in Scorpio are especially prone to UTIs, herpes, STDs, yeast infections, genital infections, issues of all kinds, and many more of Scorpio's classic maladies.

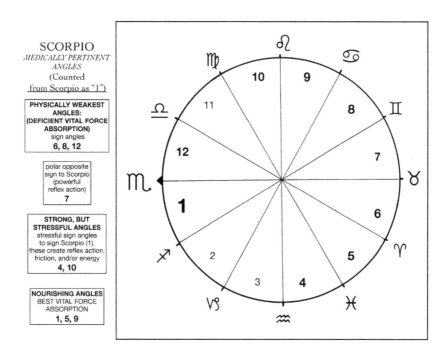

SCORPIO
MEDICALLY PERTINENT
ANGLES
(Counted
from Scorpio as "1")

PHYSICALLY WEAKEST ANGLES: (DEFICIENT VITAL FORCE ABSORPTION) sign angles 6, 8, 12

polar opposite sign to Scorpio (powerful reflex action) 7

STRONG, BUT STRESSFUL ANGLES stressful sign angles to sign Scorpio (1). these create reflex action, friction, and/or energy 4, 10

NOURISHING ANGLES BEST VITAL FORCE ABSORPTION 1, 5, 9

SYMPTOMS OF SCORPIO SYNDROME

Please note that I am not discussing "Scorpio people" per se, but those born with prominences in this sign that actually do suffer the syndrome. These symptoms can occur in seriatim, first one symptom, then weeks, months or years later, another. However, two or more of these symptoms are frequently observed clustered together at the same time. Not all symptoms occur - most typically a handful are observed in the strongly Scorpionic chart. These symptoms are not listed in any order, but simply as a list of collected observations common to natives of Scorpio. Please be sure to balance with Scorpio's Superpowers. As with any sign, there are just as many positives!

- foul smelling sweat
- large pores on back of hand (Davidson)
- acne, pock marks
- intense body odor
- hypersensitive sense of smell
- obsessed with personal hygiene (usually to prevent body odor)
- gravel voice, usually low, hypnotic
- nasal infections (chronic)
- nosebleed
- nose and nasal anomalies, such as deviated septum, cleft, broken,
- very low voice
- disorders of larynx
- diarrhea
- thyroid issues
- hernias, especially inguinal
- chronic issues of the colon, such as ulcerative colitis, Crohn's, and SIBO
- chronic constipation
- addiction or craving of strong-tasting foods, such as peppers, kimchi, spices, black chocolate, or hard liquors
- anomalies and diseases of the colon, rectum, and anus
- bladder problems
- enuresis
- hemorrhoids
- volvulus, intussusception
- anomalies of the genital organs
- twisted fallopian tubes.
- ectopic pregnancy
- ureter anomalies
- urethra issues and anomalies
- miscarriage (though a fertile sign)
- issues related to abortion
- sexual extremes (celibacy included)
- exceptional nose size, chronic sinusitis, chronic nosebleed, and polyps
- "dirty blood"
- excessive blood androgens
- excess testosterone (females), virilization
- excess of any sex hormone
- disorders of the ductless glands
- buboes (a lymph node pathology)

- enlarged prostate
- scrotal problems, priapism
- urethra issues
- hydroceles, orchitis, epididymitis
- testicular tumor, or issues
- fistulas, hernias
- uterine polyps, fibroids
- misplaced uterus, falling of uterus
- issues with seminal emission
- syphilis, AIDS, herpes, other STDs
- overworked kidneys
- ovarian cysts or other ovarian problems (with Libra)
- endometriosis
- uterine anomalies and other uterine problems
- vas deferens issues
- hypnotic power (fearless)
- exceptional transformative powers
- emotional fixations and obsessions with intense, scary or dangerous topics
- attracted to dirty jobs or dangerous work (heroic)
- hirsuteness
- excessive dumping of toxins into lymphatics, blood
- obsession with past wrongs and betrayals
- obsessed with bowel habits
- fascinated with death
- fascination with sex
- bacterial, fungus or candida infection, especially to throat, tongue, nasal, genital, anal, colon, anal, rectal regions (but anywhere)
- sepsis
- parasites, worms, flukes, lice, ticks
- colon microbiota imbalance
- psychic parasites
- tongue infection
- tremendous powers of healing and suggestion
- ear-nose-throat infection
- tumors
- hemorrhage, typically from nose, uterus, colon, uterus, bladder, or rectum
- need for blood transfusion
- troubles caused by blood transfusion

- menorrhagia
- possibly blood and marrow disease
- tendency to serious, self-inflicted accidents, such as falling
- appendicitis
- tonsilitis
- preference for black, or black and red clothing,

scary images; aggressive, extreme, sexy, or political footwear, haircuts, jewelry, or tattoos

- attracts mosquitos (Davidson)
- excessive sweating, especially in armpits

REMEDIATION TIPS

Please note that these remedial tips are for interest only. The author is not suggesting that any person use these without the evaluation and consent of their personal healthcare practitioner.

- *Poke Root*, a strong lymphatic cleanser
- *Mullein*, excellent for orchitis and swelling glands
- *Yellow Dock*, specific for ulcerative colitis
- *Red Raspberry*, a traditional for preventing miscarriage
- *Sassafras*, for nosebleed. Also, a traditional blood cleanser
- *Sarsaparilla*, a hormonal balancer and blood cleanser
- *Spearmint*, proven to mop up excess blood androgens (useful for hirsutism)
- *Chaste Tea Berry*, for excessive libido
- *Red Clover*, gives copper and is an excellent lymphatic cleanser
- *Shepherd's Purse*, for menorrhagia
- *Agrimony, Yarrow*, for internal hemorrhage, extreme indigestion (Agrimony)
- *Crab Apple Flower Essence*, cleansing

- *Holly Flower Essence*, for negative emotional fixations, obsessions
- *Olive Leaf, Clove, Black Walnut, Wormwood, Pumpkin Seed*, vermifuges, anti-parasitic
- *Horseradish*, lymphatic stimulant, antibacterial, antimicrobial
- Herbal acne protocols that address causation in colon, and/or excess androgens
- Probiotics
- Prebiotics
- Aromatherapy! (Scorpio rules the nose.)

See also Chapter 15, *The Twelve Zodiac Sign Syndromes and their Relevant Herbs.*

Chapter Eleven:
SAGITTARIUS SYNDROME

The two most important days of your life
are the day you were born and the day you found out why.
- Samuel Clemens, native of Sagittarius

Zing

Sagittarian natives are so frequently stimulating to those about them, appearing to channel and emit a uniquely positive force; let's call it "Zing." Many Sagittarians resemble both the astronomical and mythological traits of their sign's ruling planet, the benefic, grand, joyous, generous, yet turbulent Jupiter. The more typical natives of this sign are noted to run rapidly, laugh loudly, travel afar, take risks, seek knowledge and truth, and sometimes gamble! I still remember coming home after school to my Sagittarius grand-mother's delighted outbursts of "Yahtzee!" (This is the name of a once popular gambling game. When you win, you yell "Yahtzee"!) She was born with the Sun closely conjunct Jupiter in Sagittarius.

In character, Sagittarians are famously independent, protective, generous, truth-seeking, and trend toward mental and behavioral extremes. These qualities perfectly reflect this sign's dynamic rulership of the neuromuscular and arterial systems, and the higher visionary prophetical regions of the mind. Let's find out how!

Fundamentals Refresher

Sagittarius Syndrome is a set of collaborative symptoms, consistently appearing together, which are typical for natives of the sign Sagittarius. The symptoms associated with Sagittarius Syndrome can be experienced by people with other sun signs when there is a particular emphasis in this sign. Zodiac sign syndromes can occur in seriatim, first one symptom, then weeks, months or years later, another. Few experience all symptoms. However, two or more of these symptoms are frequently observed clustered together at the same time.

A Sagittarius native may have few if any of the symptoms associated with Sagittarius Syndrome. Indeed, many Sagittarius natives are specimens of perfect health. However, this symptom set often, but not always, evinces itself when the native's Sagittarius Sun, Moon, or Ascendant displays certain astrological conditions which are discussed at length in this chapter.

This chapter describes the astrological conditions that may aggravate the syndrome. With this knowledge, practitioners can explore the underlying condition when symptoms consistent with the syndrome present themselves in a patient. Understanding the energetic cause is the first step in remediation.

THE SIGN SAGITTARIUS

In Classical Western Astrology, with use of the Tropical Zodiac, a Sagittarius is someone born between 240-269 longitudinal degrees after the spring equinox, or the 30 days before the winter solstice.

As with all other signs, we cannot think of Sagittarius as an isolated single entity or a static constant. "Sagittarius" is a gestalt of strengths and weaknesses based on its angular relationship to the other signs of the interconnected solar cycle. In turn, each of the twelve phases of this cycle is influenced by the unique planetary configurations at birth and throughout the life. Sagittarius is a unique phase-state, with its interactions peculiar to the ninth stage of the twelve-fold cyclical process.

Life Cycle Phase: Sagittarius represents the ninth stage of the twelve-fold human life cycle. The infant is born (Aries), feeds (Taurus), speaks (Gemini), emotionally sensitizes and shields (Cancer), and flowers at adolescence (Leo). Come Virgo, we perfect the body, sharpen our skills, serve, discern, and labor hard to maintain the physical world. In Libra, the soul takes pause, while Scorpio brings the struggle of purging and transformation.

Freedom and independence arrive at Sagittarius. The battle-weary soul arises from Scorpio's bloody field and races freely off, seeking either meaning or excitement. The centaur's arrow points the soul towards a quest. This is the sign of the philosopher, adventurer, traveler, world-bridger, teacher, and seeker of either truth or excitement.

Element and Mode: Sagittarius is of the element *Fire*. As the transitional sign from autumn to winter, it belongs to the *Mutable* quadruplicity of signs. Here we have Fire-in-motion, a wildfire! Notably, both rock stars who were infamous for lighting stage fires during their performances were both born in this sign: Jim Morrison and Jimi Hendrix.

The Fire Triplicity: Aries and Mars rule the motor nerves in the brain and adrenal axis. Leo and Sol rule the heart. Sagittarius rules the large voluntary muscles of the legs, while it shares the outflowing arterial circulation with Jupiter. Sagittarius also largely governs the coordinative function of the entire spinal cord and holds a specific governance over the lower spinal nerves and Cauda Equina. See sections on *The Distribution of the Vital Force* and *The Arterial System* in *Research Notes* later in this chapter.

Sagittarius Superpowers

Laughter: Sagittarian Samuel Clemens once said, "Humanity has a really good weapon, laughter."

Positive Thinking: This birth season gifts its natives with a positive mental and emotional outlook. The auric field of a classic Sagittarian type is uplifting and encouraging to those around them.

Zeal: Generally speaking, this is an athletic sign, with great vigor. The problem is not a lack of energy, but conversely a tendency to "burn the candle at both ends." Natives are zealous about their ideas, beliefs, and interests.

Flight: Like a horse in flight, Sagittarians are inclined to flee far from emotional entaglements. The idea seems to be that if you are not there in the first place, then you cannot be entrapped.

Luck: Although accident prone, due to foolish risk and sports, this sign is incredibly lucky in disaster. Beneficent Jupiter smiles down on his children.

Aim: Sagittarius is also the best sharpshooter, archer, and runner. The love of motion makes for a fit body.

Natural Health: While sunny, optimistic Sagittarius is viewed as naturally healthy, I've rarely met a Sagittarian who did not suffer at least one mortally threatening illness in their life. However, they seem to outlive these challenges, moving on with a smile.

Large Muscle Coordination: This sign makes noted runners, horseback riders, archers, and sharp shooters. Famed baseball star Joe DiMaggio was a Sagittarius native with Sagittarius rising, plus Mars and Venus in Sagittarius. He offers a perfect portrait of the loose jointed, athletic "horsey" physical type. (There is also the purely "Jupiterian" type Sagittarius - quite different.)

My own statistical study of Sun Signs per sport genre and sub-genre demonstrated a statistical significance for Sagittarius amongst baseball's number one "Who's Who." Studies such as this help us sort out what parts of human physiology are prominent, or dominant in each season of birth.

Physical Appearance

Exhaustive detail with illustrations is provided in this author's *The Astrological Body Types*.

SAGITTARIUS BODY RULERSHIPS AND FUNCTIONS
Sagittarius, Body Zone 9

As described in Chapter One, a body zone is a general box that overlays many organs, functions, vessels and their sub-rulerships.

Sagittarius, Body Zone 9, rules hips, hip bones and sockets, iliac crest, thighs, femurs gluteals, iliac arteries, sciatic nerve, locomotion, and considerably influences the muscular system and ligaments. In concert with its opposite sign Gemini, Sagittarius governs the voluntary nervous system (discuss in-depth later in this chapter). The large muscle functions of throwing, running, and kicking appear largely under the auspices of this sign. Thus, Sagittarius dominates the large muscles of the body and their coordination. This is especially noted for the hip and leg muscles. Sagittarius and Aquarius co-govern the great saphenous vein and spinal cord (whereas Leo governs the spinal sheath). Cornell assigns the sacrum and coccyx to the co-rulership of Scorpio and Sagittarius.

Sagittarius Functions
Universal Coordination

My teacher taught me that Gemini and Sagittarius work constantly in reflexive polarity and can only be fully comprehended in this regard. Gemini rules *personal coordination*. Gemini symbolizes the *branching outward from center*, whereas Sagittarius governs *universal coordination* and the *unification of multifarious branches*. Gemini seems to govern the small neural processes, and Sagittarius the large. We see how Sagittarius influences the global coordinative function of the spinal cord, whereas the peripheral nerves are allotted to the general overlordship Gemini, (and Mercury), with specific signs co-influencing the nerves within each their personal body zones.

This division of labor is apparent in the complimentary vocations typical of these two signs, given below for fun.

MUNDANE COMPARISON	
GEMINI	**SAGITTARIUS**
Writer	Publisher
City connections	International connections
Bicyclist	Pilot of large airline
Short journeys	Long journeys to foreign lands
Blogger	The internet
Individual computer	The internet
Student	The college and teachers
Flautist	Symphonic conductor

MUNDANE COMPARISON	
GEMINI	**SAGITTARIUS**
Ad writer	Advertising agency, publicity, promotion
Journalist	The newspaper
The letter and mailman	The postal service
Open questioning	Religion, theologies, paradigms
One mind	Group think, religion
Debate, argument	The law
The book (individual knowledge)	The library (group knowledge)
Books	The distribution network (Sagittarius rules all distribution networks)

This comparison also leads us into a deeper understanding of how universal coordination might function *physically*, in the human neuromuscular, arterial, and prana distribution systems. As a revealing example, consider the following juxtaposed Gemini-Sagittarius functions that truly allow us to unpack all the rest.

Capillaries are governed by Gemini (and its ruler Mercury). Whereas *arteries* are governed by the opposite sign Sagittarius (and its ruler Jupiter)!

Inspiration of the breath is ruled by Gemini, whereas *expiration* of the breath is governed by Sagittarius.

Symbols: The Twins vs The Centaur-Archer

We already have seen that Sagittarius' partner Gemini is symbolized by the twins and rules the arms and hands, plus all bilateral branching processes, including the dendritic networks of the brain. We can say that Gemini is twins, *two branching forth from one.*

Conversely, Sagittarius governs *one coming forth from two.* One arrow comes forth from the double beast of a man-horse satyr. I regret that I cannot remember the author of that idea, read somewhere in my bookstore perusals.

The Nervous System: How then does this depiction pertain to the nervous system? That is the problem because there are *many* neuro-muscular pairings and divisions that this imagery could suggest. We must ferret out an answer from a study of Sagittarian people, their character, health, choice vocations, and lives.

Please see the section on *Research Notes* later in this chapter for a full discussion of these ideas. In that section we will explore the Sagittarian role in neuro-muscular communication and coordination, the spinal cord's coordinating function, the efferent and afferent nerves, and the horns of the spine. We will also explore Sagittarius' possible influence on the ligaments, fascia, thyroid, and its role in the distribution of vital force throughout the body.

The Arterial System: Sagittarius governs the arterial system. The arteries carry the warming blood from the heart, (Leo, Sol), and distribute this life-giving substance throughout the body. The capillaries (governed by Sagittarius' partner Gemini) take the oxygen home to the cells via the tiny, fractal resembling capillaries. We know that the pumping of the legs (Sagittarius) helps to circulate the blood!

Sagittarius Syndrome and the Mental Life

Sagittarius is a sign of vision and prophecy. At extremes, this sign is also implicated in grandiose mental states, bi-polar disorder, and religious manias. Schizophrenia, and other states that are colloquially described with the notion of being "out there," are typical of Sagittarius-Pisces squares and Sagittarius-Gemini oppositions, with input from Jupiter, Neptune, Uranus and the Nodes.

Perhaps this mental expansion is due, in part, to an excessive influx of cosmic and/or solar pranas from the galactic center (see discussion under Research Notes). This may be an interesting clue for healers working with Sagittarian cases.

This sign behaves like a horse when stressed - run! Distressed natives of this sign are infamous for fleeing off, abandoning their spouses, children, families, or jobs. A good Saturn and a few earth signs in the birth chart will nicely corral this equine instinct! Panic-anxiety disorder is common to those born with Sagittarius-Virgo squares, or afflictions to Moon and Mars in this sign.

RESEARCH NOTES ON SAGITTARIUS FUNCTIONS

Here are some optional ideas - some being posed as questions.

Sagittarius clearly holds a significant influence over the spinal cord's coordinating function, the entire voluntary nervous system, neuro-muscular communication and coordination, motor nerves serving of the large voluntary muscles (with Aries), and leg muscles.

Could Sagittarius also rule the coordination of the muscles, nerves, and fascia? Or the coordination of muscles, fascia, and information received from the ECM? Co-ordination of the whole, the mind, muscles, and all nervous systems?

Fire sign Sagittarius is akin to the *muscular system*, whereas its opposite, Air sign Gemini, relates more exclusively to *nerves*. However, Sagittarius clearly influences the spinal cord as the "central post office". Opposite sign Gemini, being the peripherally branching nerves, acts as the "postal carrier". Together, they govern the *voluntary* neural axis. Virgo and Pisces stand at square angles to Sagittarius and Gemini. Those signs appear to strongly influence the sympathetic and enteric nervous system (Virgo) and the parasympathetic system (Pisces). All four are flexible Mutable signs, existing at the transition points of one season to another. The planet Mercury is involved in all nervous systems!

In character, fidgety Sagittarius is demonstrably the "nervous fire sign." Both Sagittarius and Gemini reflexively partake considerably of each other, allowing several possibilities for how these signs operate together throughout the voluntary nervous system. Sagittarius has long been recognized as the singularly nervous Fire sign!

Below are sets of postulated complimentary functions for the Gemini-Sagittarius polarity. However, I am not yet clear as to which of these pairs is the correct set of complimentary functions. Personally, I feel that Sagittarius governs the spinal portion of the CNS because the spinal cord is the coordinator of the nervous systems - and this aptly reflects the Sagittarian principle of universal coordination (and their traditional careers).

In this book, we describe how the spinal cord sheath is under Leo and that Aquarius also holds a strong influence over the spinal nerves. However, the coordination function of the cord appears distinctly Sagittarian, as do several of the maladies classic to this sign.

Gemini-Sagittarius Postulated Neuromuscular Inter-functions

Gemini: Consistent with the nature of this sign, Gemini likely rules the peripheral nerves, branching outward from the CNS ("many from one"), the afferent or sensory neurons and sensory nerves, and the sending of sensory data to the brain via the spinal cord. The question becomes, does Gemini rule all afferent sensory and peripheral efferent nerves too? Or just the afferent sensory nerves? Or would it be all peripheral nerves once they branch off the spinal cord? Or just the afferent sensory peripheral nerves? Yes, it's complicated. The jury is out on this one, so different options are contemplated.

Sagittarius: <u>Two options:</u> Sagittarius likely rules the efferent nerves (motor commands carried from brain to muscle), and the conscious commands between brain and muscle, plus the muscular nerves (voluntary nervous system). This system works at lightning speed in tandem with the postulated Gemini and Mercury ruled afferent (sensory) nerves. However, it is equally possible that Sagittarius rules the spinal cord, while opposite sign Gemini governs both the sending and receiving nerves moving to and from the spinal cord (enroute to or from the brain).

Options for the Grey Columns of the Spinal Cord: We have some fascinating alternatives as to how the Gemini-Sagittarian polarity works within the horns of spinal cord grey matter.

One optional view is that Gemini governs the posterior horns of the spinal cord. These receive several types of sensory information from the body to be conducted towards the brain. Conversely, the "universal coordinator" of the zodiac, Sagittarius would absolutely govern the anterior horns of the spinal cord, which contain the lower motor neurons that are the final pathway for motor commands to skeletal muscles.

A second option offers that Gemini only rules the nerves themselves that arrive at the posterior horn of the spinal cord. In this case, Sagittarius would rule <u>both</u> *posterior* and *anterior* horns, consistent with its role as our universal coordinator.

Options for the Efferent and Afferent Nerves: While Gemini is a natural for ruling the afferent (sensory) nerves, perhaps the body zone topography would dictate that it rules both the efferent and afferent (motor) nerves of the upper body (arms, hands), while Sagittarius rules the efferent and afferent nerves of the <u>lower</u> body (hips, legs).

Alternatively, Gemini could rule all peripheral efferent and afferent nerves, while *Sagittarius rules the spinal cord and the global coordinative functions of the sensory and voluntary efferent nerves.*

Finally, Gemini could rule the neural side of the neuro-muscular system and its coordination. It is interesting to observe how so many Gemini natives appear fascinated with personal, small muscle coordination, usually with an emphasis on the upper body (e.g., juggling, unicycling, skateboards, ping pong, and puzzles). In this scenario, Sagittarius would rule the muscular side of the neural-muscular system and its coordination. Sagittarian natives are noted to excel at large muscle sports including running, throwing, and aiming.

These inter-relationships are interactively complex! From the neurological perspective, all four mutable signs (Gemini, Virgo, Sagittarius, Pisces) interact and fluctuate continuously between one another and are often horoscopically indicated for all manner of neuromuscular problems.

Distribution of Vital Force

Leo and Sagittarius are both Fire signs, and within that trine, Leo leads into and towards the sign Sagittarius. The Renaissance physicians accepted that a type of Vital Force battery resides within the heart (Leo and Sol). The solar Vital Force and the element Fire are either light or akin to it. Traditionally, light is the province of the Fire element.

This solar Vital Force must be distributed via various channels and networks to the rest of the body. This seems all so similar to the Sagittarian ruled distribution of arterial blood, described earlier. We also know that, vocationally, Sagittarius governs all large distribution networks, such as the post office, internet, and world trade networks.

Is Sagittarius the primary distributor/mover of the Vital Force? This could certainly explain one reason for the highly kinetic and energetic nature renowned to this birth season. Additionally, the Fire signs govern physical energy and caloric burning. In astrology, Fire knows *three rates of motion:* cardinal, fixed and mutable. As seen prior, Sagittarius is mutable or *moving* fire. Moving Fire is moving energy, prana, qi, or vital force.

Those that study the invisible pathways of the life current in the body speak of chakras and nadis. Chakras are the receiving sets of various cosmic forces, and the nadis are their subtle channels, reminiscent of the body's more visible arteries. And where we have arteries, we have capillaries. If Sagittarius governs the main distribution *arteries* for solar prana, wouldn't Gemini govern the smaller *capillaries* for this same energy? Tradition cites that that there are three primary nadis and, although sources wildly disagree, 72,000 is the highest number cited of branching nadis.

As discussed earlier, the Centaur is depicted as aiming an arrow from a bow. The ancient Hindu Rig Veda may offer a curious insight into this symbolism. Although there is no known *horoscopic* astrology in the Vedas (no chart, houses, signs, or aspects), we do have physical descriptions of the planetary gods. For instance, the glorious Sun God Surya carries a bow and arrow for his icon. This supposedly symbolizes the Vital Force or Prana (the arrow) rushing through the spinal cord (bow). As Dr. William Davidson said of Mars, when in Sagittarius: "too much life".

Breath: Medical astrology holds that Sagittarius governs the *expiration* of the breath, and Gemini the *inspiration*. Yogis avow that at least one type of prana enters the body partly through the inspiration of the breath. Such is the basis for the science of pranayama.

There are several traditionally suggested entry points for the Vital Force, as well as alternate storage sites. Extant texts also claim diverse types of Vital Force, including those distinct to Sun, Moon, each planet, and other cosmic rays.

The solar prana, stored in food, enters our body through the mouth (Taurus) and is distributed through the blood stream, via the arteries and capillaries. Our questions now become, "Does Sagittarius have a hand in the distribution of all Vital Forces? Or only that of the solar prana and Fire element?"

Unfortunately, until we develop methods to actually view these subtle forces, we require the help of high-quality clairvoyants to solve these riddles. For now, we can only observe the outward effects of this sign. A good detective can construct the hidden through the apparent.

Kinetic Motion Through Space: True to traditional lore, the Sagittarian natives I've known really do love travel and enjoy driving. One also notices a *love of motion through space*, particularly with young Sagittarians. Speeding tickets are common, especially for those with Mars in this sign. One woman I know born with a natal Moon-Mars conjunction in this sign, hoped to be a race car driver!

This delight in fast motion through space extends to skiing, running, pole vaulting and sky diving. A childhood friend springs to mind, who at fifty, and quite overweight, decided to try her hand at sky diving. Her birth chart shows the Moon rises in Sagittarius, a *double-Sagittarius* influence! One must ask, what is it about kinetic motion that is so thrilling and enjoyable to most Sagittarians (contrary to most Cancer natives). Is this a need for fresh experience? Is there some thrill in shocking the adrenal glands? It is interesting to note that the sign's ruling planet, Jupiter, was the hurler of thunderbolts. There are still many mysteries about this sign.

Spinal Cord and Motor Nerve Issues: Postulated above is the idea that Sagittarius governs the anterior horns of the spinal cord which process motor activity. To discover if this idea holds merit, I

have pulled nine charts of ALS victims. There was no cherry pick-
ing! I omitted football players so as not to confuse the results with
head injury causation. ALS is a disease that disintegrates these
motor neurons. The true cause of this disease is mysterious, often
cited as genetic. Maybe astrology can help!

Nine cases hardly constitute conclusive research, although it is
potentially revealing. My hypothesis would be that non-head injury
induced ALS sufferers would have a strong natal accent in Sagittarius and Gemini. This would occur through natal tenancy within this
sign of either malefics (Mars or Saturn), genetic issues (Luna
Nodes), or the nerve planets (Uranus, Mercury). Sun, Moon, and
Ascendant sign position in Sagittarius might be represented at numbers higher than chance.

Secondly, there could be affliction from Virgo, Taurus, Aries,
and an emphasis in Leo-Aquarius. Yes, that's half the zodiac! This is
why this list should be slimmed down by studying groups of *specific
types* of ALS, of which there are three types. However, for our immediate purposes here, let's look for an accent in Sagittarius-Gemini
and a mutable accent for Mars (the attacker, which also governs the
muscles).

Let's briefly compare these famous cases and see what we find.
Sun, Moon, and Mars can have extra points. For fun, I will bold all
**emphasized planet positions in Gemini or Sagittarius, underscor-
ing Mars.** However, no tenancy of Mars on these two signs doesn't
imply a non-prominent Sagittarius-Gemini polarity. Au contraire.

(1) Ady Barkan: <u>Sun, Jupiter, Neptune, Uranus, and South
Node in Sagittarius, opposing Moon in Gemini</u> (seven bodies
in this polarity).
(2) Jason Becker: <u>Mars in Sagittarius</u>

(3) David Bradley: <u>Mars and Jupiter in Gemini,</u> Sun in the Sagittarius decan of Aries.

(4) Esteban Bullrich: <u>Mars retrograde in Sagittarius opposing Sun and Mercury in Gemini, Jupiter in Virgo.</u>

(5) Stephen Hawking: Does not fit the hypothesis. Mars is in the Sagittarius decanate of Aries. No planets in Sagittarius or Gemini.

(6) Lou Gehrig: <u>Sun, Mercury, and Pluto in Gemini,</u> opposing Uranus in Sagittarius (four celestial bodies across this polarity), with Jupiter squaring from Pisces.

(7) Charles Mingus: <u>Mars rising in Sagittarius.</u>

(8) Simon Fitzmaurice: <u>Mars in Sagittarius, squared by Mercury in Virgo</u>

(9) Stephen McDannell Hillenburg: <u>Mars in Gemini opposes Jupiter stationing (super strong) in Sagittarius.</u>

RESULT: <u>*All charts,*</u> *except for Stephen Hawking, showed prominent accents in Gemini or Sagittarius.* **Mars tenants either Gemini or Sagittarius in *six of nine charts.*** If the disease is caused by an unknown antigen, virus, or bacteria, this would make sense, because Mars governs attacks on the body!

Curious, I peeked at three charts I found of football players who developed ALS. They showed a greater brain emphasis (Aries) and a quite different looking signature than this group. If you are doing your own research, please study football related ALS as a distinct data set.

Thyroid-Parathyroid Connection: For years I have noticed something neglected in previous medical astrology texts. Sagittarians with certain specific chart signatures are prone to hyperthyroidism! All three cases I have of women who suffered the medical removal of their thyroids (to save their lives) were Sagittarian natives. Not just this, but they were all born when the Sun conjoined

Jupiter in this sign, with these planets also afflicted by Mars in Virgo. Exciting as this may be, more research is needed.

However, there are plausible explanations for this relationship. We know that iodine is ruled by the Sun (Nauman, Jansky, Zain). The Sun is a friend to Jupiter, so perhaps lends a too-generous supply of this mineral. Taurus, the thyroid's body zone, is, as said, located at quincunx to Sagittarius, in this sign's malefic 6th house of health. This alone could explain the effect, except one would assume hypothyroidism, not hyper!

Edgar Cayce says that Uranus rules this gland, while Nauman and Cornell in-volve Taurus and Mercury or Mercury / Venus. Additionally, *the South Node of Uranus is in Sagittarius* (yes, planets have their personal north and south nodes). If Uranus governs the thyroid, then this fact presages a weakness of the gland in Sagittarius.

Davidson said that Mars in Sagittarius gave "too much life", and it so often does! Are we observing this effect? A visionary might explain how the intense cosmic rays spewing forth from our galactic center (located in Sagittarius) excite the thyroid glands in Sagittarius' children!

A further explanation jumps to mind relevant to hyperthyroidism and the Taurus-Sagittarian quincunx. The Taurus-zoned thyroid and parathyroid glands produce our blood calcium regulating hormones. Some people with hyperthyroidism have high blood calcium levels. Perhaps the calcium-regulating role of these Taurus-zoned glands is one remote cause behind the high incidence of hyperthyroidism in some Sagittarian people, especially those born in this sign, with strong Jupiter-Mars aspects to the natal Sun.

Ligaments and Tendons? Cornell gives ligaments to both Saturn and Mars, noting also how Pisces strongly influences the fibro-ligamentous system. My own few cases of chronically slippery ligaments support his Pisces observation. However, Sagittarius is the sign that sews multiple strands of nerves (or thoughts!) together. Could Sagittarius also influence the ligaments? I have seen multiple cases of slippery ligaments in the hips in birth charts of afflicted natal *Neptune in Sagittarius.* This positional outcome is so consistent that I was able to correctly guess the last two cases! I have also observed hyper mobility syndrome in Pisces people with Sagittarian squares or other health indications (such a Sagittarius 6th house). This malady can affect the knees, elbows, shoulders, thumbs, and other joints. Both signs are governed by Jupiter.

In support of the sewing threads together (nerves, the ligaments and bone, CNS, et al), I have noted that people addicted to weaving and knitting frequently have a strong natal Sagittarius-Virgo square. My grandmother was a Sagittarius native born with Mercury, North Node, Jupiter, and Sun in Sagittarius, square the Moon and Mars in Virgo. She was a master weaver of cloth, with her own loom and weaving shop. One would never think a restless sign inclined to large muscle movement could tolerate tedious weaving. Nevertheless, the last two weavers in my office possessed this strong Sagittarian component combined with the Virgo accent square.

The Spinal Fire and "too much life"

Let us wander afar, Sagittarius-like, into the realm of the visionary imagination. A study of Sagittarius natives, and their maladies, fills me with a palpable sensation that a species of pranic "fire" zips more fully and freely through the spinal cord of many Sagittarians. This *spinal fire* provides zip and zing to their auric field, enlivening them and cheering others. Negatively, it can run too strong, leading to toe-tapping restlessness, panic, neuroses, and flight.

Cornell describes something called the *spinal spirit fire*, allotting this to Neptune. This Sagittarian "zing" doesn't feel lazy like Neptune energy should, so I doubt that Cornell and I are talking about the same thing. However, spiritual sight is said to occur when this spinal spirit fire vibrates the pineal gland. That does sounds both Neptunian and Sagittarian!

Recall Davidson's observation of "too much life," noted for Mars posited in Sagittarius. Perhaps the fire element itself runs too fast and free in Sagittarius. After all, *the galactic center sits at approximately 26-27 degrees of this sign.* This region of space is said to produce surges of intense cosmic energy!

We know that Sol is a great friend of Jupiter, and both rule fellow fire signs. We also note that Leo, the Sun's sign, co-rules the Vital Force and shares with Sagittarius one full decan (ten-day period) of this sign. Does this give new meaning to Davidson's comment referring to Mars in Sagittarius as having "too much life"? Certainly, an excess of "life" is noted for Sagittarius' birth natives too!

It would be my unproven postulation that the otherwise unexplained hyperthyroidism common to this sign is due in fact, to an excess of life force rushing through the spinal channel, overstimulating the nerves, muscles, mind, and thyroid! We could refine this by considering that maybe the responsible party is the hot, red solar force flowing through the channel on the right side of the spinal canal, the Pingala. Next time you encounter a Sagittarian with hyperthyroidism, discover whether or not they breathe through only the right nostril.

Influx of Cosmic Energy: Let us return to the fact that from Earth's point of view, our galactic center is located in Sagittarius. In visionary thinking, this explains the Sagittarian's observable excess of spinal fire. The galactic center in Sagittarius may well be a point of intense influx of cosmic energy. Those born in this season may well receive a surplus cosmic influx! (See *Distribution of Vital Force*, above)

The Muscular System: More than any other sign, Sagittarius appears to govern the whole body large voluntary muscle system, with an emphasis on the legs and the arterial network (Gemini governs the capillaries). There is some tendency to pull tendons and ligaments. Spinal and hip complaints due to uneven load and mismatched leg growth are common. The muscular system seems to pull the vertebrae off course. It is hard to see a bed-bound athletic Sagittarian with a bulging disc!

The Need for Exercise: No sign requires more leg movement than does Sagittarius. Receiving "too much life", the sedentary Sagittarian runs the risk of their excess fire prana *migrating from the muscles into the nerves*. This results in anxiousness, neurosis, frustration, and nervous complaints. Enough leg motion is essential.

The Fascia: Astrologically, the fascia remains unassigned. Although fibrous, a Saturnian quality, the fascia is a *whole-body* envelope surrounding the muscles (think of a body suit). It is characteristically reflexive, highly responsive, mutable, and composed of not only fiber, but with *small tubes of both water and light!* This is hardly Saturnian. Pisces is our most wholistic sign, and well fits these qualities. I vote for Pisces as the sign ruler of the fascia but am also considering a combination of the two fellow Jupiter-ruled signs Sagittarius and Pisces.

Another idea might be that Pisces governs the fascia, and Sagittarius, as the zodiac's universal coordinator, somehow coordinates the fascia, ligaments, tendons, muscles, and nervous system.

SAGITTARIUS SYNDROME

As discussed in Chapter Two, a Zodiac Sign Syndrome is a cluster of symptoms associated with the body zones and functions of a zodiac sign and the signs positioned on the seasonal wheel opposite (180°) and quincunx (150°, 210°, 330°) the sign. Remediating and supporting these body zones and functions act to bring the body into balance, diminishing the syndrome. These symptoms may manifest when there is an emphasis in one or more of these signs. Planetary dignity plays an important role.

The Weaker Signs for the Sagittarius Vital Force
Quincunx signs

Taurus, Cancer, and Scorpio are quincunx Sagittarius, being positioned 150°, 210° and 330° distant from it on the seasonal wheel. These signs represent the *averted* 6th, 8th, and 12th angles from the sign Sagittarius (see the illustration for this chapter). This condition makes it difficult for Sagittarius to absorb the cosmic rays or the vibrational and light nutrients that feed these signs. Likewise, these signs may have trouble absorbing the rays from Sagittarius.

Scorpio rules Body Zone 8 which includes the sacrum, coccyx (with Sagittarius), colon, bladder, rectum, genitals, nose, sweat glands, and excretions. Sagittarius, the satyr, is hardly known for lagging libido. However, see the Addendum to this chapter, below, for a detailed explanation "The Scorpion and the Horse".

Taurus rules Body Zone 2 which includes the centers in the medullary brain stem which govern the grace and balance of the muscular system, gait, and locomotion. There is also a mysterious relationship between Sagittarius and the thyroid, positioned in Body Zone 2, Taurus. Sagittarians are prone to hyperthyroid, particularly if Jupiter is in Sagittarius, squared by Mars in Virgo. See previous section "The Thyroid-Parathyroid Connection".

Cancer rules Body Zone 4 which includes the breast, sternum, thoracic duct, upper lymphatics, rib cage, diaphragm, lower esophagus, stomach, epigastric region, and many organ coverings (e.g., pericardium, pleura, meninges, and womb when pregnant). Cancer holds a significant influence over personal and familial memory, attachment-bonding mechanism, and nurturing instincts.

The nurturing instinct function appears weak in independent Sagittarius. The sentimental memory and bonding mechanism seen in Cancer is nowhere to be found in Sagittarius. Cancer is inward and looking to the past, whereas Sagittarius escapes away from or disregards its past. This hints at how the brain centers activated in Cancer are muted down at the Sagittarius time of year. We also see some diminishment of the motherly impulse of Cancer. While often excellent parents, the classic Sagittarian is neither indulgent of, nor clinging to their offspring. Nor do they encourage dependency in their young. Of course, there are exceptions to every rule. Mother issues seem common: lack of mother, sick mother, distant mother, dislike of mother, etc. Sagittarians are infamous for abandoning home and family, or when young, becoming "runaways" and truants. (Of course, not all Sagittarius natives do this, and multiple planetary, house, and sign testimonies must accompany a Sagittarius emphasis).

Cancer also influences the posterior pituitary. At the time of this writing, I have not worked out the remote-causation issue that may be due to a deficiency in one or another of its roles. For instance, why is there a higher incidence of Sagittarians deficient in oxytocin?

Sagittarius is the apex of a *Yod*, or two quincunxes delivered from Taurus and Cancer. These signs govern the first process of food intake (mouth) and digestion (stomach). What is the association here? Many Sagittarians frequently eat on the run, in hotels, airports and pubs, drink alcohol to excess, and, although often health conscious, forget to eat in a consistent manner. But what else can this deficit at the top of the alimentary canal indicate? This is not yet sorted out and fertile ground for empirical research! We also see the bonding and nesting instincts so strong in Cancer and Taurus are quite weak in Sagittarius, the proverbial escapee of the zodiac.

Opposite Sign, Gemini

When the Sun is in Sagittarius, the opposite sign, Gemini, appears stimulated! Sagittarius and Gemini work closely together, reflexing off each other and all too often mimicking each other's physical traits and issues. Gemini rules Body Zone 3, which includes the upper lung, bronchial tubes, inspiration of the breath, peripheral and sensory nerves, shoulders, hands, arms, and fingers. Issues common to Gemini are often shared by Sagittarius and vice versa. As discussed previously, these two signs are intensely reflexive to one another.

Signs Aggravating Sagittarius Syndrome

The two squaring signs Pisces and Virgo are positioned 90° from Sagittarius, creating friction, for good or ill. (See chapter illustration).

The Virgo-Sagittarius square is the panic-anxiety square. This square is also common in Grave's Disease and hyperthyroid. The reason for the latter is not clear to me at this time.

The Pisces-Sagittarius square produces mental wanderings far from shore. Spiritual quests, grandiose ideas, visions, mysticism, and all manner of extreme mental states are typical. This square features strongly in some types of schizoid disorders and involuntary clairvoyance.

How Planetary Dignity Contributes to Sagittarius Syndrome

Strongest Planet

Jupiter, ruler of Sagittarius, is the giant of planets and warm and moist. His nature is expansive, both mentally and physically. Jupiter's governances include the liver, pituitary gland; arterial system (with Sagittarius), and thighs (with Sagittarius). This planet strongly influences the blood itself. Jupiter rules fat, and the metal tin. This is the veritable king of planets, the 'Great Benefic' and protector of the earth plane.

Weakest Planet

Mercury is in detriment in Sagittarius, as it rules opposing sign Gemini. Mercury's astute, everyday thinking functions become overly expansive in Sagittarius, losing focus, and sometimes, reality. However, this sign lends both scope of vision and breadth of knowledge to the intellect, reversing Mercury's more tedious tendencies.

Astrological Conditions that Enhance Sagittarius Syndrome

(1) **Sun, Moon, or Ascendant sign in Sagittarius**

(2) A weakness in a body zone governed by the signs opposite or quincunx Sagittarius on the seasonal wheel (Gemini, Taurus, Cancer, Scorpio). See discussion above under *The Weaker Signs for the Sagittarius Vital Force.*

(3) <u>Any</u> natal planet, luminary, or lunar node in Sagittarius, compounded by the testimonies below:

- Sun, Moon, Ascendant, Jupiter, Mars, or Lunar Nodes in Sagittarius.

- Sagittarius inhabits the 1st, 6th, 8th, or 12th houses of the natal chart.
- Saturn in hard angle to Jupiter.
- Jupiter afflicted by Mars or Uranus. Close trines can work too!
- Saturn, Mercury, Uranus, and especially Mars in Sagittarius or Gemini.
- Mercury conjunct or afflicted by Mars and/or Uranus with natal Sun in Sagittarius.
- Fire sign emphasis (Leo, Aries, Sagittarius)

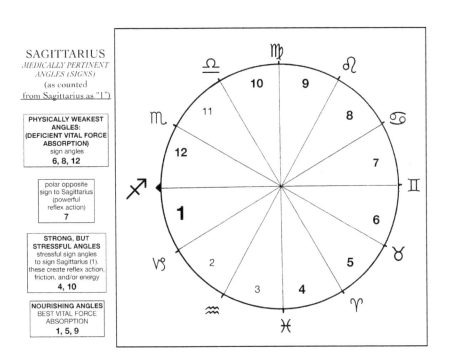

SAGITTARIUS
MEDICALLY PERTINENT
ANGLES (SIGNS)
(as counted
from Sagittarius as "1")

PHYSICALLY WEAKEST
ANGLES:
(DEFICIENT VITAL FORCE
ABSORPTION)
sign angles
6, 8, 12

polar opposite
sign to Sagittarius
(powerful
reflex action)
7

STRONG, BUT
STRESSFUL ANGLES
stressful sign angles
to sign Sagittarius (1).
these create reflex action,
friction, and/or energy
4, 10

NOURISHING ANGLES
BEST VITAL FORCE
ABSORPTION
1, 5, 9

SYMPTOMS OF SAGITTARIUS SYNDROME

The following is a list of symptoms and traits associated with Sagittarius Syndrome. Sagittarius Syndrome is a set of collaborative symptoms, consistently appearing together, which are typical for natives of this sign. *Zodiac sign syndromes* can occur in *seriatim*, first one symptom, then weeks, months or years later, another. However, two or more of these symptoms are frequently observed clustered together at the same time.

These do not pertain to "Sagittarius people" per se, but those born with prominences in this sign that actually do suffer the syndrome. These symptoms are not listed in any order, but simply as a list of collected observations common to Sagittarius. Please be sure to balance with Sagittarius Superpowers. As with any sign, there are just as many positives as potential negatives!

- restlessness, great need to walk or move around
- restless leg syndrome
- caffeine addiction
- nicotine addiction
- coffee jitters
- sciatica
- neuralgia, neuritis, or *sudden* attacks of intense nerve pain
- femur or hip injury
- restricted locomotion
- insomnia
- intense or prophetic dreams, or visiting "the other side" during sleep, "astral projection"
- sleepwalking
- religious euphoria, or religious mania, political religiosity
- schizophrenia and schizoaffective disorders
- compulsive traveling
- addiction to "uppers", caffeine, cocaine, methamphetamine, et al
- alcoholism (excess intake follows, or accompanies a day of excess caffeine)

- addiction to "downers," nicotine, sleeping pills, or alcohol (after a day of excessive caffeine or uppers)
- bi-polar diagnosis
- gambling addiction
- panic disorders
- arterial engorgement, hypertension, stroke, heart attack
- hyperthyroid
- hyper mobility syndrome
- forgetting to eat
- locomotor ataxia, diseases of motor nerves
- tremors, palsy, diseases of the spinal cord
- asthma, bronchitis, pneumonia, lung complaints
- scoliosis
- spinal injury
- slipped discs
- slippery ligaments
- sudden back or hip "out" with inexplicably intense pain
- generalized back or hip pain
- muscular tension, need to move
- claustrophobia
- fear of emotional entanglement
- paralysis
- epilepsy (with other indications)
- contributes to Parkinson's, MD, MS and various brain and spinal cord diseases
- diseases and malfunction of the CNS
- loss of vision (in one eye typical, often stroke related)
- thrill seeking and physical risks *("let's go hang gliding")*
- accidents due to horse, speeding, racing, sport, hunting, and gunshot accidents
- promiscuity or satyriasis
- fleeing, traveling off, and/or abandonment of spouse, children, family, job, (or, conversely parents abandoning them) This is the sign of flight, separations, emigration.

- "military child syndrome," bonding mechanism continually interrupted in childhood or undeveloped
- self-destructive behavior
- slippery, strained, or torn ligaments and/or tendons
- leg length issues
- unbalanced skeletal system
- various forms of paraplegia
- epilepsy (with full signature)
- lameness of legs (conversely, great runners)
- hypertension
- asthma, pneumonia, bronchitis (from opposite sign Gemini)

- carpal tunnel
- irritation of shoulder and arm nerve
- Sagittarius is a sign involved in planetary and sign signatures for schizoid disorder panic disorders, bipolar, ADHD, and religiomania, political extremism, megalomania
- secret bigamy, polyamory
- excessive talking or rants
- ghosting, bolting and vanishing acts
- involuntary clairvoyance, or prophecy

REMEDIATION TIPS

Please note that these remedial tips are for interest only. The author is not suggesting that any person use these without the evaluation and consent of their personal healthcare practitioner.

Turquoise: The Horseman's Stone

You fall, it breaks instead of you, or so goes tradition. This stone increases luck for the risk-taking Sagittarian.

Herbal Remedies for Sagittarius Syndrome

Muscular sedatives are best, especially those that relax both nerves and muscles. Secondly, the nutritive nervines are excellent because the nerves require greater support in this sign. Avoid uppers, stimulants, and psychotropics.

- Sedative Nervines such as Blue Vervain, Valerian, Passionflower, and Hops. Kava Kava and Valerian are more specific to muscles.
- Nervine nutritives, such as Oat Straw, Alfalfa (horse food!)
- Skullcap for restless leg syndrome.
- Bugleweed for hyperthyroid.
- Prickly Ash for muscle spasm and severe neuritis.
- Burdock for sciatica (Dorothy Hall).
- Neuralgia, neuritis: St John's Wort essential oil (and oil infusion) with Lavender essential oil

See also Chapter 15, *The Twelve Zodiac Sign Syndromes and their Relevant Herbs.*

ADDENDUM

The Scorpion and the Horse
The Adder that Biteth the Horse's Heels
(This addendum, lightly edited, was first published on Judith Hill's blog in December 2022).

A closer examination of the classical Zodiacal Man reveals that within his bodily trunk, some signs co-mingle their zones in interesting ways. This zone variation diverts somewhat from the usual straightforward stacking, from head to toe, of the classical melothesian Body Zones 1 12. Previously, we discussed the unique interactions of the Cancer and Leo body zones. Here, we introduce the intertwining zones of Scorpio and Sagittarius.

This is a cursory view of how Sagittarius' upper zone both encircles and is "bitten" by its preceding zone, Scorpio. Medical astrologers and chiropractors may find this ancient discovery of considerable interest.

A curious Biblical statement is hypothesized to cryptically describe a relationship between the signs Scorpio and Sagittarius. David A. Womack's book 12 Signs, 12 Sons, attests that each of the twelve Hebrew tribes was Biblically correlated with one specific zodiac sign! His compelling arguments sold me. If true, this compelling statement by the Hebrew patriarch Jacob, (said in the act of describing the character of his twelve sons), appears relevant to today's medically oriented quest. Here is the partial quote:

"Dan shall provide justice for his people... Dan shall be a serpent by the way, an adder in the path, that biteth the horse's heels so that his rider shall fall backward". Genesis 49:17

Womack correlates Dan, the venomous "adder" with the zodiac sign Scorpio. Jacob's depicted horse and rider is likewise equated with Sagittarius, the celestial centaur. This seems apt (providing that Womack's hypothesis is correct) because serpents are attributed to Scorpio, whereas the horse-rider team closely resembles the Sagittarian symbol of the centaur, a horse and man joined as one being.

Within the great patriarch's description of his twelve sons, this is the only co-mention of two sons, acting one upon the other. Does 'Zodiacal Man' mirror this co-action within his body? Can the adder really bite at the horse's heel, causing the rider to fall backward? Let's put the body zones of Scorpio and Sagittarius under our magnifying glass.

Scorpio, Body Zone 8, includes the organs in the lesser pelvis: lower colon, rectum, genitals, uterus, and bladder. It also governs the sacral plexus. Sagittarius, Body Zone 9, includes some of the bones that encircle the pelvic cavity: the crest of the hip bone, or ilium, and the ischium. However, the coccyx and sacrum are allotted to both Scorpio and Sagittarius.

Dr. H. L. Cornell states, "The Os Coccyx is under the structural rulership of the Scorpio sign. The Coccygeal Region of the Spine, the Coccygeal Vertebrae, is ruled by the Sagittarius sign."

In my handful of case studies, coccygeal pain and injuries appear to involve *both* Scorpio and Sagittarius, equally relevant to both signs!

The trochanter, femur, thighs, femoral artery, and sciatic nerve are also firmly assigned to Sagittarius. Thus, we see that although the great bulk of Body Zone 9 is indeed below Zone 8, as it should be, these two zones appear to share space in the upper portion of Zone 9.

Here we see that the Sagittarius-ruled hip bones in Zone 9 are partially sharing a horizontal body zone with the internal pelvic organs, governed by the previous zone (Zone 8). It is here in the pelvis area where we find these two zones confined together. All medical astrologers should contemplate this fact.

We see how the cleanly Sagittarian-ruled sciatic nerve originates in the largest and terminal branch of the Scorpio-ruled sacral plexus. However, there are many other nerves that originate under Scorpio's province that directly impact the function of Sagittarius' hip and thigh locomotion and comfort.

Sagittarius is our prime sign governor of the motor function of voluntary nerves, especially for the large, striated muscle groups specific to the hips and legs. I found this useful list on the web:

The Scorpio-governed sacral plexus provides motor and sensory innervation through the following nerves:

1. Sciatic Nerve (L4 - S3)

2. Pudendal Nerve (ventral divisions of S2 - S4)
3. Superior Gluteal Nerve (dorsal divisions of L4 - S1)
4. Inferior Gluteal Nerve (dorsal divisions of L5 - S2)
5. Nerve to Obturator Internus (ventral divisions of L5 - S2)

Hence, we see how the adder (Scorpio) might indeed "biteth the horse's heels," sending the rider backward, or perhaps to the chiropractor in search of relief! Sagittarian natives I've known, and those with malefics in this same sign and/or in Scorpio, all too frequently attest to this truth.

A happy balance between Scorpio (pelvis, sacrum, coccyx, sacral plexus), and Sagittarius (hip bones, coccyx, lower spinal nerves, sciatic nerve, femur, and large hip and leg muscles) is essential to pain-free locomotion!

Those with persistent spinal, hip, and thigh pain, and/or lower locomotive issues, might well study their natal charts for evidence of malefic planets, eclipses, or other stressors occurring either natally, or by current transits, within the two signs Scorpio and Sagittarius.

Chapter Twelve:

CAPRICORN SYNDROME

Peaceful, regular toil, the vigorous mountain air,
frugality and, above all, serenity in the spirit had
endowed this old man with awe-inspiring health.

- Jean Giono, *The Man Who Planted Trees*

Saturn's Children

How can we begin to describe Saturn's children? An intrepid Capricorn friend wandered off alone into the cold desert night and got lost. The alarmed sheriff alerted her mother, who apparently wasn't much concerned. Sure enough, my friend wandered into camp the next day, none the worse, having mysteriously survived the freezing temperatures. She proved the Capricorn legend of *practical efficiency* in the face of famines, long treks, or enforced hard labor. This is one tough sign!

Another Capricorn lady I know well, lived happily for seven years alone in the woods, chopping wood and caretaking a remote outpost. Stories like this abound amongst members of the celestial goat's fraternity.

These characteristics reflect Saturn's homeostasis-maintaining role combined with the Earth element's astringency, plus an innately "dry" and debilitated Moon, reflecting a stoic nature that requires little coddling to survive.

Fundamentals Refresher

Capricorn Syndrome is a set of collaborative symptoms, consistently appearing together, which are typical for natives of the sign Capricorn. The symptoms associated with Capricorn Syndrome can be experienced by people with other sun signs when there is a particular emphasis in this sign. Zodiac sign syndromes can occur in seriatim, first one symptom, then another, weeks, months or years later. However, two or more of these symptoms are frequently observed clustered together at the same time.

A Capricorn native may have few if any of the symptoms associated with Capricorn Syndrome. Indeed, many Capricorns are specimens of perfect health. However, this symptom set often, but not always, evinces itself when the native's Sun, Moon, or Ascendant tenants Capricorn and displays certain astrological conditions which are discussed at length in this chapter.

This chapter describes the astrological conditions that may aggravate the syndrome. With this knowledge, practitioners can explore the underlying condition when symptoms consistent with the syndrome present themselves in a patient. Understanding the energetic cause is the first step in remediation.

THE SIGN CAPRICORN

In Classical Western Astrology, with use of the Tropical Zodiac, a Capricorn is someone born *approximately* between 270 and 300 longitudinal degrees after the spring equinox, or 0-29 days after the winter solstice.

As with all other signs, we cannot think of Capricorn as an isolated single entity or a static constant. "Capricorn" is a gestalt of strengths and weaknesses based on its angular relationship to the other signs of the interconnected solar cycle. In turn, each of the twelve phases of this cycle is influenced by the unique planetary configurations at birth and throughout the life. Capricorn is a unique phase-state, with its interactions peculiar to the tenth stage of the twelve-fold cyclical process.

Life Cycle Phase: Capricorn represents the tenth stage on the twelve-fold human life cycle. The infant breathes its first breath (Aries), nurses (Taurus), speech centers awaken (Gemini), emotionally sensitizes and grows a protective shield (Cancer), then achieves adolescence (Leo). Come Virgo, we perfect the body, sharpen our skills, serve, discern, and labor hard to maintain the physical world. In Libra, the soul takes pause. Then Scorpio brings the struggle of purging and transformation. The advent of Sagittarius brings freedom, independence, and a quest for knowledge.

Capricorn arrives as the moment of initiation. Capricorn symbolizes the mountain top of the life cycle. This is, then, a life of seriousness, consolidation, and achievement (positive or negative). At this stage, we soberly accept our worldly, or spiritual mantel. As with Capricorn's ruler, Saturn, we reap as we have sown.

Applying reincarnation theory, in both the spiritual and material realms the soul now achieves a pinnacle of whatever it built into itself throughout its long cycle of lives. It has been said that at the Capricorn phase, the soul either attains a crystalline purity, discipline, self-mastery and wisdom, or a brittleness and density of materialism that can proceed no further without a crisis termed *The Fall of Capricorn* (e.g., Elvis Presley and Richard Nixon).

Element and Mode: Capricorn is of the element Earth. As the initiating sign of winter, it belongs to the Cardinal quadruplicity of signs.

Earth Triplicity

Capricorn is one of the three Earth signs. Taurus is the fertile earth, Virgo the winnowing and harvest, and Capricorn the baker or stored grain in the barn.

One might also conceive the three earth variations in this manner: *Fixed Taurus* is Gaia and earth magnetism. *Mutable Virgo* is moving earth, such as mud, harvesting, winnowing, preparing foods, and gathering. *Cardinal Capricorn* represents the Earth element at its greatest density, such as granite and mountains. Capricorn is astringency at its best! Or we might conceive of Capricorn as *the pinnacle of achievement for the earth element:* wheat grows under Taurus, is winnowed in Virgo, and becomes the loaf of bread in Capricorn (or barn stored for winter use).

Cardinal Mode and the *Lord of Time*

Capricorn is one of four Cardinal signs, those that initiate a season: Aries, Cancer, Libra, and Capricorn. Consistent with being initiators, their common emphasis is to produce acute conditions. However, among the Cardinal signs, Capricorn is most noted for chronic conditions. Let's explain further.

The Capricorn-Cancer polarity represents our main *time partners,* along with their ruling planets Saturn and the Moon. Capricorn and Saturn govern the longer cycle internal physical clocks. These regulate the approach of menarche, menopause, andropause, old age, death, and the like. Conversely, Cancer governs the constantly changing daily, weekly, and monthly rhythms, such as appetite and sleep cycles.

Saturn ruled Capricorn natives are noted to maintain a remarkable homeostasis of appearance for decades. But when they finally shift under Saturn's irresistible dial, it can be wholesale. Capricorns often look like a little old people at age six, holding that same face well into mid-life, when they finally catch up with it!

I've never agreed with that well-worn idea that Capricorns age backwards. I've just not seen it. A mature appearance in early youth is more typically observed. I recall one sixteen-year-old Capricorn girl in my high school who everyone thought was thirty! Perhaps it is this phenomenon that started the myth of aging backward. Occasionally you see beautiful skin in some Saturn-positive types; and an upright, never-aging dignity in the Capricorn yogis. But no, they don't look "young". This is the sign of the wise old sage.

Unremediated, afflicted Capricorns are noted for one or more chronic issues of the following types: rheumatic, arthritic, knee, liver, gallbladder, stomach absorption, uterine, and skin disorders, as well as malnourishment and mucus membrane dryness. As explained later in this chapter, these afflictions pertain more to Capricorn charts with certain astrological afflictions.

Capricorn Functions and Energetics

Capricorn's influence is primarily astringent, pulling molecules together, forming hard, identifiable structure, maintaining form through time, and pressing out fluid; hardening, drying, and consolidating. Capricorn is "cold" in that it slows atoms and hardens. This is quite different than the wet cold of Water signs, or the cold, electrically spastic nature of Aquarius. Indeed, many Capricorn issues are derived from internally trapped heat, blocked from escaping at the surface.

The actions of Capricorn are nearly identical to those of Saturn, although a few of their distinct bodily rulerships are not shared.

Capricorn's Superpowers

Stamina and endurance: This sign can survive famines, work gangs, and long mountain treks.

Efficient calorie burning and nutrient use: Capricorn gifts its natives with the ability to live off deficient calories and dietary restrictions better than any other sign, except perhaps Virgo.

Isolation: Although there is a social version of the sign, the classic "Saturnian" Capricorn can live a solitary monk's existence without complaint. It may even be their preference.

Strength: Capricorn natives often surprise others with their significant muscular strength. When happy, Saturn builds strong bones, ligaments, and tendons. The planet that governs the muscles, ligaments, and tendons, Mars, is happiest in this sign, being exalted here. Mars and Saturn, together, govern strength, toughness, and stamina.

Toughness: In hard times, hard places, and famine, Capricorn natives can outlast the more outwardly dynamic signs.

Patience: Long-time health or dietary regimes are no problem.

Resistance: Although not the longest-lived sign, Capricorns are famous for not dying when anticipated. They can cling to this earth plane of existence for years in an ancient and decrepit body. Cornell makes an amusing comment about this.

Earth Affinity: Capricorns love the Earth, and the Earth loves them. They make exceptional botanists, herbalists, farmers, and bakers. This is a strongly inclined medical sign, many become nurses or doctors (Capricorn Moon excels at nursing!) They can pull a significant amount of Vital Force from the Earth itself and from plants (see the quote at the top of this chapter!). A gardening Capricorn is a happy one!

Physical Appearance

Exhaustive detail with illustrations is provided in this author's *The Astrological Body Types.*

The Capricorn Affect

Capricorn types have a serious, self-possessed dignity so easy to interpret as depressed. This does not mean that they are depressed. "Cappy can be happy" without any need to smile. Continuous smiling is a modern American cultural artifact, appearing insipid to outside cultures. That being said, Capricorn is a sign prone to depression.

CAPRICORN BODY RULERSHIPS AND FUNCTIONS

As described in Chapter One, a body zone is a general box that overlays many organs, functions, vessels and their sub-rulerships.

Capricorn, Body Zone 10

Capricorn influences all bones, muscles, and vessels within the knee region. Capricorn is so perfectly aligned with its ruler Saturn, that we see a general influence over all joints, skin, cuticles, and teeth. Capricorn also influences the skeletal system and is the most mineral emphasizing sign. The gallbladder is shared between Leo, Virgo, and Capricorn, and planets Saturn (the organ) and Mars (the bile and its precipitation).

Keep in mind that Capricorn governs some items that Saturn doesn't share, such as the anterior pituitary. Jupiter is our planet governor of the pituitary (Cayce, confirmed by Hill). Conversely, Saturn governs the right ear, while Capricorn does not. It's so essential to not unwittingly mix up sign and planet rulerships.

Are Bones, Ligaments, Tendons, Cartilage really all ruled by Saturn?

Some books give all the above to Saturn. Others share tendons and ligaments between Saturn and Mars, or just Mars. What about cartilage (often assigned to Saturn)?

It would seem counter-intuitive that both the bones and what buffers them (cartilage) would both be Saturn-ruled. Similarly, why should elastic cords that attach bones to muscles (tendons) or bone to bone (ligaments) be ruled by the same planet, Saturn, that rules the bones themselves? These essential questions have not been sufficiently investigated yet by modern medical astrologers.

As discussed more fully in the Sagittarius chapter, Cornell firmly gives cartilage to Saturn and ligaments to both Saturn <u>and</u> Mars, noting also how Pisces strongly influences the fibro-ligamentous system. My own few cases of chronically slippery ligaments (hypermobility) support his Pisces observation, but not that of Saturn. Sagittarius, being the sign that sews multiple strands of nerves (and thoughts) together, likely also influences the ligaments that attach bone to bone. I've observed multiple cases of slippery hip ligaments for Neptune in Sagittarius, in square to Mars, or some other planet positioned in Pisces. A case of disabling slippery ligaments was noted in a Pisces native with Sagittarius at the 6th house, and Mars opposing Neptune.

Considering Saturn's domicile, Capricorn, we must view this sign, as we do all signs, in reference to its opposite sign, Cancer. If Capricorn and Saturn rule the bones, why wouldn't Cancer and its ruler, Luna, govern the serous and synovial fluids that lubricate the joints and perhaps the cartilage as well? We also have different densities of cartilage. Some cartilage has a high percentage of water - this appears more Cancerian in nature.

Or, if Saturn governs bones, is it Jupiter that governs the cartilage and shock absorbing intervertebral discs? Jupiter is the great planetary protector of the pantheon, and cartilage protects the bones.

In determining if this was so, I found a handful of clients who had severely ground down their knees or hips early in life. Not only was their Capricorn-Cancer axis prominent, but something else of interest stood out. In most of these cases, Saturn and Jupiter were typically in quincunx formation, or aversion, and sometimes in square or opposition.

Conversely, the two cases I recalled with "bones of a thirty-year-old" well into their sixties, had close trines between these two planets. Naturally, we need to have more involved in these signatures, as whole birth years share these formations. However, my suspicion that Saturn-Jupiter and Capricorn-Cancer influence cartilage-bone imbalances, cannot yet be dismissed. We must certainly consider the density and strength of cartilage as related to the Cancer-Capricorn axis.

One standout case was that of a young woman, who required full double knee replacements by thirty. She was born as the Moon and Jupiter were conjunct in Cancer, with a Cancer Ascendant. There was no balancing planet in Capricorn. As we know, the Moon rules Cancer, and Jupiter is exalted in this same sign! To have both rising in this sign screams "emphasis."

Saturn, Capricorn's ruler, couldn't balance this strong Lunar emphasis because he was in soft Pisces, plus afflicted by Mars. This lady's pattern suggests that Cancer (the watery system) greatly dominated Capricorn (the skeletal system). I was unable to inquire if the bad knee joints resulted from soft, osteoporotic knee bones or soft cartilage, too easily ground down by hard bones!

Seeing cases like this recalls the nutrient balances required to produce good bones. Calcium (Saturn), Phosphorus (Mars), Magnesium and Iodine (Sun), Potassium (Moon), Vitamin A and D (Sun), and Vitamin C (Saturn) (Nauman, Jansky).

Davidson offers a fascinating observation: "... *If you study Capricorn carefully you will again see the significance of this type of metabolism. You will find that they cannot stand chilling because they have a ready crystalizing point in their blood. Sugar put into a glass of hot water disap-*

pears, melts, but as soon as the water cools the sugar crystallizes again. So the Capricorn needs to learn how to live as regards temperature. It is unfortunate that these subtle laws of are nature are completely overlooked in all healing systems." - Davidson's Medical Lectures

CAPRICORN SYNDROME

As discussed in Chapter Two, a Zodiac Sign Syndrome is a cluster of symptoms associated with the body zones and functions of a zodiac sign and the signs positioned on the seasonal wheel opposite (180°) and quincunx (150°, 210°, 330°) the sign. Remediating and supporting these body zones and functions act to bring the body into balance, diminishing the syndrome. These symptoms may manifest when there is an emphasis in one or more of these signs. Planetary dignity plays an important role.

The Weaker Signs for the Capricorn Vital Force
Quincunx Signs

Gemini, Leo, and Sagittarius are positioned 150°, 210° and 330° distant from Capricorn on the seasonal wheel. These signs represent the *averted* 6th, 8th, and 12th angles from the sign Capricorn (see the illustration for this chapter). This *averted* condition makes it difficult for Capricorn to absorb the cosmic rays or the vibrational and light nutrients that feed these signs. Likewise, these signs may have trouble absorbing the rays from Capricorn.

Sagittarius rules Body Zone 9 which includes the hips, thighs, sciatic nerve, locomotion, Central Nervous System, expiration of breath, and the arterial system. Do Capricorn's proverbial knee complaints might originate in the misalignment of Sagittarius ruled hip and pelvis?

Gemini rules Body Zone 3 which includes the upper lung and bronchial tubes. Capricorns frequently pair skin conditions with asthma or bronchitis. Should the Gemini-ruled capillaries lack permeability, or be fragile, we might expect some calcification or nutritive delivery issues leading to the various rheumatic and arthritic problems infamous to Capricorn.

Leo rules Body Zone 5. Capricorn is prone to Leo ruled heart and spine issues. However, both signs co-govern the gallbladder! Although certainly a cold sign, Capricorn suffers almost as much as does Leo from an excess of internal heat in the liver and/or gallbladder, but for different reasons! In Capricorn, the life force slows, wastes build, and inflammation follows. Also, Saturn may prevent trapped heat from escaping. Here we observe the slowly building smoldering heat, deep in the bones or liver. Conversely, the Sun-ruled Leo produces an excess of internal heat all on its own accord! In Capricorn, we also may see mineral deposits in the heart vessels, and gallstones. Astrologically, these are related issues. There may be a weakness in older age, possibly connected to stiffening arteries or veins. I have noted some tendencies in this sign to heart failure.

Capricorn sits at the apex of a Gemini-Leo Yod. The apex of the heart (Leo) can suffer from deficient capillary circulation (Gemini). Does this contribute to Capricornian skeletal stiffness? Or does this Yod reflect some other remote causation of arthritic complaints between the gallbladder (Leo-Capricorn), and the bronchial tubes and breath's inspiration (Gemini)? This sign trio is worth investigation because as Dr. Davidson asserted, astrology was never wrong. Heart failure is not uncommon in this sign, or some congenital weakness of this organ, especially should Saturn be in Leo or afflict the Sun in Capricorn. Watch for calcium or cholesterol deposits in the vessels serving the heart - hardened arteries.

Opposite Sign, Cancer.

When the Sun is in Capricorn, the opposite sign, Cancer, "sleeps." Cancer rules Body Zone 4 which includes the stomach and breasts and influences the mucus membrane, gums, synovial fluid (Hill), fertility, and the womb (when pregnant). Cancer's moistening function upon the stomach, mucus membrane throughout, and joints is so often deficient in the Capricorn type. One might say that everything Cancer is, Capricorn is not. However, being opposite signs, they partner as the nutritive, shape building duo. Capricorn-Saturn maintains the skeleton, while Cancer brings the waters (with Pisces).

Although Capricorn is traditionally listed as moderately fertile, it is prone to uterine fibroids and is certainly not as fertile as is its opposite sign, Cancer. That said, some books associate all female signs with heightened fertility, including Capricorn. I have personally noticed a high incidence of uterine fibroids and hysterectomies for women born with the natal Moon in Capricorn, though not always. Some have lots of kids!

Cancer loves eating, while Capricorn fusses, observing great care with food. Cancer rules the stomach and breasts, while every so often Capricorn requires stomach or lactation support.

The native with Capricorn Sun, but more typically the Capricorn Moon, evinces poor stomach absorption. This is a traditional vomiting sign, and the Moon governs the stomach. One so often sees the, emaciated, atrophied Capricorn Sun or Moon, with either trouble eating, or highly restricted and specific preferences. This type is also seen in Virgo. Capricorn, with strong Virgo accent, can do it, or Capricorn with strong Saturn, and/or Saturn-Mars afflictions. Traditionally, laxatives are useless when the Moon transits through this sign!

One often finds the Capricorn Sun or Moon type devoted to a long-term fat-extremes diet. Either "I eat exactly one teaspoon of Avocado oil daily, and no other fats"; or "I'm Keto"; or "I eat mostly fat and protein, but no fruit or carbs." Although I can't opine on the merits of either extremity, my empirical observation is that both types appear malnourished and underweight, typically suffering from several of the symptoms listed in this chapter for Capricorn Syndrome, including severely restricted diets.

This sign evinces an unexamined issue with fat absorption, utilization, and the lipid pathways. The right kind of oil, and enough of it, would seem essential for this type! Dry hair, skin, and nails are typical. Note that one sees the same issues with fellow Earth sign Virgo.

Signs Aggravating Capricorn Syndrome – Squaring Signs

Libra and Aries are positioned 90° from Capricorn, squaring this sign (see chapter illustration). The effect of a square is to create friction, for good or ill. Capricorn can reflex with these signs, as well as its opposite sign, Cancer.

The Aries-Capricorn square may relate to the pituitary adrenal function. This square is quite drying and dehydrating in action, especially upon the stomach, giving nausea. We may also observe headaches and dry eyes due to brain and overall tissue dehydration. This square is also prone to joint inflammation and accidents. However, it's great for career building and realizing ambitions!

The Libra-Capricorn square may relate to the kidney's influence on calcium and mineral balance. Minerals, especially calcium, are Saturn's domain, Capricorn's ruler. Blood calcium concentrations are maintained through the kidney's regulation of the excretion of calcium (in response to the thyroid hormone calcitonin, or parathyroid hormone), plus the conversion of Vitamin D into a useful form essential to calcium absorption. Libra rules the kidneys.

A good web article exists, aptly entitled *Evidence for a Novel Calcium-Regulating Bone Kidney Axis* by Rajiv Kumar and Volker Vallon. However, astrology already teaches us that bones (Saturn-Capricorn) have a strong relationship with fellow Cardinal sign Libra, because Saturn (bones) is exalted in Libra!

How Planetary Dignity Contributes to Capricorn Syndrome

Strongest Planets

Saturn Rules Capricorn: Cold, astringent, dry, and slow. It pushes water out or traps it. It prevents heat from rising or traps it inside. Saturn rules skin, bones, teeth (with Taurus), gallbladder, right ear, peripheral sympathetic nerves (Cornell), the timing of larger body changes, and the bringing of old age. Saturn maintains homeostasis, constancy, and endurance. Its character is rigid and slow, like Capricorn symptoms.

Mars is Exalted in Capricorn: The Capricorn governed anterior pituitary secretes several hormones supporting many traditional Mars ruled functions. For instance, the adrenocorticotropic hormone, produced in the anterior pituitary, stimulates the traditionally Mars-governed adrenals! Curiously, the Martian hormone-gland pathway has only been established in modern times. Mars governs phosphorous (Jansky, Nauman), and possibly silica (Hill), all necessary support for good bone (Saturn).

Capricorn also slows Mars' energy use, providing legendary stamina to those either born in this sign or with natal Mars placed herein.

Thyroid stimulating hormone (TSH) is directly related to our felt energy levels (Mars). The Capricorn-ruled anterior pituitary gland (together with the thyroid) strongly influences our metabolism and caloric burn rate, both profoundly Martian functions.

The anterior pituitary also secretes Follicle-stimulating hormone (FSH), exciting the testes and ovaries to produce sperm and eggs. For sure, the male reproductive functions are ruled by Mars.

We also have growth hormone, another hormone on a timer. Children grow, and adults maintain healthy bones, muscles, and fat. Instead of being Mars ruled, this may relate more to the growth planet Jupiter and maybe Saturn (bones). We do see that Capricorn suffers weight extremes. Most Capricorns I have observed are either extreme ectomorphs or extreme mesomorphs. Both types are very strong!

Please note that the Capricorn ectomorph is not the frail, thin type we think of when hearing that word! Rather, the boney structure remains dominant, and although the body is without fat, and even emaciated, one sees the large and prominent knuckles, knees, and the like. What we truly have is not the classic ectomorph, but rather, the Saturnian type.

Mars governs muscles, and Saturn bones. This planetary partnership thus benefits Capricorn, providing this sign exceptional muscular strength. It is notable that two of the greatest heavyweight boxers who ever lived were Capricorns: Muhammed Ali and George Foreman.

Weakest Planets

Jupiter falls in Capricorn: The Jupiter-governed liver is notoriously slow and dry in this sign. Perhaps we can sum up many of Capricorn's maladies to this astrological fact!

Jupiter governs fat, generosity, and joy. Capricorn people have an interesting relationship with fats, lipids, joyfulness, and expenditure. As discussed above under Mars, there are two physical Capricorn types. The classic Saturnian is hard and dry, lacking fats, and sometimes emaciated. Then, we have the heavyweight Earth type with massive bones, large muscles, and a covered layer of hard fat. Both types may suffer from lipid distribution problems, with dry, problematic skin, brittle nails, compromised hearing, retreating gums, and creaking joints.

Although Capricorn can have a sense of humor, one rarely hears the loud belly laugh or protracted teenage laughing fit. (Nor wild expenditure!)

Luna is in detriment in Capricorn: As Saturn's partner, Luna guides our opposite lunar functions. Therefore, their lack is a prime precursor of Capricorn Syndrome. Luna governs the waters of the body, their flux and flow. She governs change, elasticity, emotional receptivity, lactation, and fertility.

The Moon's nature is moistening, cooling, rhythmic, and unstable. The entire mucus membrane is strongly Lunar, as are the bodily lubricants (with Venus and Jupiter). The Moon governs absorption, the stomach, breast, and womb. Lack of fluid absorption is a major issue for Capricorn Sun and Moon natives, as is dry membranes and general stiffness. There may be some deficiency of synovial fluids, saliva, skin lubrication, lipid distribution to the skin and hair, and the like.

Planetary and House Positions that Contribute to Capricorn Syndrome

(1) **Sun, Moon, or Ascendant sign in Capricorn**

(2) A weakness in a body zone governed by the signs opposite or quincunx Capricorn on the seasonal wheel (Gemini, Leo, Cancer, Sagittarius). See discussion above under *The Weaker Signs for the Capricorn Vital Force.*

(3) Sun, Moon, Ascendant, Jupiter, Mars, Saturn, or Lunar Nodes in Capricorn, and to a lesser extent any other planet, compounded by any of the testimonies below. The first two are the most important:

- Capricorn inhabits the 1st, 6th, 8th, or 12th houses of the natal chart. This is especially true if a natal Capricorn Sun or Moon is in the natal 6th or 8th houses.

- Saturn in hard angle to Jupiter (fats), Sun, Moon, Venus, or Mars.
- Excess or deficient natal Saturn (by sign placement and house). Both conditions contribute to the syndrome, but for opposite reasons! **Excess Saturn** creates stiffness and build ups of calcium gravel, causing inflammation and eventual joint breakdown or deficient nutrient delivery. Conversely, **deficient Saturn** produces deficient mineral absorption and assimilation at onset, leading to weakened teeth, joints, and bones. This in turn causes inflammatory skeletal conditions quite similar to those seen for excess Saturn.
- Saturn closely conjuncts *either* natal Lunar Node (South/ North). For instance, Saturn on the North Node can signal mineral buildups, often depositing problematically in the muscles or joints; over time, minerals irritate the joints, causing inflammation, trapped heat, and gradual joint damage. Saturn conjunct North Node can over time, grow excessively hardening and drying to the bones, skin, and to any body zone tenanted by natal Saturn, or the signs it afflicts. One notes all manner of dry, hard skin issues, ligaments, et al.
- Conversely, Saturn on the South Node can indicate poor mineral absorption with consequential bone and connective tissue issues such as osteoporosis or spongey gums.
- Saturn in hard angle to the Sun or Moon will increase the astringent nature of this sign, as will a natal Capricorn Moon.

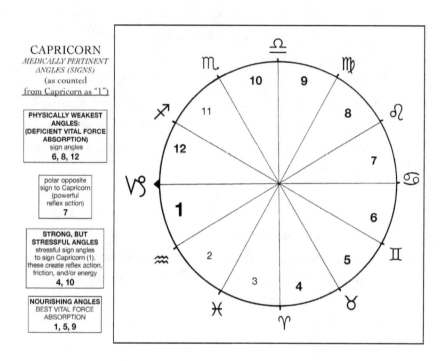

CAPRICORN
MEDICALLY PERTINENT
ANGLES (SIGNS)
(as counted
from Capricorn as "1")

PHYSICALLY WEAKEST
ANGLES:
(DEFICIENT VITAL FORCE
ABSORPTION)
sign angles
6, 8, 12

polar opposite
sign to Capricorn
(powerful
reflex action)
7

STRONG, BUT
STRESSFUL ANGLES
stressful sign angles
to sign Capricorn (1).
these create reflex action,
friction, and/or energy
4, 10

NOURISHING ANGLES
BEST VITAL FORCE
ABSORPTION
1, 5, 9

SYMPTOMS OF CAPRICORN SYNDROME

Please note that I am not discussing "Capricorn people" per se, but those born with prominences in this sign that <u>actually do suffer the syndrome.</u> These symptoms can occur in seriatim, first one symptom, then weeks, months or years later, another. However, two or more of these symptoms are frequently observed clustered together at the same time. These symptoms are not listed in any order, but simply as a list of collected observations common to natives of Capricorn. Please be sure to balance with Capricorn's Superpowers. As with any sign, there are just as many positives!

- moles, warts, skin tags, skin issues
- itchy, dry skin (especially with Mars and/or Mercury in Capricorn)
- eczema, psoriasis
- dandruff
- brittle nails, cuticle issues
- nail fungus
- thinning, brittle hair, lacking shine or body
- brittle teeth (or strong teeth)
- soft or receding gums
- nausea or overactive vomiting response
- slow stomach digestion
- poor appetite/poor digestion
- insufficient stomach acids
- insufficient/thin mucus membrane protection of stomach wall
- dehydration / disinclination to drink water
- lactose or gluten intolerance
- excess or deficient hydrochloric acid
- difficulty laughing freely
- affectless expression
- stoic in public but weeping spells in private (especially with moon in Capricorn)
- taciturn
- fear of spending money
- dry esophagus or easy choking
- xerostomia (dry mouth)
- gallstones
- jaundice
- GERD
- heat trapped in digestive organs or joints.
- inflammation (joints, stomach, intestines)
- dry ligaments and tendons
- long term weight extremes, such as being underweight or obesity.
- stubborn emaciation or under-weight or conversely, obstinant obesity
- muscle atrophy, emaciation
- orthorexia, anorexia, hyporexia, bulimia
- severely restrictive diets
- compulsive dieting
- malnourishment (too few fats, proteins, or calories)

- poor lactation
- fertility issues
- stiff or creaking joints, knees
- arthritis, rheumatism
- joint inflammation
- poor quality cartilage
- poor quality collagen (or very good!)
- osteoporosis and osteopenia
- bone spurs
- rickets, in deficient Saturn and Sun charts
- mineral deposits where they ought not be, such as mineral deposits in muscles, joints, arteries, ear canal, or as gravel in the gallbladder or kidneys
- bursitis, tendonitis (dry, hot, inflamed, stiff, lacking moisture or lubrication)
- knee issues or anomalies
- trick knee
- asthma
- bronchitis
- deafness, or compromised hearing
- calcium deposits in ears, stiffening ear bones
- uterine fibroids, especially with Capricorn Moon (sometimes hysterectomy)
- menstrual issues: amenorrhea/menorrhagia
- voluntary celibacy (more typical in females)
- breast cysts and lumps
- receding and bleeding gums
- dry, inelastic ligaments or tendons
- poor lipid distribution
- weak sebaceous glands
- deficient sweating
- dehydration
- deficient moisture in the extra cellular matrix (ECM)
- poor memory, memory decline, dementia
- rigidity of habits
- OCD
- acidic system
- life timing anomalies (early/late menarche or menopause)
- growth pattern anomaly, such as the short kid who has the enormous growth spurt at age 21

- lack of libido (or high libido for Mars in Capricorn, especially in males)
- disinterest in babies
- cold extremities
- solitary nature
- liver cirrhosis
- internal dryness
- constipation
- stomach, duodenal, or colon ulcers
- insufficient pancreatic enzymes
- insufficient vaginal lubrication
- insufficient ear wax
- fear of getting fat and of fats
- compulsive exercising
- obsession with muscle strength or bodily perfection
- workaholism
- indigestion
- intestinal/colon dryness and consequent issues
- poor secretions
- skin cancers (rare)

- intense preference for same chair
- undisclosed chronic depression
- shouldering excess duties
- preoccupation with life accomplishments or spiritual perfection (either/or)
- disinclination to leisure, play, fun
- stiffness
- osteoporosis (or very dense bones!)
- bleating sound in voice, weak voice
- dislike of spontaneous hugs, singalongs, holding hands in group circle, sudden intrusions, guests, people dropping by, unplanned phone calls
- dislikes disruption of daily routine

REMEDIATION TIPS

Please note that these remedial tips are for interest only. The author is not suggesting that any person use these without the evaluation and consent of their personal healthcare practitioner.

Heat: One fine herb specific for "heat that has baked down into the bones" (Matthew Wood) is Dandelion Root (*Taraxacum officinale*). This bright, plentiful weed provides double duty as a cleanser of breast tissue, assistance for acne and other skin issues, and as a first-rate liver-gallbladder assist. Some herbalists report that with the help of Dandelion Root, a significant improvement has been witnessed in arthritic conditions, and weak ligaments. This root is often paired with Burdock Root (*Arctium lappa*).

Skin: Herbs for skin conditions abound, including Burdock, Oregon Grape Root (*Mahonia aquifolium*), Turmeric (*Curcuma longa*), Yellow Dock (*Rumex crispus*), and the vast array of alternate herbs for the epidermis. The cellular moistening qualities of Chickweed (*Stellaria media*) may be of inestimable value for external and internal use. Wood notes that few herbs penetrate and moisten through the layers of the dermis as nicely as this little herb. It's a traditional favorite for rough, dry skin, and cradle cap.

Capricorn benefits from cellular hydration through pure water and memory enhancing herbs, such as Sage, *Salvia officinalis* (which also prevents fluid loss), Gingko (*Gingko biloba*), Periwinkle (*Vinca*), Gotu Kola (*Centella asiatica*), Rosemary (*Salvia Rosmarinus*), and Holy Thistle (Cnicus benedictus). Gotu Kola also help open the capillaries, which is often needful here. In this regard, my preference for Capricorn leans to the Holy Thistle (*Cnicus benedictus*). This herb not only may reduce amyloid plaques (thus being preventative to Alzheimer's Disease) but is renowned to protect both the liver and memory. Better still, this plant sports a glorious purple flower, and violet is the color of Capricorn on the artist's color wheel.

Stomach: The stomach is fussy in Capricorn, for various reasons detailed in this chapter. One must first find if the classic Capricornian hyporexia is due to excessive or deficient stomach acid; or a weak, dry mucus membrane; or caused by an excess of heat building in the liver or gallbladder. Different herbs would be best in each case.

Chickweed (*Stellaria media*), Chamomile (*Matricaria chamomilla*) and Marshmallow Root (*Althaea officinalis*) are all noted as cooling, softening, and soothing to a hot, dry stomach.

The vomit reflex is traditionally thought enhanced at the Moon's monthly passage through this sign. It is said that cathartics won't work at the reverse end of our alimentary canal. Clearly, Capricorn rejects entry at the top and hangs on at the bottom!

Pituitary: Pituitary support would seem essential, although so little is known regarding herbal support of this tiny, master gland. Poke Root is known to stimulate pituitary function. However, be sure to request your physician's opinion on all herbs discussed here, especially Poke Root, an herb known for dose cautions.

Kidney and Gallbladder: Many herbs assist with gravel in the kidneys or gallbladder. Gravel Root (*Eutrochium purpureum*), Stone Root (*Collinsonia canadensis*), and your kitchen Parsley all activate the gravel out of the kidneys, sometimes too fast in the latter case! Professional care is necessitated in the known presence of stones. Greater Celandine (*Chelidonium majus*) is a noted specific for the health of the Capricorn-sensitive gallbladder.

Mineral Absorption: Capricorns need to assess their vitamin and mineral intake, as calcium requires Vitamin C, D, A, plus Potassium, Magnesium, and Phosphorus to build good bones. Calcium is Saturn's main mineral, whereas Potassium belongs to Capricorn's opposite sign, Cancer. This might suggest that Capricorn natives are prone towards Potassium deficiency. Astrology is rarely wrong!

Our mineralizing herbs include Alfalfa (*Medicago sativa*), Oat Straw (*Avena sativa*), Nettles (*Urtica dioica*), Dandelion (*Taraxacum officinale*), and Red Clover (*Trifolium pratense*). The latter possesses red tops due to the presence of copper, Venus' metal. Because Venus assists Saturn, it is possible that Copper may be helpful to the Saturn influenced Capricorn. The classic and pioneering works by Susan Weed on menopause are suggested.

Fats: It's important for Capricorn natives to assess their fat intake and distribution. Cold Pressed Olive Oil would seem preferential because of its liver and gallbladder assisting properties! Always remember that a slow, dry liver is associated with this sign! Borage (*Borago officinalis*) is noted for assisting lactation.

Other Herbs: Canadian herbalist and acupuncturist Francis Bonaldo reports from his experience that orange peel tincture, or tangerine, will reliably cure an inability to digest gluten or dairy. We learn from Traditional Chinese Medicine that bitter and sour flavors both are relevant for those needing liver assist.

Pleurisy Root (*Asclepias tuberosa*) is beneficial for bursitis (Wood). In fact, this herb appears the perfect herb for a multiple array of Capricorn's complaints. Michael Moore cites this herb's penchant for stimulating both sebaceous and sudoriferous secretions, and generally stimulating the mucosal circulation. This plant is noted for assistance with dry skin and hair, asthma, bursitis, exanthematous (eruptive) diseases, and fluidic restrictions of the pleura. An impressive power is Pleurisy Root's ability to move dampness and stagnation in the lower lung, while moistening a dry bronchial tract. See Matthew Wood's fantastic description in *The Earthwise Herbal*.

See also Chapter 15, *The Twelve Zodiac Sign Syndromes and their Relevant Herbs.*

Chapter Thirteen:

AQUARIUS SYNDROME

Thought allied fearlessly to purpose becomes creative force: he who knows this is ready to become something higher and stronger than a mere bundle of wavering thoughts and fluctuating sensations; he who does this has become the conscious and intelligent wielder of his mental powers.

- James Allen, *As A Man Thinketh*

The Center of Humanity

This is the sign of vision, forward thought, and creative imagination, also known as the zodiac's center of *humanity*. Indeed, my Aquarian friends are happily engaged in creative or philanthropic concerns that have little relation to personal profit. Shaking the hand of one famous astrologer, I accurately guessed her birth sign as Aquarius from the friendly, yet impersonal way she shook my hand, while focusing instead on the larger group scene going on behind me.

Medically speaking, Aquarius is arguably the most puzzling sign of the zodiac. Does this have something to do with this sign's dominant connection with the unseen electro-magnetic bodies, chakras, and forces we know so little about, and are not yet medically recognized in clinical-institutional practice?

This medical propensity is also reflected in other areas of life. For example, does that Aquarian you know decide to prune the trees at midnight, conceive oddly imaginative meals, mismatch clothes, or have trouble arriving on time? Are they inventing something in the garage? Do they have unexpected laughing fits, make friends with the old folks, or avidly study something you find truly weird?

What has all this to do with Aquarius' oxygenation or venous functions, or perhaps its rulership of the lower leg? Maybe we can discover this together!

Fundamentals Refresher

Aquarius Syndrome is a set of collaborative symptoms, consistently appearing together, which are typical for natives of the sign Aquarius. The symptoms associated with Aquarius Syndrome can be experienced by people with other sun signs when there is a particular emphasis in this sign. Zodiac sign syndromes can occur in seriatim, first one symptom, then another, weeks, months or years later. Few experience all symptoms. However, two or more of these symptoms are frequently observed clustered together at the same time.

An Aquarius native may have few if any of the symptoms associated with Aquarius Syndrome. Indeed, many Aquarians are specimens of perfect health. However, this symptom set often, but not always, evinces itself when the native's Sun, Moon, or Ascendant tenants Aquarius and displays certain astrological conditions which are discussed at length in this chapter.

This chapter describes the astrological conditions that may aggravate the syndrome. With this knowledge, practitioners can explore the underlying condition when symptoms consistent with the syndrome present themselves in a patient. Understanding the energetic cause is the first step in remediation.

THE SIGN AQUARIUS

In Classical Western Astrology, with use of the Tropical Zodiac, an Aquarian is someone born between 60 to 30 days (or longitudinal degrees) prior to the spring equinox.

As with all other signs, we cannot think of Aquarius as an isolated single entity or a static constant. "Aquarius" is a gestalt of strengths and weaknesses based on its angular relationship to the other signs of the interconnected solar cycle. In turn, each of the twelve phases of this cycle is influenced by the unique planetary configurations at birth and throughout the life. Aquarius is a unique phase-state, with its interactions peculiar to the eleventh stage of the twelve-fold cyclical process.

Element and Mode: Aquarius is the mid-winter sign and of the *Fixed* quadruplicity. Aquarius is of the element Air.

Life Cycle Phase: Aquarius represents the eleventh stage of the twelve-fold human life cycle. The infant breathes its first breath (Aries), nurses (Taurus), speech centers awaken (Gemini), emotionally bonds with family (Cancer), and achieves adolescence (Leo). Come Virgo, we perfect the body, sharpen our skills, serve, discern, and labor hard to maintain the physical world. In Libra, the soul takes pause, then Scorpio brings the struggle of purging and transformation. Freedom, independence, and a quest for knowledge arrive with Sagittarius. Capricorn is the time of reaping what we have sown, achievement, the mountaintop of the life cycle.

In Aquarius the soul, having reached the mountaintop, moves past personal ambition to a consciousness of humanity, the greater good, universal ideals, engagement in causes, expression of genius, or simply a release to a lifetime of floating and "taking one's measure." This is the state of creative leisure. The soul having arrived at a state of *"what do I want to do now?"*, creates for a lifetime a phase of open possibilities and the consequent unfolding of genius. Hence, the old moniker for the 11th house, or stage in the life cycle, "The house of hopes and dreams." Ah, but so much more.

About Aquarius

The Aquarian type is an unusual, "evolved" human - fascinated, if not obsessed, with all manner of odd subjects and often possessing a terrific sense of the absurd regarding the human condition. Typically, they experience a life of at least some degree of emotional-social isolation, yet they are often friendly to strangers and popular with acquaintances. They avoid what they see as the more mushy, gooey social attachments or obligations.

It is rare to encounter a deceptive Aquarian because this independent type does not prefer to cheat or manipulate others. They do like their freedom! The inventive, and imaginative faculties are outstanding. Yet they can sometimes morph into extreme mental states. This is the sign of genius!

Aquarians are typically not well grounded in happy family life, warmth, or practical work like gardening or cooking. Aquarian women are often disinclined to infant care. However, Aquarians often enjoy coaching and mentoring children and young adults.

Aquarius Superpowers
Vision, Overview, Imagination, Humor

In the Aquarian phase, the mind is drawn away from ego and centered more on the larger themes and problems of humanity at large, or on intellectual fascinations, mental pleasures, creative invention, and leisure.

Aquarius as *mental* creativity stands opposite to Leo's *physical* creativity. Their consequent maladies represent the extremes of cold vs hot.

The Aquarian looks at the greater community, often drawn to idealistic, progressive causes and organization, such as civil rights, child welfare, socialism, or equality. They can be tolerant, altruistic, charitable, humane, and philanthropic. They are drawn to enlightenment movements and are concerned with the evolution of man and society, new teachings, and the great works.

Aquarius is a wisdom sign, ruled by Saturn, wisdom of the old. They can view human drama with interest and are less inclined to be governed by reactive instincts. The forebrain is very strong in Aquarians. The Saturnian Aquarian type may prefer to be alone with a dislike or disdain for crowds. Often these attributes contribute to humanity through a great novel or invention!

Aquarians are often geniuses or polymaths; inventive or holding big dreams. They can have a highly developed sense of the socially absurd and an unpredictable sense of humor. Conveniently, laughing greatly contributes to preventative health. Interestingly, Aquarians resist hypnosis.

Physical Appearance

Exhaustive detail with illustrations is provided in this author's *The Astrological Body Types*.

AQUARIUS BODY RULERSHIPS AND FUNCTIONS
Aquarius, Body Zone 11

As described in Chapter One, a body zone is a general box that overlays many organs, functions, vessels and their sub-rulerships. Anything within Body Zone 11 will feel the influence of Aquarius.

Aquarius, Body Zone 11, includes the lower legs, tibia, Achilles tendon, saphenous vein, ankles, calves, venous circulation, fibula, neurotransmission, oxygen-carbon exchange; and the body's electrical system (with Leo and possibly Sagittarius). Aquarius influences vision and the spine. Aquarius and Venus co-rule the venous system. Aquarius, (with Sagittarius, and opposite sign Leo), governs the entire circulatory system.

It is possible that Aquarius holds dominion over the interfacing between the subtle energies entering the body, via the chakras, and the nervous and electrical systems of the body. This would explain some of the more mysterious and "undiagnosable" neuromuscular symptoms noted to this sign.

Aquarius Body Functions
Oxygenation

Although Aquarius is the sign of oxygenation of the blood, experience demonstrates that Aquarian types are notoriously *sub-oxygenated*. This is perhaps the major issue of this sign! We know that there are several considerations that produce oxygen starvation. Fellow air sign Gemini governs the bronchial tubes, upper lungs, and inspiration of the breath. Inspiration is not an Aquarius function but is ruled by Gemini. The oxygen molecule must bind to the hemoglobin in blood cells (turning them red), and subsequently be carried along in the blood stream to their destination. This process involves Aquarius, but also involves the arterial rulership (Jupiter, Sagittarius, and the heart ruler, Leo). A surprising number of Aquarian women are anemic.

It is my suspicion that Aquarius sub-oxygenation is also caused by anomalous cellular respiration - the process of oxygen uptake within the cells themselves. Cells use oxygen and glucose to burn energy and release the byproduct, carbon. Could Aquarius types suffer deficient oxygen uptake at the cellular level? Or conversely, are they either releasing or holding too much carbon in the bloodstream, thus suffering autointoxication? This could explain the Aquarian disdain for sleeping with gas on, craving fresh air, sleeping with windows open (Davidson), taking spontaneous hikes, the tendency for altitude sickness, Caisson's disease (the "bends"), extreme fatigue, and stiff muscles. These are all useful considerations. Traveling Aquarians so often crawl out of bed to block the hotel heat vent or crack a window!

We also have the possibility of lack of oxygen to the brain occurring at birth. Extreme cases, known as "blue babies," often present through life with Cerebral Palsy. However, one can have "a little" CP without the physician necessarily identifying this condition. The Achilles heel will be contracted, and the toddler will toe-walk. Muscles and tendons may be hyper-stiff and inelastic throughout life.

Electrical Flow of the Body

Astrology offers ancient wisdom regarding electro-magnetism, the seasons, and the body. The opposite sign Leo and its ruler Sol govern the heart, the body's major electrical generator. The Aquarius body zone (lower leg, ankles) stands in reflex position to Leo on the scheme of the year, replicated in Zodiacal Human. Could the ankles be a center of electro-magnetic regulation, working in reflex action with the electrical generating function of the heart?

The Sun governs opposite sign Leo. We are all made of solar photons. Thus, physicists realize that we are all, in essence, made of light. Mid-winter's Aquarius stands opposite on the season wheel to the mid-summer Leo. If you are sensitive enough, you can palpably feel the electrical stirring in the air and ground on mid-winter's day! Perhaps a mysterious energy, balancing to sunlight, is necessary to life on earth, and its source is the vibrational frequency connected with mid-winter, and the lower leg. (I call this energy "zing" because it feels that way). Could this relate to the electro-magnetic field of the Sun, earth, or the body?

Related to electrical impulse, we have spasm. Aquarians are famous for muscle spasms of mysterious origin. Also observed is a heightened tendency for shock when opening car doors, switching on light switches, petting cats, and the like. The native Aquarian Sun or Moon so often appears to be a bit more "electrical" than other signs. Spasm and/or electrical storms can occur anywhere, including the brain. However, leg and foot spasms seem typical.

The Aquarian needs to pay attention to their electrolyte and salt balances, as minerals balance electricity and sodium is a neurotransmitter! Medical astrologers have noted how Aquarians so often suffer "undiagnosable" complaints which puzzle the medical professionals. These problems might not be so puzzling should one consider electrical sources or problems with electrolytes, minerals, salts, or actual electricity. One should also consider the oft ignored positioning and nerves of the Achilles heel and lower leg.

To reiterate from above: Is it possible that Aquarius holds dominion over the *interface* between the subtle energies entering the body through the chakras and the nervous and electrical systems of the body? The Aquarius icon of the water-bearer (or angel) pouring water from an urn is as intriguing in this context as is the two "electrical" looking lines selected as the Aquarius glyph.

Cornell opines that Aquarius governs the spinal nerves, although Sagittarius clearly plays a dominant role there. Both signs are implicated in planetary signatures for many types of spinal cord diseases. I have observed some Aquarians display a heightened neural sensitivity, becoming tense and sensitive with too much noise, EMF, or crowd exposure. There is often a high degree of psychic reception in these types - as if they were a human radio. Wild nature is beloved by Aquarian types.

The Circulation and Quality of the Blood

Aquarius reigns supreme over venous circulation. However, we often see a sluggishness here, possibly due to a weakness in the opposite sign Leo, the heart. Low blood pressure with cold extremities is a great problem of this sign. The blood can hang at the ankles, sometimes purplish in hue, and varicosities are standard. One key is to check for a weak or insufficient heart muscle. I have also noted cases of high blood pressure for this sign, due to atherosclerosis. Generally speaking (one must view the entire chart), Aquarius and Leo are equally prone to cardiac complaints, but from opposite energetic sources.

Aquarius is also prone to all manner of blood cell diseases and insufficiencies.

Fatigue and Poor Absorption

This is the Saturn-ruled, mid-winter sign, standing opposite mid-Summer and the Sun! Perhaps more than any other sign, Aquarius is prone to vitamin and mineral deficiencies. The Sun ruled nutrients are especially suspect, including A, D, Magnesium and Iodine. Look also to C and Calcium, ruled by Saturn.

Aquarians typically crave sodium. Do Aquarian types require more sodium because neurotransmission is hypothetically minutely more active than in most other signs (except possibly Gemini and Sagittarius). Fatigue is common to the sign, so look to heart weakness, nutrient deficiency, and sub-oxygenation.

Depression

Aquarius is one of our sign types most prone to this malady. More so the night born Aquarian, and especially if also born during the Moon's waning phase. They need light, light, and more LIGHT!

I discovered this depressive tendency in "dark" charts long ago, implying a form of depression caused by astral light deprivation. Years later, the doctors announced their new discovery that yes, light deprivation caused some forms of depression. Curative light machines are now on the market.

Repetitively, I have witnessed many cases of Aquarians born at night, near the dark of the Moon who suffered this complaint. The Aquarian Sun or Moon alone can produce depression when in hard aspect to Saturn! This frozen astrological condition is traditionally assisted with warmth, spices, oiling, love, touch, pleasant music, nutrients, and light.

AQUARIUS SYNDROME

As discussed in Chapter Two, a Zodiac Sign Syndrome is a cluster of symptoms associated with the body zones and functions of a zodiac sign and the signs positioned on the seasonal wheel opposite (180°) and quincunx (150°, 210°, 330°) the sign. Remediating and supporting these body zones and functions act to bring the body into balance, diminishing the syndrome.

These symptoms may manifest when there is an emphasis in one or more of these signs. Planetary dignity plays an important role. These body parts and functions will occur either in strength, excess, deficiency, or disturbance, except solely in deficiency as seen for the opposite and quincunxing signs.

The Weaker Signs for the Aquarius Vital Force
Quincunx signs

The signs Cancer, Virgo, and Capricorn are positioned 150°, 210° and 330° distant from Aquarius on the seasonal wheel. These signs represent the 6th, 8th, and 12th *averted* angles from the sign Aquarius (see the illustration for this chapter). This condition makes it difficult for Aquarius to absorb the cosmic rays or the vibrational and light nutrients that feed these signs. Likewise, these signs may have trouble absorbing the rays from Aquarius.

Cancer rules Body Zone 4 which includes the stomach, bodily nourishment, breasts, fertility, thoracic duct, mucus membrane, gums, spleen (with Virgo), and moisture. Aquarius syndrome involves a lack of Cancerian nurturance and nourishment, both emotionally and physically. Perhaps some insufficiency in stomach enzymes contributes to the poor assimilation of vitamins and minerals common to this sign? Or perhaps, a lack of mother's milk in infancy? Or similarly, a neglect of motherly hugs and affection in early life? Cancer and Virgo govern the spleen (see below).

Virgo rules Body Zone 6 which includes the upper intestinal organs, spleen, digestion, sympathetic nerves, immune system (with Pisces and Mars), and gut efficiency. Aquarius syndrome may involve a lack of breakdown, absorption, and assimilation of nutrients.

Aquarius sits on the apex of a Yod between Cancer and Virgo. This elicits many ideas inclusive of poor nutrient absorption and assimilation. The spleen has a shared rulership between Cancer and especially Virgo. Could it be an impaired spleen function contributes to the blood cell quality issues typical of Aquarius?

Capricorn rules Body Zone 10 which includes the knees, gallbladder (with Leo), skin, teeth, bones, and bone building. Capricorn is the sign standing immediately behind Aquarius and therefore occupies the mysterious twelfth angle to it. Thus, Aquarius syndrome involves *fear of Capricorn*, a disdain for authority or outside control. Aquarius profoundly dislikes authority, timed regimens, and hierarchy, which are all hallmarks of Capricorn. The twelfth house position of Capricorn to Aquarius signals the psychological issues behind some of the physical health problems of the syndrome. Capricorn is also our sign of nutrient assimilation - deep to the bones. Perhaps we can blame some of Aquarius' nutrient deficiencies on its weak 12th angle being positioned at Capricorn!

Opposite Sign, Leo

When the Sun is in Aquarius, the opposite sign, Leo, "sleeps." **Leo rules Body Zone 5** which includes the heart, thoracic spine, aorta, gallbladder, and spinal sheaths. When there is a deficiency in Leo, it appears to fuel the syndrome. So often, we see the lazy heart muscle in Aquarius, with consequential low blood pressure and fatigue. This is a major key to the remediation of Aquarius Syndrome! (See also *The Circulation and Quality of the Blood*, above).

Signs Aggravating Aquarius Syndrome – Squaring Signs

Taurus and Scorpio are positioned 90° from Aquarius squaring this sign (see chapter illustration), creating friction, for good or ill. Aquarius can reflex with these signs, as well as its opposite sign (Leo).

Taurus rules Body Zone 2 which includes the thyroid, neck, brain stem, ears, throat, the upper esophagus, cervical vertebrae, mouth, lower jaw and teeth, vocal cords, and trapezius.

Scorpio rules Body Zone 8 which includes the coccyx, colon, bladder, nose, urethra, rectum, large intestine, excretion, sweat glands, and genitals. This square can produce autotoxicity.

How Planetary Dignity Contributes to Aquarius Syndrome

Strongest Planets

Saturn, Mercury, and Uranus are the strongest planets. They produce an excess of their color rays in this sign.

Saturn, the traditional ruler of Aquarius, and Uranus have an assumed co-influence over this sign. Modern Western astrologers give Aquarius as Mercury's exaltation. All three planets strongly influence the nerves.

Saturn 's cold and dry influence is prominent, especially in the highly focused, fixed intellect observed in this sign. It also influences the nerve bulbs, which appear to lack moisture in this sign, producing "static".

Uranus is the electrical planet, whose excess in this sign produces the spasms and odd electrical symptoms that Aquarius is so famous for.

The Weakest Planets

The Sun is weakest because it rules the opposite sign Leo and is therefore in *detriment* in Aquarius. A weakness of solar ruled functions and parts contributes to Aquarius Syndrome. The Sun primarily governs the Vital Force and heart, though influences the brain and eyes. A weak heart muscle, fatigue, poor circulation to the brain, and low blood pressure are typical manifestations. Over time, poor oxygenation and waste removal within the brain can lead to dementia. As said above, the remediation of the lazy heart muscle is key to Aquarius Syndrome.

Everything solar is in short supply: light, sun, color, warmth. Aquarius does well to imbibe these life-giving forces plus plenty of seeds, nuts, and color-rich foods, all high in Sol's essential Vital Force.

The Moon rules quincunx sign Cancer and is also notably weak in Aquarius. Poor nutrient absorbtion is one potential outcome.

Planetary and House Positions that Enhance Aquarius Syndrome

(1) **Sun, Moon, or Ascendant sign in Aquarius**

(2) A weakness in a body zone governed by the signs opposite or quincunx Aquarius on the seasonal wheel, as discussed above under *The Weaker Signs for the Aquarius Vital Force.*

(3) The Aquarius symptom cluster is accentuated when one or more of the Sun, Moon, Ascendant, Ascendant Ruler, Saturn, and the South or North Node is in Aquarius in the native's birth chart. This is compounded by the testimonies below:

- Aquarius inhabits the 1st, 6th, 8th, or 12th houses.
- Saturn square an Aquarius Sun or Moon.
- Saturn in Aquarius, especially in the 1st, 6th, 7th, 8th, or 12th houses.
- South Node rising in Aquarius or conjunct the Sun or Moon in Aquarius.
- Night birth, with the waning Moon in Aquarius, especially the Balsamic Moon.
- Mars, Jupiter, either Node, and sometimes Venus in Aquarius in difficult aspect to the Sun, Moon, Saturn, or Ascendant (especially if located in the 1st, 6th or 8th houses). This last is sometimes seen for Aquarian anomalous blood conditions, varicosities, and thrombosis.

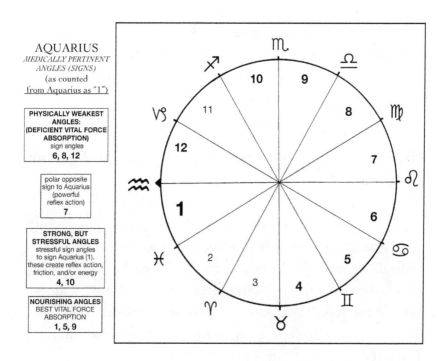

SYMPTOMS OF AQUARIUS SYNDROME

Please note that I am not discussing "Aquarius people" per se, but those born with prominences in this sign that actually do suffer the syndrome. These symptoms are not listed in any order, but simply as a list of collected observations common to natives of Aquarius. Please be sure to balance with *Aquarius's Superpowers*. As with any sign, there are just as many positives!

- sub-oxygenation, wants window open when sleeping
- craves salt
- haphazard or flipped meals like breakfast for dinner
- so absorbed in their project that they forget to eat
- bitterly cold extremities, cannot warm up
- difficulty maintaining internal heat (hypothermia prone)
- dementia
- fatigue
- anemia or other blood cell conditions
- weaker upper body with stronger legs, mostly in females. This occasionally reverses

- weak heart muscle
- deficient electrical-magnetic forcefield about the heart
- deficient oxygen to heart
- low or high blood pressure
- hypothyroid
- androgyny in females
- poor breast development in females
- poor circulation, especially the venous
- venous sluggishness, 'low blood' or varicose veins
- waterlogged ankles (typically minor)
- varicose veins, thrombosis, hemorrhoids
- cold sweats (Davidson)
- eyes sometimes set very far apart
- mental obsessions

- mental extremes and fixations
- is "a walking dictionary"
- annoys friends by being an authority on everything
- chronic depression
- political extremism
- verbal or written rants (more observed in males)
- excellent creative imagination, sometimes ungrounded
- "dry nerves"
- extremely sensitive nerves
- feels vibrations and thought atmospheres
- terror of electricity, (or works with it)!
- easily shocked (opens car door, turns on light switch)
- EMF sensitive
- most sensitive sign to barometric changes (Davidson and possibly Jansky).
- fatigued by bad lighting. Needs full spectrum light.
- sudden, powerful muscle spasms (lasting minutes or months!)

- very odd neurological and neuromuscular complaints that confound the physicians
- conditions that are hard to diagnose
- weak wrists or forearms
- deficient vitamins and minerals (no matter what they eat!)
- chronic depression
- feels neglected, unloved, different
- disinterest in babies, though loves coaching young people
- flees from the sound of screaming babies (Aquarius moon)
- sensitive knees
- may not have been nursed or cuddled as a baby
- intestinal stasis, low peristalsis, internal dryness.
- some tendency toward arthritis and rheumatism
- stiff, inelastic ligaments or tendons
- restricted Achilles tendon

- eccentric, mismatched, nonbinary or shocking fashion sensibilities
- attraction to blue, violet and purple clothing
- extreme muscular stiffness
- low or irregular libido (extremes)
- thinks sex is silly or stupid
- blood cell anomalies and deficiencies, blood diseases (rare, requires multiple testimonies)
- alcoholism in males
- experiences family ostracism or is a loner
- when young, has elderly friends, when old, has young friends
- can truly be friends with the opposite gender
- genius, but perceived as the family "nut" and misunderstood
- bone fragility, osteopenia, osteoporosis driven by mineral deficiency
- fine, thin, flyaway hair, sometimes balding
- scurvy, or symptoms of it
- insufficient digestion, absorption, poor assimilation of nutrients
- something outstanding about the shin, calf, or ankle, such as extreme length or width, multiple fractures, extra ankle bone, or bowed legs
- laughing fits, highly developed sense of the absurd
- dislike of crowds or conversely adores a crowd or an audience
- intense dislike of authority and bureaucracy
- great love of wild nature

REMEDIATION TIPS

Please note that these remedial tips are for interest only. The author is not suggesting that any person use these without the evaluation and consent of their personal healthcare practitioner.

What to strengthen?

Astrologically, one wants to strengthen the Sun, and the body zones governed especially by the opposite sign Leo, and Body Zones 4, 6, 10 (see previous section on quincunx signs). Consider strengthening the heart, quality of the blood, venous circulation, arterial circulation, oxygenation uptake, cellular respiration, and spinal sheaths. Bring warmth to the circulatory system. Improve moisture and the uptake and assimilation of minerals, salts, vitamins, and food.

The heart: The opposite sign, Leo, rules the heart, so this organ may need fortification. A traditional Renaissance method for strengthening a weak heart, imparted to me by late Aquarian native Dave Roell, was to hang a nugget of gold over the heart. This makes sense because the Sun governs the heart, and Sol's metal is gold. Renowned Renaissance physician and medical diarist Joseph Blagrave mentions the hanging of a small bag with three or five solar herbs as a treatment for a deficient heart. Hawthorne and Rosemary are my favorite solar herbs.

I've discovered that Turquoise works quite well. Turquoise contains both copper and iron, two metals that together are capable of generating an electro-magnetic field. One, two or five large beads hung over the heart appear to work wonders in some cases of heart weakness. If useful, a rise in energy is noted within three days. Amber also did the trick in one case. It is possible that both substances increase the magnetic field of the heart, which is the largest electrical generator of the body. *It may be unwise to hang these substances over the thyroid gland!*

Aquarian Syndrome fatigue and overall bodily stiffness: The stiffness appears in the muscles, rather than joints (this is more marked for fellow Saturnian-ruled Capricorn). Possible reasons include lack of oxygen, moisture, or nutrients to the muscle, poor cellular respiration, muscle contraction, low electrolytes, restricted circulation, excessive neural tension. I have observed the following items to work well together: A small handful of organic black raisins soaked in water until plump or cooked in cereal every day; nettle tea; beet powder; or a small to large handful of seaweed several times weekly.

Depression: As the midwinter sign, Aquarians need LIGHT! Perhaps no sign is as vulnerable to seasonal affective disorder as is Aquarius. The Aquarian type does well to exercise in the open air and often loves it.

Mineral and Vitamin Deficiencies: So often, Aquarian types present with a chronic deficiency of various vitamins and minerals. They can complain about how they include these in their diets to no avail! These deficiencies may constitute a significant cause of many of the Aquarian syndrome symptoms.

Some minerals (Saturn) are naturally grounding for electrical current. Copper and silver assist electrical flow through wires, so why not nerves? The body better absorbs and assimilates minerals ingested through herbal infusions and decoctions. For those that have no glucose issues, raw honey possesses many micro-nutrients. The right kind of table salt is essential for Aquarian natives. Homeopathic sodium (Nat Mur) may be worthy of evaluation. Aquarians love salt, often heavily salting their food. **Do they utilize it faster, thus needing more? Or are they somehow deficient?**

Aquarian type muscle spasms can come on suddenly, seemingly without warning or cause, being experienced almost like a muscular seizure, intense and quite painful. Once set in, they contract the muscle, causing the hapless victim to limp, or twist. These spasms can last days or months, before mysteriously relaxing. Here are some interesting ideas for treatment.

Along time ago, a wise man suggested to me that if these cases were due to an electrical "stutter" in the nerves, one might try applying the shock of a hot/cold/hot/cold shower applied to the spine. When comparing this reasoning to ancient European methods of curing epilepsy, we see a hint of the same reasoning. The idea is to somehow shock the electro-magnetic field into returning to normalcy. This idea was attempted once, and worked, though was reported as quite uncomfortable.

As an aside, strange cures for epilepsy included pouring water over crystals, then drinking it; or drinking water collected in a copper bowl under a Lunar Eclipse (do not try this)! Obviously, the ancient ones knew something about working with nature's electro-magnetic currents to cure epilepsy. Intuition suggests that this ancient methodology could also work for intense electrical surges and outages in the muscles, or the quick delivery of deficient cell salts, so typical of Aquarius.

Along these lines, I've discovered an herbal formula that simultaneously provides intense stimulation and relaxation. This reminds me of the hot/cold water technique that somehow resets the electro-magnetic flow. This formula has been entirely successful in two out of two trials, halting attacks of sudden onset, violent, muscle spasms. Prickly Ash tincture made strong in Apple Cider Vinegar. One-two tablespoons followed immediately by a classic sedative ("sleeping") tincture, such as Valerian, Kava Kava, Hops, Passion-flower, Skullcap, or St. John's Wort.

With Aquarius, one must always consider the ankle, calf, and shin. Always check if a misalignment of the lower leg is responsible for the spasms higher up the body chain! Stretching the Achilles tendon twice a day for two minutes has been found to alleviate one case of ongoing, lifelong Aquarian syndrome spasm of the hips, waist, thighs and sometimes the neck. The homeopathic cell salt Magnesium Phosphoricum is specific to muscle spasm.

Blood Quality: So often the Aquarian Type has poor blood cell quality. Sesame seeds are traditionally believed (in India) to help cure leukemia, a fact I've witnessed once. It is thought that they assist the integrity of blood cell walls. I understand that cancer is a very complex and intelligent disease, and we are making no claims for a cure.

Black raisins plumped in water (some prefer gin or vodka), beet powder and nettles are excellent blood builders. The People's Pharmacy gives ten golden raisins soaked overnight in gin daily. I have not found that necessary. The black raisins in oatmeal work great, as described above under *stiffness*. These cures take about three months. I have witnessed the blood improvement foods resolve lifelong stiffness conditions! It makes one consider if the stiffness is due to a lack of oxygen delivery to the muscles! (Note: Please obtain your physician's approval before attempting any "People's" cures!)

Venous Insufficiency: Nettles with Rue, *Ruta graveolens* (from Dorothy Hall – Rue is now considered obsolete by some modern herbalists due to its toxicity), Gingko, Gotu Kola, Rosemary, Cayenne (contraindicated if fragile capillaries), Sage, and Mullein. Daily leg activity and raising the lower legs. Varicose veins, hemorrhoids, thrombosis seem rather common for those born with an Aquarian emphasis. Mars in Aquarius often gives anemia. Thrombosis cases, especially of the lower leg, are often observed with Mars, Jupiter, either node, and sometimes Venus in this sign.

Fatigue: Davidson recommended a chilling cold-water dip for sub-oxygenated, fatigued, cold people! Their ensuing shocked response was thought to reboot the oxygen metabolism. In some cases, it would seem extremely dangerous to submit a frozen, low vital force person born in mid-winter to cold water. Especially if they were older and it was winter! However, I know one case of a classic Aquarius syndrome twenty-year-old, ever exhausted, who claims great energy obtained from her summertime swims in a live, flowing river. I believe this works to jump start a sagging electrical system! For Aquarius Syndrome, weird cures are often fruitful. (See disclaimer in front of book).

Fine Energy and Vibrational Cures: These may work well for some Aquarians, though be wary of oscillation. I've personally witnessed one Aquarian type temporarily paralyzed (for no discernible reason) through use of an oscillation machine; and a second case of sudden, inexplicable paralysis delivered by a homeopathic remedy administered at the precise minute of an eclipse! Because Aquarius is so strongly linked to electricity, one never knows what might occur when using strange vibrational remedies. However, the Jyotish have fascinating gem remedies that work through the application of various cosmic color rays.

There is a specific use of the blue sapphire, for the application of the cosmic violet ray that is used for specific cases of extreme neurological conditions. However, only experts should apply the blue sapphire, following analysis of the natal chart. In fact, this gem is rarely applied because it is considered dangerous unless there exist many testimonies in the natal chart in support of its use.

Food Color: Purple is the color of Aquarius on the color wheel, and sodium is the Aquarian salt. Dulse! Consider foods that are purple, violet, black, and yellow (opposite sign Leo). Orange and yellow-green foods treat the lost quincunxing rays of Cancer and Virgo. They also assist the eyesight, so useful for this sign.

Herbs

For poor Venus Circulation, low oxygenation, and insufficient capillaries: Nettles (*Urtica dioica*) with Rue (*Ruta graveolens*) (Hall) balances aerial and venous circulation and varicosities; toxic with incorrect use (see earlier note). Gingko (*Gingko Biloba*) and Gotu Kola (*Centella asiatica*) increase oxygen delivery and capillary strength. Rosemary (*Salvia Rosmarinus*) and Cayenne (*Capsicum*) used for warming and lifting sluggish, cold circulation; these are contraindicated if fragile capillaries. Sage (*Salvia officials*), Mullein (*Verbascum thapsus*), and Horsetail (*Equisetum arvense*) are used for varicosities.

Blood Quality: Beets, soaked black raisins, legumes, tahini (ground sesame seed, black preferred).

Spasm: Magnesium Phosphoricum (homeopathic), Prickly Ash (*Zanthoxylum americana* - endangered), Valerian Root (*Valeriana officinalis*), and Blue Vervain (*Verbena hastata*).

See also Chapter 15, *The Twelve Zodiac Sign Syndromes and their Relevant Herbs.*

Chapter Fourteen:

PISCES SYNDROME

C'est l'amour, l'amour, l'amour, qui fait tourner le monde
It is love, love, love, that makes the world go around.

The Saxophone

Years ago, I discovered that the classically unambitious Pisces appeared to be the least represented sign in those huge *Who's Who* compendiums published each year. However, there was an exception found. Pisces achieved a statistical significance above that of all other signs amongst famous jazz saxophonists. This makes perfect sense to me. The many Pisces natives I know care little for the limelight, preferring instead the sea, music, spiritual life, or romance (with the saxophone being a notably sexy instrument)!

Neither does this sign have the inner stamina for ambitious, high intensity lives. It seems almost "traditional" for that lone Pisces Sun (or Moon) member of a known rock band to be that one who dies young by overdose or suicide. However, those Pisces who learn to cherish their Vital Force will live to bless many. The mystically thoughtful and spiritual nature of this sign is easily observable in the sweet, wise, and twinkling eyes of Piscean natives Linus Pauling, Meher Baba, Ramana Maharshi, and Albert Einstein.

Fundamentals Refresher

Pisces Syndrome is a set of collaborative symptoms, consistently appearing together, which are typical for natives of the sign Pisces. The symptoms associated with Pisces Syndrome can be experienced by people with other sun signs when there is a particular emphasis in this sign. Zodiac sign syndromes can occur in seriatim, first one symptom, then another, weeks, months or years later. Few experience all symptoms. However, two or more of these symptoms are frequently observed clustered together at the same time.

A Pisces native may have few if any of the symptoms associated with Pisces Syndrome. Indeed, many Pisceans are specimens of perfect health. However, this symptom set often, but not always, evinces itself when the native's Sun, Moon, or Ascendant tenants Pisces and displays certain astrological conditions which are discussed at length in this chapter.

This chapter describes the astrological conditions that may aggravate the syndrome. With this knowledge, practitioners can explore the underlying condition when symptoms consistent with the syndrome present themselves in a patient. Understanding the energetic cause is the first step in remediation.

THE SIGN PISCES

In Classical Western Astrology, which uses the Tropical Zodiac, a Pisces is someone born during the thirty days (or longitudinal degrees) prior to the spring equinox.

As with all other signs, we cannot think of Pisces as an isolated single entity or a static constant. "Pisces" is a gestalt of strengths and weaknesses based on its angular relationship to the other signs of the interconnected solar cycle. In turn, each of the twelve phases of this cycle is influenced by the unique planetary configurations at birth and throughout the life. Pisces is a unique phase-state, with its interactions peculiar to the twelfth or last stage of the twelve-fold cyclical process.

Element and Mode: Pisces is the late winter sign of the mutable group. It is of the element Water.

Life Cycle Phase: Pisces represents the end, the twelfth stage of the twelve-fold human life cycle.

The infant breathes its first breath (Aries), nurses (Taurus), speech centers awaken (Gemini), emotionally matures and shields (Cancer), and achieves adolescence (Leo). Come Virgo, we perfect the body, sharpen our skills, serve, discern, and labor hard to maintain the physical world. In Libra, the soul takes pause, then Scorpio brings the struggle of purging and transformation. Freedom, independence, and a quest for knowledge arrive with Sagittarius. Capricorn is the time of reaping what we have sown, achievement, the mountaintop of the life cycle. In Aquarius the soul, having reached the mountaintop, moves past personal ambition to a consciousness of humanity, engagement in higher ideals or causes, or simply a release and floating through life.

In Pisces the incarnate soul prepares for dissolution. Having traversed the expansion of youth and the hard work, struggles, and ambition of worldly life, the soul now develops a consciousness of universal emotion, the unseen, the limitless. This stage also symbolizes the process of the soul's passing from the body, back to the astral world (or to nonexistence for those that do not believe in an afterlife.) This is the sign of entropy and universal feeling.

About Pisces

Nearing the end of the life cycle, there is a growing awareness of and sometime identification with the vastness of an infinite, unbound, universal consciousness and the expanse of universal love. Often the Pisces native can absorb themselves in religious practices of the devotional or the ascetic (life denying) variety. The "veil" is sometimes porous in natives of this sign, allowing involuntary visions, and psychic insights, both welcome and sometimes not.

The Piscean temperament can translate into mundane life as a practical lack of boundaries or organizational skills; an attraction to the whimsical, the ethereal, the gentle fluctuations of a flute, or the rise and fall of ocean waves. The harshness of worldly life is grating. The Pisces native does not relish battling the world for their piece of the pie. Rather, they are attuned to sacrifice. They are also attuned to the sensation of eternity, so the native may not be deadline prone.

The sense of self is weak in Pisces, which can cause the native to struggle to adapt to the pressures of worldly life. An understandable response is to withdraw from this unnatural fit and seek more comfortable terrain, such as monastic life, sleep, drugs, perhaps their own small apartment or hideaway (often at the beach), or a quiet nighttime job. Some Pisces appear "born tired".

Occupying the twelfth and final sign of the zodiac, the native shoulders what some might understand as "past life karmas", or for non-believers, the burden of involutionary and/or psychological issues. The native, who is more attuned to universal themes, may nevertheless face confinements, darkness, and depression. Positively, Pisceans often choose monastic, poetic, musical, or service-oriented lives.

Boundary Dissolution and the "War with Entropy"

As much as Pisces' opposite sign Virgo discerns, designates, and maintains boundaries, *Pisces dissolves them!* Metaphorically, Virgo says "no", Pisces says "maybe". My teacher said *"with Pisces, there is always some kind of boundary problem"*. One friend who permitted a stray cat to commandeer her clothes closet for a cozy kitten birthing nest, was aptly born with Moon, Jupiter and Ascendant all in Pisces. You might also note that Pisces types are either gigglers and chatterboxes, or remotely silent, sometimes alternating between these verbal extremes. Pisces types usually eat, sleep late, or romance to excess. I remember Linda Goodman's astute comment about how the wife of a wandering spouse hates it most for the 'other woman' to be a Pisces!

Pisces types experience life as a continual "war with entropy". In crude layman's terms, entropy is the universal law that returns all forms to disorder. In other words, without proper maintenance, everything eventually breaks down and becomes a mess. *This law of entropy appears speeded up in this sign!* You can readily observe this fact by observing how fast a new jacket or car will break down around natives of this sign! Clothes, shoes, objects... always fraying at the edge, or getting lost ("where is that sock?"), or falling off the table yet again, or perhaps their picture frames are always tilting on the wall! Unless a Piscean chart includes a strong Virgo, Capricorn or Saturn component, there is typically an issue with keeping hair, desks, and objects in consistently straight order. These themes of boundary dissolution and entropy (speeded up!) reflect in the physical symptomology of this sign. We will soon learn how!

Acceptance

Pisces is proverbially the most compassionate and accepting of all signs! These qualities reflect the Pisces-governed functions of the ECM, (extracellular matrix) and also, the gut porosity. The blood outlets nutrients into the "accepting" ECM. The cells dump their wastes into the "non-judgmental" waters of the ECM. In general, the opposite sign Virgo governs the discernment function of the intestinal wall and villi, whereas Pisces its accepting porosity.

Pisces Superpowers
Universal Access, Faith

For all its inherent delicacies, Pisces has extraordinary superpowers!

Pisces rules *the great oneness*, being the most universal of the twelve signs. Pisceans are at home in the universe, though not necessarily at home in the world. Natives of this gentle sign can have the ability to "grok" (comprehend) the entire gestalt with or without the intellect.

Piscean types can access the great universal source of knowledge when needed! For these natives, health direction can easily arrive through intuition or dreamtime experience, such as Grandma appearing at the foot of the bed.

A Pisces native with spiritual training may exhibit a unique ability to absorb needed Vital Force from Universal Supply. This is the perfect antidote for an innately weaker Vital Force. The field porousness of this sign works both ways! They only need to find the way.

Pisceans can demonstrate the ability to attract miraculous healings through prayer, angelic assistance, homeopathy, music, and other vibrational remedies. Angels seem to have a special affection for the natives of this sign! Yes, this can also hold true for those born with Moon or Ascendant in Pisces.

Natives of this season also evince an ability to access past life talents, often learning languages or musical instruments quickly through absorption, stunning those about them.

Pisces is the most sure-footed sign of the zodiac, often showing a fantastic talent for running around junk covered floors or obstacle festooned areas without falling! This trait also shows itself in the strange ability to emerge from horrific falls and crashes without damage, smiling. Despite some outer frailties, Piscean types possess a pliability that provides them with a considerable inner strength that prevents breaking in a storm. The strong pine breaks before the flexing willow!

Photographic memory for specific subjects is common, even while suffering brain fog in the present time!

To Encompass All Things

Pisceans are often gifted chameleons, readily blending into a social or cultural landscape as necessary or being invisible to the world. Some are even gifted linguists, readily adopting the dialect and mannerisms of their current environment.

Spiritual Protection

Pisceans are famous for strange luck, large inheritances, and somehow being supported with little effort. Perhaps all this is a product of their proverbial faith in Universal Provision, "Daddy will take care of it."

Physical Appearance

Exhaustive detail with illustrations is provided in this author's *The Astrological Body Types.*

PISCES BODY RULERSHIPS AND FUNCTIONS

As described in Chapter One, a body zone is a general box that overlays many organs, functions, vessels and their sub-rulerships. Anything within Body Zone 12 will feel the influence of Pisces. For example, Capricorn rules the bones, but Pisces natives are more prone to break them in the foot.

Pisces, Body Zone 12

Pisces famously governs the feet. Pisces will typically be noted in natal charts, or by current transit, when one observes accidents or symptoms in this area. Davidson states uniquely that Pisces governs the duodenum and cecum, although these are within the opposite sign Virgo's body zone - let us then consider these as co-ruled by this sign polarity. Cornell gives to Pisces the omentum and the serum of the peritoneum. These are also well within Virgo's auspices. Giving the omentum to Pisces makes some sense, it being a fatty, protective curtain, quite Jupiterian in nature, and unlike anything Virgo in character or function. Let us add to the Piscean influence within Virgo's zone by adding the lacteals (lymphatic vessels) stationed within the intestinal villi. Here, we would see the Pisces-Virgo polarity in perfect action within Virgo's Body Zone 6.

The Extracellular Matrix

This author assigned the *extracellular matrix* (ECM) to Pisces. Matthew Wood who wrote the breakthrough work *Holistic Medicine and the Extracellular Matrix* agrees with this assignment. This can be further updated. The ECM comprises the great ocean within - the various fluids, nutrients, and wastes drifting between the capillary walls and the cell membranes. The lymphatic fluids move from the capillaries into the matrix. The cells are nourished, and they in turn, dump their wastes back into this inner sea, to be pressed up into the lymphatic vessels with more, or less, success. Because Pisces governs wastelands and abandoned houses, I would postulate that this sign also *governs the wastewater within the matrix*. Further astrological rulerships and the immune system's cells, chemicals, and attack-defense strategy are postulated later in this chapter and also in the chapter on Virgo.

The Lymphatic System and the Three Water Signs

Let's explore how water signs Cancer, Pisces, and Scorpio have a role to play within our remarkable lymphatic system.

Neither ancient physicians nor modern medical astrologers have comprehended the lymphatic system well. Is the entire lymphatic system exclusively ruled by Pisces, with help from the lymphatic planets Moon, Venus, and Neptune?

Obviously, the thoracic duct and lymph nodes of the armpit are powerfully influenced by Pisces' fellow water sign Cancer because it rules the axillae (armpits). We have discussed above how Pisces most likely governs the extracellular matrix, and the interstitial fluids (outside the cells). The ECM engages 26% of our body's extracellular water.

It is my conjecture that the intracellular fluids (inside the cells) and the cellular membranes are under Cancer's auspices, as this sign pertains to hollow containers, cottages, protective walls, shells, wells, and enclosed spaces. Why then wouldn't the sign Cancer rule the cellular walls and their contained water within? Intracellular water is clearly a water sign "thing" as 67% of our bodily water is contained within the cells (intracellular fluid)!

And wouldn't Cancer then lord over the **lymph nodes** themselves, being that these lymphatic organs are enclosed containers for lymphatic tissue, actively serving as centers for lymph flow and filtration? Cancer is after all, the sign that *draws towards the center.*

To understand lymphatic flow from the astrological perspective, we might envision the tiny lymphatic capillaries as "streams" connecting to larger "rivers, the lymphatic vessels. These vessels in turn direct the "dirty" return lymph to pathogen and toxin sifting lymph ducts.

Individual sign and planet rulerships for these multifarious processes have not been established in medical astrology because the ancients did not understand this system and its parts. We will give a tentative stab at immune component assignment below and, more specifically, in the chapter on Virgo where possible sub rulerships for the immune cells are discussed.

It behooves us to consider how Pisces' fellow water sign Scorpio is involved in the defensive and attacking cells of the lymph nodes, welcoming drifting pathogens. The awaiting B cells bind to foreign substances and recruit other cells to help destroy invaders. The killer T cells attack and destroy pathogens. Scorpio is a martial sign! Although frontal attack is Aries, binding and destruction are both Scorpio specialties, as is waste removal. Passive Pisces does not reflect these qualities. Perhaps Pisces governs the ECM and the lymphatic fluids themselves (with the help of the Moon, and perhaps Venus, Neptune), whereas Scorpio governs the function of the lymph nodes? At any rate, we see how all three water signs have a role to play within our remarkable lymphatic system.

Sleep, Parasympathetic and Glymphatic Systems, Serous fluids, Lacteals

Pisces also governs the *parasympathetic nervous system*, as opposite sign Virgo governs the *sympathetic nervous system*. Pisces governs sleep, while opposite sign Virgo governs useful work. Pisces governs the processes necessary during sleep and dreaming. A possible Pisces rulership is the recently discovered *glymphatic system*, which is thought to cleanse the brain of cellular wastes during sleep, partially explaining the need for sleep.

Cornell notes that Pisces governs the *serous fluid* of the peritoneum (abdominal lining) and pleura and, with Venus, the intestinal mucus. Studying cases, it looks as though Pisces may in fact strongly influence the omentum and peritoneum, in balance with opposite sign Virgo, that governs the upper intestinal zone. The peritoneum does show some Piscean style functions through lubrication and by acting as a conduit for fluids, blood, and lymph through the intestinal zone.

Gut Permeability

In studying cases of leaky gut syndrome, I found that Pisces is almost always involved. Pisces rules porousness of boundaries, whereas opposite sign Virgo governs the upper intestines and boundary enforcement. We can thus readily speculate that Pisces governs the permeability of the gut lining, whereas Virgo rules the nutrient selective function. In addition to leaky gut, you might also see non-absorption issues with non-assimilation and malnutrition within the Pisces-Virgo polarity.

Though positioned in Virgo's body Zone 6, Dr. Davidson held that the duodenum was governed by Pisces, and that the cecum might also be influenced by this sign as well in certain planetary combinations. I've not uncovered his reasoning for this opinion but will watch for corroboration in case horoscopes.

Psychic Porousness

Pisces also governs our degree of psychic porousness and is strongly implicated in all manner of psychic problems, including what I submit may be past life memory hangovers, spirit interference, control by suggestive hypnosis, and so much more. Cornell notes issues of psychic mediumistic origin.

Glandular Coordination: Medical astrologers have cited Pisces' influence in coordinating the glands. That is interesting, considering that its ruling planet Jupiter was said by Edgar Cayce to govern the pituitary gland, which is the control center for many glands.

Other Possible Rulerships

Could Pisces govern the fascia? The fascia is structural (Saturn), but also flexible, fluidic, responsive, and a whole-body communication system. None of these qualities are Saturnian, but rather, Piscean to perfection!

Does Pisces rule the synovial fluids? Cornell says yes. One could speculate that all fluidic substances that allay friction between parts have a Piscean quality (also Lunar and Venusian) and, if oily, a Jupiter connection.

Ligament influence? Cornell noted something that I have independently stumbled upon in my work: that Pisces, with Neptune and Sagittarius, influence the ligaments. I have repeatedly witnessed these three indicators implicated in slippery ligaments! Cornell places the *fibro-ligamentous system* under Pisces. It is possible that Pisces may hold some co-rulership over the ligaments with Mars and Sagittarius (Cornell). More research is needed.

Cornell also notes Pisces strongly influences the matrix of the womb (Scorpio and Moon also govern the uterus). According to Cornell, Pisces governs the fibrin of the blood. However, the function of fibrin (to make boundaries) appears distinctly Virgo, the opposite sign. It is interesting in this regard to note the bleeding tendency of Pisces.

PISCES SYNDROME

As discussed in Chapter Two, a Zodiac Sign Syndrome is a cluster of symptoms associated with the body zones and functions of a zodiac sign and the signs positioned on the seasonal wheel opposite (180°) and quincunx (150°, 210°, 330°) the sign. Remediating and supporting these body zones and functions act to bring the body into balance, diminishing the syndrome. These symptoms may manifest when there is an emphasis in one or more of these signs. Planetary dignity plays an important role.

The Weaker Signs for the Pisces Vital Force

Quincunx signs

The signs Leo, Libra, and Aquarius are positioned 150°, 210° and 330° distant from Pisces on the seasonal wheel. These signs represent the 6th, 8th, and 12th *averted* angles from the sign Pisces (see the illustration for this chapter). This condition makes it difficult for Pisces to absorb the cosmic rays that feed these signs. Thus, Pisces natives may have trouble absorbing the vibrational and light nutrients of these signs. Likewise, these signs may have trouble absorbing the rays from Pisces.

Leo rules Body Zone 5 which includes the heart, thoracic spine, aorta, gallbladder, spinal sheaths. When there is a deficiency in Leo, it appears to fuel the syndrome. Many Pisces suffer some form of delicacy, combined with fatigue, leading one to wonder if a weak heart muscle is involved.

Libra rules Body Zone 7 which includes the kidneys, ovaries, lumbar spine, acid-alkaline balances, salt-water balances; and adrenal axis (with Aries, Mars). Is the ademic tendency of Pisces linked to poorly functioning kidneys? It is known that having sore feet (Pisces) is one symptom of weak kidneys (Libra).

Aquarius rules Body Zone 11 which includes the venous circulation, lower legs, ankles, oxygenation of the blood, cellular respiration (oxygen-carbon exchange), quality of blood, and electrical circulation. Pisces shares with Aquarius a tendency for sub oxygenation, and fatigue.

Aquarius stands behind Pisces and is therefore the twelfth house to this sign. Thus, Aquarius signals the psychological issues behind some of the Pisces-style physical health problems. Pisces syndrome involves *fear of Aquarius* - a disinclination for large, milling crowds or a purely intellectual approaches to knowledge.

Opposite Sign, Virgo

When the Sun is in Pisces, the opposite sign, Virgo, "sleeps." Virgo rules Body Zone 6 which includes the upper intestine, liver, duodenum, spleen, and pancreas. It influences the sympathetic nerves. When there is a deficiency in Virgo, it appears to fuel the syndrome. The Pisces natives I've studied definitely exist on the parasympathetic side of this continuum. They love to eat heartily, laugh, relax, and sleep late! The dishes can always wait.

Signs Aggravating Pisces Syndrome – Squaring Signs

Gemini and Sagittarius are the two Signs positioned 90° from Pisces squaring this sign (see chapter illustration). Squares create friction, for good or for ill. Pisces can reflex with these signs, as well as its opposite sign Virgo.

Gemini rules Body Zone 3 which includes the upper lungs and bronchial tubes, speed of synapses, peripheral nerves, capillaries, and speech. Pisces and Gemini are both noted for pneumonic tendencies and weak lungs. Is there a connection between slow lymphatic clearance, excess waste in the ECM (Pisces) and bronchial infection (Gemini)? This square also influences the mind, bringing either exceptional linguistic abilities and similar skills or stuttering or confusion.

Sagittarius rules Body Zone 9 which includes the coccyx, hips, thighs, locomotive nerves of lower spine, ligaments, CNS, and arterial system. This square greatly excites the higher mind, vision, religiosity, great largess, intellectual breadth, and imagination. This square is also noted in schizoid symptoms, and bipolar disorders. One also notes *hypermobility syndrome* (slippery ligaments),

How Planetary Dignity Contributes to Pisces Syndrome
Strongest Planets, Jupiter, Neptune, and Venus

The expansive planet Jupiter is Pisces' traditional ruler. The recently discovered and profoundly diffuse Neptune is a modern co-ruler of the sign, and a lovely fit! Sweet Venus, the planet of love, is exalted in Pisces, the sign the universal love. She bequeaths her relaxed, compassionate and romantic ways to natives of this sign and just as often, an excess of mucus! Jupiter governs the pituitary (Cayce), an assignment that explains the height, weight and size extremes so often noted for this sign. Jupiter governs expansion, fat, and too much of anything. Both Jupiter and Neptune lack boundaries and with Venus contribute to the atonic, phlegmatic, sleepy, and sexy excesses of this sign.

Weakest Planets

Mercury: Mercury rules the opposite sign Virgo, placing this tiny planet in detriment in Pisces. This is not surprising, as this is the planet of the everyday, practical mind.

Because Mercury is in detriment in Pisces, a weakness of Mercurial ruled functions and parts contributes to Pisces Syndrome. Mercury governs the alert, everyday mind, and efferent sense reception. Pisces natives are renowned for their sleepy ways. In this sign, the parasympathetic nervous system dominates the sympathetic and voluntary nervous systems.

Saturn: Saturn the ruler of boundaries (not a Piscean trait) is notably weaker in this sign, unless very well aspected in the natal chart. Saturn's tonifying, astringent, boundary defining, and strengthening functions are weakened in the season of Pisces, explaining many of the symptoms in reverse of these qualities (prolapse, hyper flexibility, running fluids, and the like).

Planet and House Conditions that Enhance Pisces Syndrome

(1) **Sun, Moon, or Ascendant sign in Pisces**

(2) A weakness in a body zone governed by the signs opposite or quincunx Pisces, as discussed above under *The Weaker Signs for the Pisces Vital Force.*

(3) The Sun, Moon, Ascendant, Ascendant Ruler, Saturn, or South Node is in Pisces, compounded by the testimonies below:

- Pisces inhabits the 1st, 6th, 8th, or 12th houses (See discussion in Chapter Two on Weak Houses).
- Saturn square or conjunct a Pisces Sun or Moon.
- Saturn in Pisces, especially in the 1st, 6th, 7th, 8th, or 12th houses.
- Jupiter, Venus, or Neptune are in Pisces in the 1st, 6th, 7th, 8th, or 12th houses. This is compounded when the Sun, Moon or Ascendant are also in Pisces.
- South Node rising in Pisces or conjunct the Sun or Moon in Pisces.
- Night birth with the waning Moon in Aquarius or Pisces, especially the Balsamic Moon.
- Neptune dominating the chart of a Pisces native, such as when Neptune is closely conjunct Ascendant, MC, Sun, or Moon.
- The Sun in Pisces, with the Moon or Ascendant in Cancer.
- The Sun in Cancer, with the Moon or Ascendant in Pisces.

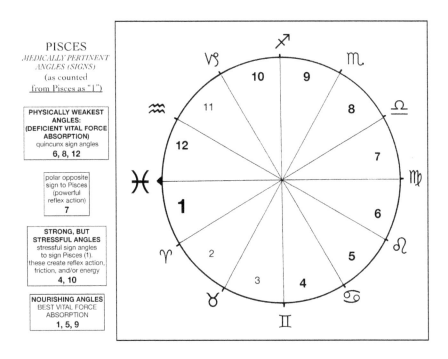

PISCES
MEDICALLY PERTINENT
ANGLES (SIGNS)
(as counted
from Pisces as "1")

PHYSICALLY WEAKEST ANGLES:
(DEFICIENT VITAL FORCE ABSORPTION)
quincunx sign angles
6, 8, 12

polar opposite
sign to Pisces
(powerful
reflex action)
7

STRONG, BUT STRESSFUL ANGLES
stressful sign angles
to sign Pisces (1).
these create reflex action,
friction, and/or energy
4, 10

NOURISHING ANGLES
BEST VITAL FORCE
ABSORPTION
1, 5, 9

SYMPTOMS OF PISCES SYNDROME

Please note that I am not discussing "Pisces people" per se, but those born with prominences in this sign <u>that actually do suffer the syndrome.</u> These symptoms can occur in seriatim, first one symptom, then weeks, months or years later, another. However, two or more of these symptoms are frequently observed clustered together at the same time. These symptoms are not listed in any order, but simply as a list of collected observations common to natives of Pisces. Please be sure to balance with *Pisces Superpowers.* As with any sign, there are just as many positives!

Please note that there are two quite different Pisces types. The delicate, graceful "yogi" type Piscean is less represented here. We are mostly describing the phlegmatic Piscean. However, both types suffer the mental, psychic, and psychological issues of the syndrome.

- hypothyroid
- pituitary extremes
- all manner of glandular and hormonal extremes
- growth extremes (rare), dwarfism, gigantism
- tired feet or foot issues
- large feet, foot anomalies
- dislike of enclosed shoes - prefers open toe shoes, loose shoes, or barefoot.
- shoe collections, or no shoes!
- slow healing of wounds
- weak immunity: easily catches bugs and slowly recovers from colds and flus.
- waterlogged, atonic tissues, edema, phlegmatic
- atonic, lazy heart muscle, or leaky valves
- slippery or hyper flexible ligaments
- elastic facial expressions (good at making faces)
- prolapse of various organs due to lack of tone
- atonic muscles appear to inadequately process proteins
- sleepy (sleeps for 9-12 hours)
- dislike of morning hours, prefers night
- intense dream life
- extreme sensitivity to sounds and noises
- depression and suicidal ideology
- sweet cheerfulness combined with neglect of worldly tasks and self-care
- low motivation or ambition
- very messy house, disorder, objects out of order (books on staircase, etc.)
- collects or hoards (adores books, antiques, photos etc.)

- oversexed (Pisces is the sign of sexual pleasure)
- financial dependency
- weak to temptations, poor boundaries, passivity
- remarkably sure footed
- past life memory hangovers,
- preference for earlier eras
- low psychic boundaries with possible spirit interference
- weak, cold kidneys
- weak heart muscle, or waterlogged heart
- feels cold
- fatigued, chronic fatigue
- excess mucus in gut, lungs, or nose
- edema
- sluggish ECM clearance
- sluggish lymphatic system
- prone to sluggish blood and lymphatic clearance of toxins, drugs, or alcohol. One often notes purple or pink skin blotches, boils, and carbuncles. Alcohol excess shows as purple skin blotches or swollen, discolored nose.
- excess gut fermentation and moisture
- sluggish peristalsis (or the opposite)
- pancreatic issues
- duodenal sensitivity
- alcohol intolerance
- escapism
- drug abuse or alcoholism fast leads to bad results
- addiction prone (Pisces moon)
- physical and emotional delicacy
- weak lungs and bronchial tubes (prone to pneumonia and wet lung complaints). Prone to all manner of lingering and/or dangerous lung complaints
- avoidance of routine work, frequent escapes to solitude, the sea, etc.
- low blood pressure,
- leaky gut issues (prevalent with South Node or Neptune in Pisces)
- inexplicably high blood cholesterol (noted for Jupiter in Pisces)
- huge appetite

- not thrilled about "being here"
- loves the ocean
- born tired
- psychic porousness
- psychic information interfering with everyday consciousness
- over impressionable
- weak willed
- weeps easily
- long-suffering over lost love
- overeats
- weak individuality
- timid, fearful, allows abuse
- delicacy on all levels
- prefers to avoid the world and hide from, or ignore, life's problems
- frequent escapes
- requires decompression time in solitude
- ignores reality until forced
- chronic depression
- nymphomania (rare, Pisces moon)
- great love of animals
- trouble saying "no"
- shyness
- weak, soft, sweet, tired quiet, or whiney voice, soft spoken

REMEDIATION TIPS

Please note that these remedial tips are for interest only. The author is not suggesting that any person use these without the evaluation and consent of their personal healthcare practitioner.

Wholistic Treatment: Pisces is the last sign, symbolizing the culmination of the life cycle. This oceanic sign represents the awareness of the whole universe, where all is one. It would therefore seem prudent to consider wholistic treatments for Pisces natives, attending to the whole body and psyche. Music therapy, yoga and foot reflexology are excellent. Also, decocted and infused herbs are highly compatible with this delicate water sign. Treatments that target the whole-body communication systems (such as the fascia or ECM) might be highly effective for these natives should all else fail.

What to strengthen? Problems often begin with the ankle (Aquarius) and foot (Pisces)! Stabilize the ankle. Check for pronation, inverted ankles, hammer toe, padding issues, and all manner of foot anomalies. Proper footwear is imperative (look down). Foot massage and reflexology are perfect for natives of Pisces. (Healthy Pisces have perfect feet). Should foot muscles be weak and painful, assist the kidneys and reinforce proteins (see below). Ligaments and tendons may need tightening.

Proteins: Many Piscean muscular weaknesses respond well to pre-digested amino acids and other forms of enhancing protein absorption. This season appears to have some trouble assimilating proteins.

The heart muscle: Pisceans can suffer from a lazy, fluidic heart. Improving the function of the heart muscle is imperative in these cases. Please see the *Remediation* Section of the Aquarius chapter under *The Heart* for suggestions for strengthening a weak heart muscle. These include hanging a nugget of gold, a pouch of soar herbs, or Turquoise over the heart.

Fatigue and depression: For this late winter water sign, give warmth and LIGHT! Pisces responds well to physical affection.

Stimulation: Natives of this cold-water sign do well with warming stimulant herbs, such as Ginger and Cayenne. Angelica might be particularly valuable because it does double duty with hormonal issues so prevalent with this sign. Warm food, warm drink, never ice.

Horseradish (*Armoracia rusticana*) is a superior lymphatic stimulant that is hot "to the fourth degree," containing antibacterial plus antimicrobial properties. Useful for "old" lymph stagnation, lung ailments, and UTI. Although more research is required on humans, horseradish is hypothesized as possibly preventative in stomach, lung, and colon cancer, plus possesses strong antioxidant properties. This herb seems a perfect fit for many cold, stagnant water sign issues and body parts, although it should be strictly avoided in kidney complaints.

Kidney and lumbar support: Piscean types might respond well to warming kidney herbs. In most cases, Pisces inclines toward the lazy, inefficient, wet, cold kidney. Matthew Wood mentions *Solidago* (Goldenrod) as a warming kidney remedy, and Pipsissewa (*Chimaphila*). We note a Libra-Pisces link active in the two herbs *Solidago* (Goldenrod) and *Verbascum thapsus* (Mullein) because they simultaneously assist kidney issues and tired feet (Wood). It is difficult to find warming diuretics. The lumbar spine should be kept warm and strong. For damp stagnation of kidneys: *Cnicus Benedictus* (Wood). See Matthew Wood's *Earthwise Repertory* for a significant exposition of kidney herbs by energetic imbalance.

Intestinal absorption balance: Pisceans may be prone to excessive absorption of nutrients through the gut wall (leaky gut syndrome). Conversely, food may process too rapidly through the intestine, creating a failure of nutrient uptake. South Node in Pisces in one of the health houses hints of this condition, if symptomatic.

Tonification: The phlegmatic type of Pisces Syndrome sufferer requires overall tonification. Everything seems sloppy about them, including the tissues. Herbs to consider: Horsetail (*Equisetum arvense*), Oat Straw (*Avena sativa*), White Oak (*Quercus alba*).

Slippery ligaments: Solomon Seal Root (Wood), Dandelion Root (for thumbs).

Excess mucus: Strengthen the lungs! Pisces are famous for weak lungs and should never smoke. Mullein is an herb for assisting the cilia (Wood). The warming, drying expectorants are useful in Pisces Syndrome. Wood says Gravel Root, and Golden Seal are great enemies of pus. Intestinal and peritoneal mucus may be excessive. Gravel Root, Yellow Dock (see Wood's *Earthwise Repertory*).

Cold, wet interior: Warm the stomach, intestine, and colon. Ginger and other spices may be useful for that purpose. Regular consumption of cayenne cured one case of Pisces cold colon with soggy, white coated tongue. Warm the portal circulation, the lymphatics, and the circulation.

Warm the circulation: Aquarius on the 12th angle to Pisces indicates a need in Pisces for better circulation, especially the venous.

Assist the Fascia: The fascia, though structural, has many Piscean qualities. It is flexible, adaptable, includes tiny water filled tubes, and forms a wholistic, all body, communication system. Pisces always indicates "the whole". Some Pisceans have marvelous results with Rolfing therapy.

Motion: Pisceans benefit by graceful, undulating motion! Think of the ocean. Dance, tai chi, hula, positive music are useful therapies. (Choice of music must be carefully selected to obviate psychic absorption of negative suggestions.

Depression: As the late winter water sign, give warmth and LIGHT!

Psychic Self-Defense: Pisces Syndrome is indicative of porous psychic boundaries. This also explains the Piscean requirement for extra sleep and diffusion time. Methods must be learned to strengthen the boundary to the other side, to stay alert, and to empower one's individuality. Natural herb amulets, religious symbols, various stones, flower essences (Walnut) are helpful. An education in psychic self-protection is a must! A bag of Juniper berries and leaves, worn about the neck, helps close the doors between this plane and the astral world (from a lecture by significant herbalist and teacher Deborah Francis RN). Others use pink yarrow. Various religious traditions have their methods.

Blood Quality: So often the Piscean type has poor blood cell quality, similar to Aquarius. Perhaps this is because Aquarius is on the 12th angle (quincunx) to Pisces. Sesame seeds are renowned (in India) for curing leukemia, a fact I have witnessed once. It is thought that they assist the integrity of blood cell walls. I understand that cancer is a very complex and intelligent disease, and we are making no claims for a cure.

Black raisins plumped in water (some prefer gin or vodka), beet powder and nettles are excellent blood builders. The People's Pharmacy gives ten golden raisins soaked overnight in gin daily. I have not found that necessary. The black raisins in oatmeal work great! However, beets and other magenta-colored foods may be in order.

On the color wheel, "Red-Purple" is the exact color of Pisces! I've noted that so many herbs and food of this precise color stimulate the cleansing of the kidneys, urinary tract, and colon. This is akin to Scorpio, but also useful for Pisceans, because these herbs also serve for lymphatic clearance. Hemorrhage and menorrhagia are common in this sign. Menorrhagic anemia can ensue. There are many excellent hemostatic herbs. Shepard's Purse and Yarrow come to mind. Alfalfa as a high vitamin K content. I knew one Pisces native who bled too long and freely from minor cuts. He was drinking regular Alfalfa tea for nutritive assistance. Following months on this regime, he sustained a minor cut and noticed the bleeding problem had resolved.

Lymphatic Cleansers: If anything, Pisces is the lymphatic sign (with sister water sign Cancer). The warming lymphatic cleansers would seem best, or the ones with the magenta hue. It is difficult to find warm lymphatic movers, as most are cold. However, many have the magenta-pink-violet hue we are looking for: Poke Root (*Phytolacca*), Red Root (*Ceanothus americanus*), Red Clover (*Trifolium pratense*), Sweet Violet (*Viola odorata*), Rhubarb (*Rheum rhabarbarum*),

Horseradish, *Armoracia rusticana* (hot!), and Burdock root (*Arctium lappa*). Burdock is a good candidate for Pisces Syndrome because it serves so many issues. Sassafras is a warming and hormonally balancing blood cleanser. However, if the "cold, moist" Piscean native craves the cooling, light green matrix cleansers, why not? But do not serve them ice cold and include a spice or stimulant for warming balance (with doc's approval). The highly cooling matrix cleansers include: Chickweed (*Stellaria media*), Cucumber juice, Cabbage, Green Grapes. It might also be useful to seek herbs that assist the brain's "glymphatic" system. Matthew Wood suggests Black Cohosh (*Actaea racemosa*) for "bunched up" cerebral spinal fluids. Calamus Root aka Sweet Flag (*Acorus calamus*) is famous to clear the confused mind, and strengthen the voice, (often weak in this sign).

For a short list of herbs for each sign see next chapter, *The Twelve Zodiac Sign Syndromes and their Relevant Herbs.*

Chapter Fifteen:

THE TWELVE
ZODIAC SIGN SYNDROMES
AND THEIR RELEVANT HERBS

"...Man, on the corporal side, is part of nature. Thus the key to the discrimination of physiological types in man is to be found in the correlation of men with their distinctive times and seasons, and especially with their origins in time..."

- John Addey, 1974

Several herbs per sign are entered here as "good fits" for our previously described Zodiac Sign Syndromes.

There are a great many *other* candidate herbs that have historically been used for these same health tendencies. Also, these herbs treat a multitude of conditions that may or may not have been discussed in this book. Therefore, the herbs listed here are not *exclusive* to these conditions, nor constitute the exclusive herbal repertory for syndrome remediation! In keeping with the space allotted, the author has selected a few herbs per sign that satisfy the more noteworthy issues of each zodiac sign. However, correct herbal choice varies per body type, physical examination, doctor's opinion, temperament, age, the weather, and so forth. See disclaimer, below.

The author has coined the descriptive term "Zodiac Sign Syndromes" to describe this empirically observed astrological phenomenon. Hypothetically, all syndromes can be paired to several relevant herbs - as well as to their specific zodiac signs. However, please note that the herbs listed below are not necessarily *ruled* by these zodiac signs! *Rather, these select herbs possess properties that are potentially remediative to one or more of the classic zodiac sign syndrome symptoms previously detailed in this book.* An excellent resource for assessing a wider array of syndrome-relevant herbs is *"The Earthwise Herbal Repertory"* by Matthew Wood.

Disclaimer: Herbs listed here are for educative and historic use only. The author is not providing medical opinion, direction, or advice. Herbs are medicines to be used only with the direction of your licensed health practitioner. Herbs contain phytochemicals (produced by plants)! Many herbs potentize chemical medications, or conversely, prevent their absorption. Some herbs are toxic and must be carefully dosed or taken for prescribed periods of time.

ARIES SYNDROME
Yarrow, *Achillea millefolium*
Traditional "blacksmith's herb" for "high blood", wounds, bleeding, and protection from injury.

Wood Betony, *Stachys officinalis*
Useful for headache, recovery from concussion, calming to head and nerves.

Borage, *Borago officinalis*
This herb is believed to help rebuild the adrenal cortex in cases of exhaustion due to protracted excess fight-or-flight stress. "Borage for courage."

Peach Leaf, *Prunus Persica*
Excellent candidate for irritated, hot, dry stomach membrane "Aries nausea"

St John's Wort, *Hypericum perforatum*
One of best articles for neuralgia and neuritis, abrasions, wounds, sunburn, and myalgia.

Passionflower (Maypops), *Passiflora incarnata*
Edgar Cayce's specific for epilepsy.

White Peony, *Paeonia lactiflora*
Assists recovery of mental function after injury. Also noted for use in epilepsy (in the Middle Ages a peony root was worn about the neck to prevent epileptic seizures).

Wild Bergamot (Bee Balm), *Monarda fistulosa*
Specific for tinnitus, vertigo, Meniere's Disease, and other disturbance of the cranial and sensory nerves (specific for taste and smell disturbance).

Arnica, *Arnica montana*
For shock. Used homeopathically or in spray bottles, pills, or as cream. Do not use it on open wounds. Herbalists report that Arnica works fast!

TAURUS SYNDROME
Cleavers, *Galium aparine*
Specific for draining fluidic pressure of the ear region.

Poke Root, *Phytolacca americana*
Traditional for sluggish lymphatics, clearing boils, and sluggish people (very powerful, dangerous in high doses).

Black Walnut Hulls, *Juglans nigra*
Specific for hypothyroid, reduces edema.
Plantain, *Plantago major*
Specific for swollen tongue.

Sweet Violet, *Viola Odorata*
Traditional specific for the upper lymphatic system, breast tissue clearance, anti-carcinogenic.

Blue Vervain, *Verbena hastata*
Sedative, antispasmodic, mental tension, and stubborn cases of epilepsy (not so typical of Taurus). However, for Taurus Syndrome, this herb is more useful for its famed reputation in reducing spasm and tension in the neck!

Calamus Root, *Acorus calamus*
Specific for strengthening weak vocal cords and improving vocal strength (take care with overuse).

Headache: Both the natal Taurus Sun and Moon are sometimes prone to hormonal headache or migraines related to mucus/fluid congestion. A large, detailed selection of herbal assists, listed by headache type is found in Matthew Wood's compendium, *The Earthwise Herbal Repertory.*

 Although too simplistic, favored candidates for "Taurus" headaches, might include Blessed Thistle *(Cnicus benedictus)*, Chelidonium (homeopathic), Black Cohosh *(Cimicifuga racemosa)*, Rosemary *(Salvia rosmarinus)*, Cayenne, *(Capsicum)*, Dandelion Root *(Taraxacum)*, and Pulsatilla *(Pulsatilla)*. Also see headache note for *Cancer*, below.

GEMINI SYNDROME

Sunflower seeds
Herbal specific for bronchitis and known to strengthen the lungs.

Oat Straw & Milky Oat Tops, *Avena sativa*
Nourishes the nerves (mores so the Milky Oat Tops); generally nutritive, and mineralizing (Oat Straw and Oat Water)

Coltsfoot, *Tussilago farfara*
Demulcent pulmonary herb

Lavender, *Lavandula*
Calming to mind and nerves.

Gotu Kola, *Centella asiatica*
May improve capillary circulation.

Parsley, *Petroselinum crispum*
This highly nutritive herb of multifarious properties is helpful to Gemini Syndrome because it both relaxes and assists the nervous system and strengthens the exhausted heart (sometimes caused by burnout, poor nutrition, and constant coughing).

Black Cumin Seed Oil, *Nigella sativa*
Specific to asthma, bronchitis, and stubborn hacking coughs.

CANCER SYNDROME:

Chamomile, *Matricaria chamomilla*
Gentles the stomach, calms peevish emotions.

Angelica, *Angelica archangelica*
Warming hormonal regulator

Horseradish, *Armoracia rusticana*
A superior hot lymphatic stimulant, also useful for cold, moist lung conditions and sluggish digestion. Antimicrobial, antibacterial, antiviral.

Red Clover, *Trifolium pratense*
Hormonal regulator, famous for removal, and walling off breast cysts, anti-carcinogenic.

Red Root, *Ceanothus americanus*
Traditional specific for splenic issues.

Sweet Violet, *Viola odorata*
Traditional specific for the upper lymphatic system, breast clearance.

Dandelion Root, *Taraxacum officinale*
Specific for the cleansing of breast tissue and assists liver cleansing.

Bilberry, *Vaccinium myrtillus*
Improves night vision.

Ginger, *Zingiber officinale*
Gentle stomachic and digestive stimulant, comforts stomach. Great for car, flight, and sea sickness.

Kelp, *Ascophyllum nodosum*
Specific for dyspepsia due to either duodenal ulcers or pyloric spasm. An antacid and toning effect on stomach (Eric F.W. Powell, PhD., N.D.). Also good for pancreas (co-ruled by Cancer and Virgo).

Peppermint, *Mentha piperita*
Relaxes tight and mucus choked bronchial tubes (do not take with gallbladder illness or any kind of hemorrhage). Traditionally used in combination with either Elder or Yarrow flowers for lung and bronchial congestion.

Headache: Both the Cancer natal Sun and Moon are sometimes prone to hormonal headache or otherwise fluidic pressure related migraines. A large, detailed selection of herbal assistants, listed by headache type is found in Matthew Wood's *The Earthwise Herbal Repertory.*

Although too simplistic, Cancer's hormonal headaches suggest Pulsatilla *(Pulsatilla)* for its hormone balancing properties. Whereas Yellow Clover *(Melilotus)* is best for blood congestion, being one of the strongest herbal blood thinners. Black Cohosh *(Cimicifuga racemosa) is* noted for moving congested CSF. Cayenne *(Capsicum)* is traditionally taken just as the "aura" comes on. Dandelion Root and Leaves *(Taraxacum officinale)* are liver assists and diuretics. Also see same note under *Taurus.*

LEO SYNDROME:

Hawthorn, *Crataegus monogyna*

A famous 'all purpose' cardiac herb. Regulates blood pressure up or down. Thought to increase arterial flexibility and assist in preventing clot formation.

Celandine, *Chelidonium majus* (homeopathic only)

Traditional specific for multiple gallbladder issues.

Motherwort, *Leonurus cardiaca*

Specific in some cases of heart palpitation.

Sumac, *Rhus coriaria L.*

Cooling and holds fluids in the body. Good for summer dehydration tendencies.

Yarrow, *Achillea millefolium*

Traditional "blacksmith's herb" for "high blood," flushed red face and palms, wounds, and bleeding.

Linden, *Tilia americana*

A calming cardiac herb, used in some cases of irregular heartbeat.

Ginger, *Zingiber officinale*

Helps reduce platelet stickiness and arterial plaque.

VIRGO SYNDROME

Milk Thistle, *Silybum marianum*
Assists in rebuilding damaged liver cells and in cleansing the liver.

Hops, *Humulus lupulus*
A mild sedative useful for irritability, anxiety, restlessness, and insomnia.

Yellow Dock, *Rumex crispus*
Specific for intestinal and colonic bleeding and ulcers.

Red Root, *Ceanothus americanus*
Traditional specific for splenic issues.

Gentian, *Gentiana lutea*
One of the best digestive aids and cooling, bile moving "bitters."

Skullcap, *Scutellaria lateriflora*
Assists with anxiety, insomnia, and nervous disorders.

Mugwort, *Artemisia vulgaris*
Improves function and coordination of autonomic nervous system, assists sleep and dreaming.

Black Cumin Seed Oil, *Nigella sativa*
Specific to asthma and a wide variety of stubborn intestinal complaints, gallbladder clearance, liver assistance, skin issues, eczema, and diabetes.

Kelp, *Ascophyllum nodosum*
specific for toning and assisting pancreas (co-ruled by Cancer and Virgo, clears gallbladder.

Marshmallow, *Althaea officinalis*
Soothing to dry, inflamed mucus membrane of digestive and urinary tract. Highly touted by herbalists for the Virgo malady diverticulitis.

LIBRA SYNDROME

Goldenrod, *Solidago virginiana*
An all-purpose herb for improving kidney function.

Parsley, *Petroselinum crispum*
A specific herb for nocturnal enuresis (bed wetting); high in potassium.

Royal Fern, *Osmunda regalis*
A specific herb for lower back pain.

Nettle (Seeds), *Urtica urens*
Famed specific herb for the treatment of kidney disease.

Sarsaparilla, *Smilax officinalis*
Balances out excess/deficiency of both male and female hormones; blood cleansing, acne. (Yes, also for Scorpio, below).

Lemon juice and Sea Salt
Possesses alkalizing effects, thus helping balance the blood's delicate ph. Assists in the removal of uric acid from joints. Sea salt chemically interacts with the lemon to make it easier on the teeth!

SCORPIO SYNDROME

Sarsaparilla *Smilax officinalis*
Balances out excess/deficiency of both male and female hormones; blood cleansing, acne.

Sanicle, *Sanicula europaea*
A powerful blood cleanser, anti-sepsis, assists in auto-toxicity related conditions.

Olive Leaf, *Olea europaea*
Kills many kinds of pathogens, bacteria, and viruses without bothering good bacteria (excepting in high doses).

Cranberry, *Vaccinium subg. Oxycoccus*
Specific for UTI.

Yellow Dock, *Rumex Crispus*
Specific for intestinal/colonic bleeding and ulcers.

Marshmallow, *Althaea officinalis*
Soothing to dry, inflamed mucus membrane of the digestive and urinary tracts. Highly touted by herbalists for the Virgo malady diverticulitis. May also assist irritation of the descending colon (Scorpio) and the Scorpio governed urinary tract.

Kelp, *Ascophyllum nodosum*
Tones uterus and a weak colon. Normalizes a weak or engorged prostate gland and removes pain in testicles (Eric F. W. Powell, PhD., N.D.).

Garlic, *Allium sativum*

Antiparasitic, antibacterial, antiviral. Assists in all manner of Scorpionic antigen issues. Specifically strong for ear and vaginal infection (see herbalist for correct use - do not apply directly to exposed membranes).

Horseradish, *Armoracia rusticana,* hot lymphatic stimulant, antibacterial, antimicrobial, antiparasitic. Useful for UTIs.

Lemon juice and sea salt

Possesses alkalizing effects, thus helping balance the blood's delicate ph. Assists in the removal of uric acid from joints. Sea salt chemically interacts with the lemon to make it easier on the teeth!

SAGITTARIUS SYNDROME

Blue Vervain, *Verbena hastata*

Sedative, antispasmodic, mental tension, and stubborn cases of epilepsy.

Wild Yam, *Dioscorea villosa*

Famous for assisting with hip issues.

Lemon Balm, *Melissa officinalis*

Calming, light sedative noted herb for hyperthyroid.

Burdock, *Arctium lappa*

Dorothy Hall's specific for sciatica.

Bugleweed, *Ajuga reptans*

Specific for hyperthyroid.

Valerian, *Valeriana officinalis*
Muscle relaxant, sleep aid.

Sage, *Salvia officinalis*
The Renaissance specific for "palsy."

St John's Wort essential oil and oil infusion *(Hypericum)* combined with Lavender *(Lavandula)* essential oil - excellent reputation in the quelling of neuralgia and neuritis.

CAPRICORN SYNDROME
Mullein, *Verbascum thapsus*
A specific for spinal and joint lubrication. Said to release synovial fluid into the bursa, and to help bones realign. Allays rheumatic joints and assists in dry, hacking cough where the protective cilia are worn down.

Burdock, *Arctium lappa*
Useful in dry skin conditions caused by poor lipid distribution and sluggish liver and kidneys.

Chickweed, *Stellaria media*
Perhaps the most cellular absorbing, deeply moistening herb (cooling).

Celandine, *Chelidonium magus* (homeopathic only)
The traditional specific for gallbladder issues.

Periwinkle, *Vinca minor*
Possibly reduces brain plaques that may contribute to Alzheimer's. Assists memory.

Celery Seed, *Apium graveolens*
Specific for clearing gout.

Slippery Elm, *Ulmus rubra*
Nutritive comfort for "dry" stomach, nausea, and inflamed mucus membrane through the entire digestive tract. **Endangered plant**. A less nutritive alternative is Marshmallow Root.

Black Cumin Seed Oil, *Nigella sativa*
Useful for gallbladder problems, eczema, joint pains, stiffness, and all manner of skin problems.

Ginger, *Zingiber officinale*
Gentle stomachic and digestive stimulant, comforts stomach, good for car, flight, and sea sickness.

AQUARIUS SYNDROME

Rosemary, *Rosmarinus officinalis*
Lifts low blood, useful in purple blood at ankle, low blood pressure, headache.

Ginkgo, *Ginkgo biloba*
Oxygenating.

Nettles, *Urtica dioca*
Traditional herb for anemia, weak blood, poor circulation, and iron deficiency.

Prickly Ash, *Zanthoxylum americanum*
Muscular and circulatory antispasmodic, neural pain relief, and opens capillary circulation.

Cayenne, *Capsicum*
The most potent internally heating herb, warms, vivifies, and increases blood flow to the extremities.

Gotu Kola, *Centella asiatica*
May improve and open capillary circulation.

Beet root, *Beta vulgaris*
Blood builder, anti-anemia, assists brain function.

St John's Wort, *Hypericum perforatum*
One of best articles for neuralgia, neuritis, and depression. Combines synergistically with Lavender.

Dulse, *Palmaria palmata*
When dried, possesses the purple color associated with Aquarius on the artist's color wheel.

Periwinkle, *Vinca minor*
Tests suggest this herb actively assists in the prevention or removal of brain plaques, thus possibly preventative of memory related disorders.

PISCES SYNDROME

Seaweeds (Dulse, Kelp, et al)

Hypothetically, seaweed supports the extracellular matrix. Also, many species show the magenta (purple-red) hues associated with this sign's personal Vital Force color on the artist's color wheel. Excellent whole-body remedy, serving many organs.

Ground Ivy, *Glechoma hederacea*

Noted specific for purulent wounds, chronic waste, rot, excess pus, and for strengthening the immune system.

Horseradish, *Armoracia rusticana*

A superior hot lymphatic stimulant, also useful for cold, moist lung conditions and sluggish digestion

Red Root, *Ceanothus americanus*

One of the most favored clearing herbs for the extracellular matrix and the lymphatic system. Also helps with weak immunity, making it more difficult for bacteria to settle on or penetrate capillary walls

Fenugreek, *Trigonella foenum graecum*

Convalescent herb and warming lymph cleanser.

Ashwagandha, *Withania somnifera*

Adaptogenic, strengthens the Vital Force, improves cell-mediated immunity, balances the reproductive hormones, and overall supports adapting to stress.

Beet root, *Beta vulgaris*
Blood builder, anti-anemia, and assists brain function. Beet root color provides the perfect color ray for Pisces!

Maca Root, *Lepidium meyenii*
A deep strengthening slow working herb. Assists in frailty, fatigue, low stamina, and increases libido. Sexy Pisces rarely needs the later!

Peppermint, *Mentha piperita*
Relaxes tight and mucus choked bronchial tubes (do not take with gallbladder illness or any kind of hemorrhage). Traditionally used in combination with either Elder or Yarrow flowers for lung and bronchial congestion.

Calamus Root (Sweet Flag), *Acorus calamus*
A powerful herb for clearing a confused brain, and for strengthening the weak voice. Correct dose and length of use essential. Popular in Chinese Medicine, but on "cautions" list in the West.

EPILOGUE

"...There is a curious thing if you study the human body in the zodiac. You know many think the zodiac is an accidental business. You know what the astronomers believe; they believe the zodiac as born on the banks of the Nile, that the shepherds at night were watching their flocks and they were drinking and so they began to imagine that they saw things. That is their idea. Now, the zodiac is one of the greatest mysteries, even occultly little has been said about it. As a matter of fact, invisibly every one of those great constellations has a form that has been "imagined" there, is there. Be that as it may, you notice if you start at "Taurus" the mouth, then skip Gemini, you come to Cancer, the stomach, every other sign follows the digestion, then Scorpio, the colon. And if you study a great many other things, in the zodiac, you'll soon get insight enough to reveal there is something very deep behind it, and it is not an accidental business..."

Dr. William M. Davidson
Davidson's Medical Lectures
Edited by Vivia Jayne, 1979

BIBLIOGRAPHY of
MEDICAL ASTROLOGY
Compiled by Judith Hill

This student-requested medical astrology-oriented bibliography was originally compiled for the benefit of students of *The Academy for Astrological Medicine*. It is not possible to represent all extant literature in this field, nor to include all significant authors! Neglect of any work or author does not imply that this author has done so deliberately. Furthermore, new books continue to appear frequently in this field. That being said, all but a few titles represented below are favorite books of the author! And, in some manner, great or small, each added to the knowledge bank necessary for the writing of this present work.

This list comprises a comprehensive collection of works representing most of our many sub-branches of astrological medicine. This list is categorized by sub-branches, to assist in locating books specific to an immediate need or interest.

Table of Contents
Categories of this bibliography are arranged in the following manner:

- Astro-genetics
- Astrophysiognomy (appearance and physical type)
- Astrological Herbology
- Basics (significant general books)
- Death
- Degrees
- Dictionaries and Encyclopedias
- Fertility and Conception
- Gems-Metals-Colors in Astrology; Eclipses

- Herbal Medicine in Astrology (includes flower essences, homeopathy)
- Historical Techniques and Writings
- Lunar Nodes: medical significations
- Lunar Nodes: medical transits of; Midpoints (medical)
- Nutrition and Cell Salts (medical)
- Science, Research and Testimony (supportive to physical astrology Surgery and Elections (date selections for medical procedure)
- TCM (Traditional Chinese Medicine and medical astrology)
- Transits (medical)

ASTRO-GENETICS

The Mars-Redhead Files, Stellium Press, 2000 (research compendium with astrologers, Judith A. Hill and Jacalyn Thompson)

Hill, Judith. *"Astrogenetics"* Class lecture, The Academy for Astrological Medicine, available at AcademyForAstrologicalMedicine.com

ASTROPHYSIOGNOMY (Appearance and Physical Type)

Anrias, David, *Man and the Zodiac,* E.P. Dutton and Company, New York, 1938

Barrett, F., *Astrological Physiognomy,* Aries Press, Chicago, 1941

Cornell, H. L., M.D., L.L.D., *The Encyclopaedia of Medical Astrology,* Llewellyn Publications and Samuel Weiser, 1972. (Note: this title includes a great deal of detail on physical appearance.)

Duff, Howard M., *Astrological Types,* 1948 (really good!)

Hall, Manly P., wrote a delightful, illustrated pamphlet on the zodiac facial (or planetary?) facial types. However, I cannot seem to find the title name on the web (my copy is misplaced).

Hill, Judith. *"Astrophysiognomy: Physical Appearance & The Astrological Birth."* Class lecture, The Academy for Astrological Medicine, available at AcademyForAstrologicalMedicine.com

Hill, Judith, *The Astrological Body Types*, revised and expanded, Stellium Press, 1997 (available through Book People, A.F. A. Inc.).

Hill, Judith, " *Astrological Heredity - New Evidence, New Thoughts,*" *Borderlands*, a Quarterly Journal of Borderland Research (Borderland Research Science Foundation), 1996; reprinted in the below compendium.

The Mars-Redhead Files: *A Scientific Test of Astrological Tradition*, Research of The Redheads Project 1986-1998, compiled by Judith Hill, inclusive of research by Hill and Hill and Jacalyn Thompson.

King, Chauncey, *Know Your Horoscope for Accurate Horoscope Making*, American Federation of Astrologers, Inc. Tempe, AZ, 1927

Vettius Valens of Antioch, *Anthology, Book 1*, Chapter 21, Translated by Andrea Gehrz, Moira Press, 2011

Porphyry of Tyre, *An Introduction to the Tetrobiblios of Ptolemy*, 44, 45, translated by Andrea Gehrz, Moira Press, 2011

BASICS
Medical Astrology and General. All levels represented.
Brennan, Chris, *Hellenistic Astrology*

Coppock, Austin, 36 Faces: *The History, Astrology and Magic of the Decans*

Cramer, Diane, *How to Give an Astrological Health Reading* 1983

Davidson, William, *Davidson's Medical Lectures*, Chapter 2, pg. 13, edited by Vivia Jayne, The Astrological Bureau, Monroe, New York, 1979

Frawley, David, *Sports Astrology* (this writer has some very good texts on Ayurvedic Medicine). This particular work might interest students researching what astrological indicators signify different muscle groups and functions, or nervous system dominances (as shown by different the sports represented).

Garrison, Omar, *How Medical Astrology Works*

Heindel, Max, *Astro-Diagnosis, A Guide to Healing*

Hill, Judith. "*Medical Astrology 101.*" Full Online Course, The Academy for Astrological Medicine, available at AcademyForAstrologicalMedicine.com

Hill, Judith. "*Planetary Dignity: Assessing Planetary Dignity and Strength.*" Full Online Course, The Academy for Astrological Medicine, available at AcademyForAstrologicalMedicine.com

Hill, Judith. "*Elective timing for Important Life Events.*" Class Lecture, The Academy for Astrological Medicine, available at AcademyForAstrologicalMedicine.com

Hill, Judith. "*The Art of Astrological Timing*" Full Online Course, The Academy for Astrological Medicine, available at AcademyForAstrologicalMedicine.com

Hill, Judith. "*Medical Astrology Tools & Techniques.*" Full Online Workshop, The Academy for Astrological Medicine, available at AcademyForAstrologicalMedicine.com

Hill, Judith, *Medical Astrology: A Guide to Planetary Pathology*

Jansky, Robert Carl *Modern Medical Astrology*, p. 86-90, Astro-Analytics Publications, Van Nuys, California, 1978

Jansky, Robert Carl: *Astrology, Nutrition and Heath*, Para Research, 1977

Millard, Ruth, *Case Notes of a Medical Astrologer*, Red Wheel, Weiser, 1980.

Montgomery, Ruth, *Born to Heal: The Amazing True Story of Mr. A. and the Astonishing Art of Healing with Life Energies*, Montgomery, Alabama, 1973

Morris, William PH.D. *Cycles in Medical Astrology*, 2018 (this work is a strong example of 'post modern' medical astrology. Curiously, Morris was the first person who gave this term to this author.) See 'Post Modern' in our Academy Glossary.

Nauman, Eileen, *Medical Astrology*, DHM, Blue Turtle Publishing, Cottonwood, Arizona, 1982.

Ridder-Patrick, Jane, *A Handbook of Medical Astrology*, Penguin Books, London, NY, 1990.

Starck, Marcia, *Healing with Astrology*, 1997.

Paramahansa Yogananda, *The Bhagavad Gita*, Royal Science of God-Realization, pp. 60, 365, 497-506, 573-76, 848, 670, 798 Self Realization Fellowship, 1996 3. Ibid.

Manolesco, Sir John, Count of Romagna, *Scientific Astrology, Introduction*, pp.12-13, Pinnacle Books, NYC, 1973

Waage, Erin. *"Astrology 101: Learn How to Read a Birth Chart."* Full Online Course, The Academy for Astrological Medicine, available at AcademyForAstrologicalMedicine.com

William Davidson, *Davidson's Medical Lectures*, Chapter 2, pg. 13, edited by Vivia Jayne, The Astrological Bureau, Monroe, New York, 1979

Zain, C.C. (Elbert Benjamin), *Natal Astrology: Vitality, Health and Disease*, Church of Light1924

Zain, C. C. (Elbert Benjamin), *Astral Vibrations*, Church of Light, 1923,

Zain, C.C. (Elbert Benjamin), *Stellar Healing*

DEATH

Carter, C.E.O., *The Astrology of Accidents*, Theosophical Publishing House, LTD, 1977

Hill, Judith. *"The Astrology of Death: Transit Indicators in the Birth Chart."* Class lecture, The Academy for Astrological Medicine, available at AcademyForAstrologicalMedicine.com

Hill, Judith, *The Lunar Nodes, Your Key to Excellent Chart Interpretation*, Chapter 12 "Death and The Lunar Nodes", Stellium Press, 2009

Hill, Judith, *Medical Astrology, A Guide to Planetary Pathology*, Chapter 19, Stellium Press, 2005

Hill, Judith, *Astrology & Your Vital Force: Healing with Cosmic Rays and DNA Resonance*, (includes dedicated discussion, questioning and comparison of traditional gender-based doctrines for determining the Hyleg).

Jansky, Robert Carl *Modern Medical Astrology*, p. 86-90, Astro Analytics Publications, Van Nuys, California, 1978 (nice section on the Hyleg)

Houck, Richard, *The Astrology of Death*, Groundswell Press, 1994

Davidson, William, *Davidson's Medical Lectures*, Chapter 1, p. 4, Edited by Vivia Jayne, The Astrological Bureau, Monroe, N.Y., 1979

Lilly, William, *An Introduction to Astrology*, Newcastle Publishing Company, Inc., Hollywood, California, 1972, (written in 1647) See chapter on the 8th house. (Lilly's Christian Astrology contains similar observations.)

Note: Many ancient and Renaissance writers (Ptolemy, Blagrave, Lilly, et al) have sections on assessing longevity - of great concern in times when the average lifespan was below 40!

ZODIAC DEGREES (MEDICAL)

Carter, C.E.O., The Astrology of Death, Theosophical Publishing House, LTD, 1977

Hill, Judith, (compendium of disease degrees), from observations of Donna Walter Henson, the Ebertins (below), D.E.O. Carter, Nicholas Devore plus the author's case files, *Medical Astrology, A Guide to Planetary Pathology*, pages 23-26.

Ebertin, Reinhold and Elsbeth, "Anatomishe Entssprechungen Der Tierkreisgrade".

DICTIONARIES AND ENCYCLOPEDIAS

Cornell, H. L., M.D., L.L.D., *The Encyclopedia of Medical Astrology*, Llewellyn Publications and Samuel Weiser, 1972

DeVore, Nicholas, The Dictionary of Astrology

Gettings, Fred, The Encyclopedia of Astrology

Rex, Bills, *The Rulership Book*. (This classic includes items ruled by signs, planets, houses. The knowledge of specific item rulership is useful to all astrologers.)

Jansky, Robert Carl, *Getting Your Correct Birth Data*, Astro-Analytics Publications, Venice, California, 1975

Rodden, Lois M. *The American Book of Charts*, 1982 (although the focus is not medical, this chart collection includes many bizarre medical cases)

ECLIPSES (medical influence)

Hill, Judith, *Eclipses and You: How to Align with Life's Hidden Tides*, Stellium Press, 2013

Hill, Judith. *"Lunar Nodes and Eclipses."* Full Online Course, The Academy for Astrological Medicine, available at AcademyForAstrologicalMedicine.com

FERTILITY AND CONCEPTION

Astrological Birth Control: A Report on the work of Dr. Eugen Jonas by Sheila Ostrander and Lynn Schroeder, Prentice-Hall, Inc. 1972

Hill, Judith. *"Astrology of Fertility 1: Conception Techniques."* Online Course, The Academy for Astrological Medicine, available at AcademyForAstrologicalMedicine.com

Hill, Judith. *"Astrology of Fertility 2: Prenatal Preparation & Other Essentials."* Online Course, The Academy for Astrological Medicine, available at AcademyForAstrologicalMedicine.com

Porphyry of Tyre, (234-305 CE) *Ensoulment*, Translated by Andrea Gehrz, Moira Press, 2015

GEMS, METALS, COLORS, AND ASTROLOGY

Beckman, Howard, *Vibrational Healing with Gems* (discusses lamp technique, more)

Bhattacharya, A.K. and Ramchandra, D.N., *The Science of Cosmic Ray Therapy or Teletherapy*, Firma KLM Private LTD, Calcutta, 1976

Bhattacharya, Benoytosh, M.A., PH.D., revised and enlarged by A.K. Bhattacharya, *Gem Therapy*, Firma KLM Private LTD., Calcutta, India 1992

Case, Paul Foster, *Correlation Color and Sound, B.O.T.A. Text 2*, Builders of the Adytum, 1931

Johari, Harish, *The Healing Power of Gemstones in Tantra, Ayurveda, Astrology* Destiny Books, Rochester, Vermont, 1988

Bhattacharjee, Shivaji, *Astrological Healing Gems*, Passage Press, Salt Lake City, UT, 1990 Howard Beckman, *Vibrational Healing with Gems*, Balaji Publishing House, Pecor, NM; Gyan Publishing House, New Delhi, no date given

Brown, Richard S., G.I.A., *Ancient Astrological Gemstones & Talismans*, A.G.T. Co. Ltd., Publishers, Bangkok, Thailand, 1995

Hunt, Ronald, Dr., Seven Keys to Cosmic Healing

Kapoor, Dr. Gouri Shanker, *Gems & Astrology*, Ranjan Publications, New Delhi, India, 1985

Jain, Manik Chand, *The Occult Power of Gems*, Ranjan Publications, New Delhi, India, 1988

Uyldert, M., *Metal Magic: The Esoteric Properties and Uses of Metals*, Turnstone Press Limited, UK, 1980

Davison, Alison, *Metal Power, The Soul Life of the Planets*, Borderland Sciences Research Foundation, Garberville, California,1991

Hill, Judith. *"Traditional Gem & Herbal Antidotes for Planetary Conditions."* Full Online Course, The Academy for Astrological Medicine, available at AcademyForAstrologicalMedicine.com

Kollerstrom, Nicholas, *The Metal Planet Relationship*, Borderland Sciences Research Foundation, Garberville, California, 1993

Saha, N.N., *Stellar Healing*. (a classic)

Saha, N. N., *Speaking of Healing Through Gems*

Tansley, David V., D.C., *Radionics & the Subtle Anatomy of Man*, Health Sciences Press, *Bradford, Devon, Holsworthy, England, 1972.*

HERBAL MEDICINE (ASTROLOGICAL)
Flower Essences, Homeopathy, in Practice
Allen, Cameron. *"Wellness Practice: Harnessing Your Skills to Get Started with Clients & Blinded Case Studies."* Online Class lecture and notes, The Academy for Astrological Medicine, available at AcademyForAstrologicalMedicine.com

Brooke, Elisabeth, *Traditional Western Herbal Medicine*: As Above So Below, Aeon Books, 2019

Blagrave, Joseph, *Blagrave's Physick*, p. 147, London, 1671, edited by David R. Roell, Astrological Classics, 2010 (includes a great deal of herbal information relative to the era.)

Culpeper, Nicholas, *Culpeper's Complete Herbal*, England, 1653.

Gailing, Stephanie, *Planetary Apothecary*, Groundswell Press, 2009:

Gailing, Stephanie, *The Complete Guide to Astrological Self Care*, Groundswell Press, 2021

Hill, Judith. *"Astrological Herbalism Decoded."* Full Online Course, The Academy for Astrological Medicine, available at AcademyForAstrologicalMedicine.com

Hill, Judith. *"Twelve Zodiac Signs, 36 Herbs."* Class Lecture, The Academy for Astrological Medicine, available at AcademyForAstrologicalMedicine.com

Hill, Judith. *"Lunar Secrets of Herbal Crafting."* Class lecture, The Academy for Astrological Medicine, available at AcademyForAstrologicalMedicine.com

Hill, Judith. *"Lunar Secrets of Herbal Administration."* Class lecture, The Academy for Astrological Medicine, available at AcademyForAstrologicalMedicine.com

Hill, Judith, *Medical Astrology in Action*, Stellium Press, 2019 (includes herbal tips for most transit conjunctions and chapter specifically for herbalists on how to utilize the Moon).

Muir, Ada, *The Healing Herbs of the Zodiac*, Llewellyn Publications, 1974

Nauman, Eileen, *Medical Astrology*, DHM, Blue Turtle Publishing, Cottonwood, Arizona, 1982. (Solid herbal and homeopathic sections)

Sajah Popham, *Evolutionary Herbalism* (includes traditional astrological herbalism and fantastic sections on alchemy), North Atlantic Books

Wood, Matthew, *The Practice of Traditional Herbalism*, North Atlantic Books, Berkeley, California, 2004

HISTORICAL TECHNIQUES, DIARIES AND WRITINGS
(Decumbiture, Renaissance Techniques, Medieval Medicine, Biographies, Physician Diaries)

Ashmole, Elias: His Autobiographical and Historical Notes (1600s)

Brennan, Chris, *Hellenistic Astrology: See 'Iatromathematica', 'Melothesia'* 1.

Brooke, Elisabeth, *Traditional Western Herbal Medicine: As Above So Below*, Aeon Books, 2019

Blagrave, Joseph, *Blagrave's Physick*, p. 147, London, 1671, edited by David R. Roell, Astrological Classics, 2010

Culpeper, Nicholas, *Astrological Judgement of Diseases from the Decumbiture of the Sick*, 1655

Lilly, William: *Christian Astrology*, 1647 (see 6th and 8th house questions)

Mount, Tony, *Medieval Medicine*, Amberly, 2015

Ptolemy, Claudius, *Tetrobiblios*, 140 CE, Books 111 and 1V (physical astrology references)

Popham, Sajah, *Evolutionary Herbalism* (includes traditional astrological herbalism and fantastic sections on alchemy), North Atlantic Books

Saunders, Richard, *The Astrological Judgement of the Practice of Physick*, 1677

Wood, Matthew, *The Practice of Traditional Herbalism*, North Atlantic Books, Berkeley, California, 2004

LUNAR NODES (MEDICAL, NATAL, TRANSIT AND COLLECTIVE)

Hill, Judith, *The Lunar Nodes: Your Key to Excellent Chart Interpretation*, Stellium Press (chapter on Medical Nodes)

Hill, Judith, *Medical Astrology in Action, The Transits of Health* (see chapters on North and South Lunar Nodes), Stellium Press, 2019. Includes medically interpretive sections on transits of all planets to the nodes, and transits of the nodes to all planets, and through all signs and elements.

Hill, Judith. *"Lunar Nodes and Eclipses."* Full Online Course, The Academy for Astrological Medicine, available at AcademyForAstrologicalMedicine.com

Hill, Judith. *"Moon Lore."* Class Lecture, The Academy for Astrological Medicine, available at AcademyForAstrologicalMedicine.com

MIDPOINTS (medical)

Ebertin, Reinhold, *The Combination of Stellar Influences*, AFA, Inc., 1940

Nauman, Eileen, *Medical Astrology*, DHM, Blue Turtle Publishing, Cottonwood, Arizona, 1982

NUTRITION, CELL SALTS (astrologically based)

Hill, Judith. *"Foods for the Twelve Zodiac Signs: Diet and Nutrients for the Sun, Moon & Rising Signs."* Class lecture, The Academy for Astrological Medicine, AcademyForAstrologicalMedicine.com

Hill, Judith. *"Astrological Nutrition."* Class lecture, The Academy for Astrological Medicine, available at AcademyForAstrologicalMedicine.com

Jansky, Robert Carl *Modern Medical Astrology*, p. 86-90, Astro-Analytics Publications, Van Nuys, California, 1978

Jansky, Robert Carl: *Astrology, Nutrition and Heath*, Para Research, 1977

Nauman, Eileen, *Medical Astrology*, DHM, Blue Turtle Publishing, Cottonwood, Arizona, 1982. (solid herbal and homeopathic sections)

SCIENCE, RESEARCH and TESTIMONY

(Concerning or supportive to physical and medical astrology). Note: This list is a paltry representative of extant (and future) research specifically supportive of physical astrology.

Emoto, Masaru, The Hidden Messages of Water, 2004

Emoto, Masaru, *The Healing Power of Water, 2004*

Emoto, Masaru, *The Secret Life of Water*

Gauquelin, Michel, *The Cosmic Clocks, ACS Publications, 1982*

Grey, W.E., *Know Your Magnetic Field*, p. 57 Christopher Publishing House, Boston, Massachusetts, 1947.

Hill, Judith, *Astrological Heredity - New Evidence, New Thoughts, Borderlands*, a Quarterly Journal of Borderland Research (Borderland Research Science Foundation), 1996; reprinted in the below compendium.

Hill, Judith, *The Mars-Redhead Files*, A Scientific Test of Astrological Tradition, Research of The Redheads Project 1986-1998, compiled Hill, inclusive of research by Hill and Hill and Jacalyn Thompson.

Jonas, Eugen (regarding): *Astrological Birth Control*: A Report on the work of Dr. Eugen Jonas by Sheila Ostrander and Lynn Schroeder, Prentice-Hall, Inc. 1972

Kollerstrom, Nick, *The Metal Planet Relationship*, Borderland Sciences Research Foundation, Garberville, California, 1993

Manolesco, Sir John, Count of Romagna, *Scientific Astrology, Introduction*, pp.12-13, Pinnacle Books, NYC, 1973

Montgomery, Ruth, *Born to Heal: The Amazing True Story of Mr. A. and the Astonishing Art of Healing with Life Energies*, Montgomery, Alabama, 1973

Payne, Buryl, Ph.D. *Apparatus for Detecting Emanations from the Planets*, 1982

Tansley, David V., D.C., *Radionics & the Subtle Anatomy of Man*, Health SSs Press, Bradford, Devon, Holsworthy, England, 1972

Westlake, Aubrey T., *The Pattern of Health*, M.D. Shambhala, Berkeley and London, 1973

Winston, Shirley Rabb, *Music as the Bridge*, Based on the Edgar Cayce Readings, A.R.E. Press, Virginia Beach, Virginia, 1972

Young, Arthur M. *The Geometry of Meaning*, A Merloyd Lawrence Book, Delacorte Press, 1976 Arthur M. Young, *The Reflexive Universe*, Robert Briggs Associates, Mill Valley, 1976

Young, Arthur M., *The Reflexive Universe*, Robert Briggs Associates, Mill Valley, 1976.

See: GEMS, METALS, COLORS AND ASTROLOGY section of this bibliography. Researchers and practitioners A.K. Bhattacharya, D.N. Ramchandra, Benoytosh Bhattacharyya, Howard Beckman, and Hunt have wonderful research and new devices based on the use of specific gems to treat conditions caused by the cosmic color rays, as shown in the natal chart, or influenced by transits.

SURGERY AND ELECTIONS (Date selection for medical procedures).

Hill, Judith, *Medical Astrology: A Guide to Planetary Pathology*, Chapter 22, "How to Find a Safe Surgery Date" and Chapter 23, "Let's Do Safe Surgery Dates", Stellium Press, Portland, OR, 2004

Hill, Judith. *"Selecting Surgery Dates: Electional Astrology."* Class Lecture, The Academy for Astrological Medicine, available at AcademyForAstrologicalMedicine.com

Robson, Vivien, *Electional Astrology*, Samuel Weiser, 1972

Traditional Chinese Medicine (TCM) and Astrology
Clougstoun-Willmott, Jonathan. *Western Astrology & Chinese Medicine*, Destiny Books, 1985

TRANSITS (medical influence)
Hill, Judith, *Medical Astrology in Action: The Transits of Health*, Stellium Press, 2019. (Extremely detailed, herbal and surgical timing tips included. Includes complete sections on Lunar Node transits, planetary transits, solar and lunar transits (through signs, elements, and in aspect to natal planets.) Over 82 "Field Notes".

Hill, Judith. *"The Medical Astrology Forecast Hour."* Live Class for the Monthly Transit Forecasts, The Academy for Astrological Medicine, available at AcademyForAstrologicalMedicine.com

Hill, Judith. *"The Master Sun Cycle and your Health."* Full Online Course, The Academy for Astrological Medicine, available at AcademyForAstrologicalMedicine.com

Hill, Judith, *Astrology & Your Vital Force: Healing with Cosmic Rays and DNA Resonance* (includes exhaustive section on medical timing for all herbal purposes.)

Hill, Judith, *Medical Astrology for Health Practitioners*, Stellium Press, 2019 (sections on collective transits for the healer's awareness; and specific Lunar conjunctions for the timing of herbal uses.

Nauman, Eileen, *Medical Astrology*, DHM, Blue Turtle Publishing, Cottonwood, Arizona, 1982

Bibliography of Medical Astrology

STELLIUM
P R E S S

BOOKS BY JUDITH A. HILL

Stellium Press for stellar minds

https://www.judithhillastrology.com/books

Available Through:

The American Federation of Astrologers, Inc.; Amazon, Barnes & Noble

The Astrological Body Types, revised and expanded, Stellium Press, 1997, (available through Book People, A.F. A. Inc.).

Astrology & Your Vital Force: Healing with Cosmic Rays and DNA Resonance, Stellium Press, 2017

Eclipses and You: How to Align with Life's Hidden Tides, Stellium Press, 2013

The Lunar Nodes: Your Key to Excellent Chart Interpretation, Stellium Press, 2010

Medical Astrology: A Guide to Planetary Pathology, Stellium Press, 2005

Medical Astrology for Health Practitioners, Stellium Press, 2019

Medical Astrology in Action: The Transits of Health, Stellium Press, 2019

Mrs. Winkler's Cure, (as Julia Holly), Stellium Press, Portland, Oregon, 2010

The Part of Fortune in Astrology, Stellium Press, 1998

The Twelve Zodiac Sign Syndromes of Medical Astrology. Publication due for 2024.

Vocational Astrology: A Complete Handbook of Western Astrological Career Selection and Guidance Techniques, A.F. A. Inc., 1999. This title received the Paul R. Grell "Best Book" Award 1999, for American Federation of Astrologers, Inc., publications.
A Wonderbook of True Astrological Case Files, (co-authored with Andrea L. Gehrz, Stellium Press, 2012

Statistical Research Compendiums:
<u>Note:</u> These two below **research compendiums** are available only through Stellium Press at <u>JudithHillAstrology.com</u>

The Mars-Redhead Files, Stellium Press, 2000 (research compendium with Judith Hill and Jacalyn Thompson)

Astroseismology: Earthquakes and Astrology, Stellium Press, 2000. (Research compendium with Judith Hill and Mark W. Polit)
E-file of *Astroseismology* is available to Academy subscribers in the course by that title.

The Academy for Astrological Medicine

AcademyForAstrologicalMedicine.com

This online medical astrology school contains hundreds of hours of lectures, a research discussion forum, and monthly medical astrology forecasts. All six branches of medical astrology are taught here: natal, transits and progressions, electional (surgical; fertility and protocol timing), remedials (including astrological herbology; gemology; nutrition, et al), horary techniques and mental health. The academy provides a strong foundation to those who wish to master the craft. Indeed, the Academy was launched as the most significant medical astrology educational initiative since medieval times.

About the Author

Judith Hill is a second generation, lifetime, consulting astrologer, having performed over 9,000 readings to date, having worked full time in that capacity for several decades. She is also an astrological researcher, teacher, publisher and award-winning author of thirteen books. These include her medically relevant titles: *Medical Astrology: Your Guide to Planetary Pathology; Astrology & Your Vital Force: Healing with Cosmic Rays and DNA Resonance; Medical Astrology for Health Practitioner; Medical Astrology in Action: The Transits of Health;* and the classic *The Astrological Body Types.* Some of her writings have been translated into Russian, Vietnamese, Italian, Lettish and Arabi c.

Hill is the founder and President of *The Academy for Astrological Medicine,* under the Direction of Melissa Behm.

Hill is a Chartered Herbalist with *The Dominion Herbal College,* and faculty with *Kepler College,* and *The Matthew Wood Institute of Herbalism* - where she and Wood co-created two original astrological herbalism courses.

Judith created the course "Medical Astrology 101" for the independent student and later introduced traditional Western medical astrology to students in Szechuan, China (2017-18).

She created and produced the annual "Renaissance Medicine Conference©" in Portland, Oregon, pioneering the conflation of medical astrology and herbal-alchemical topic conferences in the USA. Previously, Hill conceived and co-produced the first exclusively medically oriented astrology conferences in Portland,

Oregon: "Medical Astrology Day", with OAA board members, M. Neuner and S. Scott, with obtained sponsorship from AFAN (1992); and "Medical Astrology Day", with the assistance of Deborah Tramposh (2008).

One of Judith's contributions to medical astrology is her original documentation of the comprehensive medical and physical implications of the Lunar Nodes through both their natal and transit conjunctions to each planet and sign; and also, by detailing the medical impact of eclipses through each zodiac sign and in aspect to planets.

Judith served as the Educational Director for the San Francisco chapter of *The National Council of Geocosmic Research*. She worked for ten years in the statistical study of astrology, receiving an unsolicited research grant from *The Institute for the Study of Consciousness*; and produced two widely acclaimed research compendiums: "The Mars-Redhead Files" with Jacalyn Thompson and "Astro-Seismology" with Mark Polit. The team developed and successfully tested her method for assessing earthquake likelihood per region. Her breakthrough astrogenetic research was featured on Television's *Strange Universe.*

As a pioneer in astro-seismology and astro-genetics, she founded *The Redhead Research Project*; Stellium Press ("for stellar minds"), and San Francisco's first "NCGR Research Day" in the late 1980s. Near this time she briefly worked as an astrological research project assistant for the renowned physicist Arthur Young in Berkeley, California, and assisted KCBS radio's Editorial Director Joan Margalith with her pioneering *Infinity* radio show.

As a "road tested" astrologer, Hill successfully matched five charts to five biographies in a 1989 NCGR sponsored skeptic's challenge.

She segregated and documented the impact of eclipses according to their nodal polarity (North vs. South Node eclipses, for both solar and lunar eclipses); and published possibly the first eclipse calendar for astrological use, inclusive of stated nodal polarity. Hill also documented the potential physical and health effects of most transits in her pioneering work *Medical Astrology in Action: The Transits of Health* (2019).

Hill also created a historically first (known) lateral view of traditional "Zodiacal Man", plus more complete depictions of 'his' physical-sign correspondences.

In the 1980's, Hill authored perhaps the first serious column on real astrology outside of the popular press, entitled "Astrology, a Philosophy of Time and Space" for *Sufism Magazine*.

Judith has lectured widely for multiple conferences, groups, podcasts, radio and television shows both inside, and outside of the astrological world. A biographical interview with Judith by noted producer and astrologer Tony Howard was featured in the December 2010 issue of *The Mountain Astrologer Magazine*.

In her spare time, she is a professional musician and vocalist in multiple genres, producer, sculptor, teacher, tree advocate, illustrator, "roadside anthropologist" and Jewish heritage historian.

She can be reached at JudithHillAstrology.com or AcademyforAstrologicalMedicine.com (as of 2024).

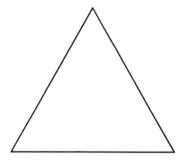

Printed in the USA
CPSIA information can be obtained
at www.ICGtesting.com
CBHW071246120524
8444CB00010B/650